The Nature of

Uncleannes

C O N S I D E R ' D :

Wherein is difcourfed of the
Caufes and Confequences of
this Sin, and the Duties of fuch
as are under the Guilt of it.

To which is added, A

D I S C O U R S E

Concerning the Nature of

C H A S T I T Y,

And the Means of Obtaining it.

By *J. F. OSTERVALD*, Minifter of the
Church of *Neufchâtel*, Author of *A Treatife
of the Caufes of the prefent Corruption of Chriftians, A Catechifm*, &c.

L O N D O N,
Printed for *R. Bonwicke, W. Freeman, Tim: Goodwin,
J. Walthoe, M. Wotton, S. Manfhip, J. Nicholfon, B, Took,
R. Parker*, and *R. Smith.* M DCC VIII.

TO THE
READER.

THE following Difcourfe was written, as the Title-Page imports, by the Learned and Judicious Mr. *Oftervald*, Preacher in *Swifferland*, at *Neufchâtel* as the *French*, or as the *Germans* call it *Newenburg*, a City with a fmall Principality belonging to it; and upon this account a Place of fome Note, efpecially at prefent, becaufe of the Difputes that have been of late, and are not yet wholly compofed, concerning the Sovereignty of it. And he is not only an Author of great Fame there, but in his neighbouring City of *Geneva*, and other Places. And in our own Nation he is not only had in great Efteem, for the particular Refpect he has fhewn to the *Englifh* Liturgy, and his Endeavours to introduce a like Worfhip amongft his Neighbours, but for his excellent Writings likewife; which have no fooner appeared amongft us, but they have been received with a general Applaufe. His *Treatife of the Caufes of the prefent Corruption of Chriftians, and the Remedies thereof,* was quickly cried up, and admired by the beft Judges of folid Reafon, and found Divinity,

and

and was prefently publifh'd in our own Tongue, for the Benefit of fuch as underftand not the *French* Language.

His *Catechetical Difcourfe* likewife explaining 𝔱𝔥𝔢 𝔊𝔯𝔬𝔲𝔫𝔡𝔰 𝔞𝔫𝔡 𝔓𝔯𝔦𝔫𝔠𝔦𝔭𝔩𝔢𝔰 𝔬𝔣 𝔱𝔥𝔢 𝔠𝔥𝔯𝔦𝔰𝔱𝔦𝔞𝔫 𝔯𝔢𝔩𝔦𝔤𝔦𝔬𝔫, did not only meet with a hearty Welcome here; but was foon Tranflated into *Englifh*, by the Ingenious Mr. *Wanly*; and Revifed by the Reverend and Learned Doctor *Stanhope* Dean of *Canterbury*, at the Requeft of *the Society for Propagating Religion*: And met with fuch Approbation from the *Corporation De Promovendo Evangelio*, that their Miffionaries are all Ordered to take their Share of its Copies along with them into the Foreign Plantations, whither they are fent. Which, confidering the Nature of this Illuftrious Society, that it confifts of Perfons of diverfe, and fome of them of the Higheft Ranks and Degrees, both Ecclefiaftical and others, all the Prelates, and many of the chief Dignitaries, and others of Note among the Clergy, and many of the Nobility and Gentlemen of Quality and great Worth, I take to be a noble Teftimony to its Value, and a fingular Recommendation of it, as highly ufeful to the Ends whereto it was defigned, the Promotion of God's Glory, and Inftruction of the Pious and Well-difpofed Readers, efpecially thofe of the Younger Sort.

And this Difcourfe here publifhed, being not only the fame Author's, but well worthy of Him too, it is to be hoped, will not meet with

a lefs

a lefs favourable Reception than thofe that have gone before it : Efpecially confidering the Subjects handled in it, *Uncleannefs*, and *Chaftity*, both of them of very great Importance, and yet concerning which lefs has been written, either in our Own or Foreign Languages, than of moft other Vices or Virtues. The moft probable Caufe of which Defect, I take to be what Himfelf affigns in the beginning of his Preface, namely, *The Nature of the Subject*, and the Difficulty of managing it with fuch Prudence and Caution, as neither to omit what is neceffary to be faid, nor to fay any thing that the Luftful and Licentious may not turn to Sport and Ridicule, or to fome farther Improvement in their Vice.

For it is too plain, as Bifhop *Taylor* obferves, in his *Rules and Exercifes of Holy Living*, Sect. 2. Chap. 2. *That there are fome Spirits fo Atheiftical, and fome fo wholly poffeffed with a Spirit of Uncleannefs, that they turn the moft prudent and chaft Difcourfes into Dirt, and filthy Apprehenfions ; like Cholerick Stomachs, changing their very Cordials and Medicines into Bitternefs, and in a literal fenfe turning the Grace of God into Wantonnefs. They ftudy Cafes of Confcience* (as he proceeds) *in the Cafe of Carnal Sins, not to avoid, but to learn ways how to offend God, and pollute their own Spirits, and fearch their Houfes with a Sun-beam, that they may be inftructed in all the corners of Naftinefs.* Hence he cautions his Reader, as I beg leave to intreat of mine, that he will make a ftop, and

A 4   not

not proceed to *the following Advices, unless he
be of a Chaft Spirit, or defire to be Chaft, or at
leaft be apt to confider whether he ought or no.*

And I doubt not but this fhameful Corruption of Mankind, and the ill Ufe that is frequently made of the moft ferious and beft-weighed Inftructions, and Exhortations, that can be given, in relation to that Purity both of Heart and Life, which our Lord requires of his Difciples, has been a principal Caufe of the Scarcity of Books upon this, above moft other Moral Duties. It is not to be fuppofed, that either Preachers or Writers have had lefs Concern for the Promotion of Chaftity, than of other Virtues ; but only that they have been difcouraged from the Confideration of it, by an Apprehenfion, that too many would be ready to pervert whatever fhould be propofed, though with all the tendernefs and caution that might be, to a wrong Purpofe.

Yet never was more need of Difcourfes of this nature than now, when Wickednefs appears bare-fac'd, and too many are neither afraid nor afhamed to glory in it ; as if it were a piece of Bravery, or a Jefting Matter, to bid Defiance to the Almighty, and daringly provoke him to his Face. When People come to this height of Impiety, it is high time to warn them of their exceffive Folly and Danger, and to intreat and befeech them to bethink themfelves in time, left the Wrath of God break forth upon them, and there be no efcaping. This is a dreadful Cafe, and may juftly be expected

to

to bring down heavy Judgments upon a People, where thefe Iniquities prevail, to make their Land mourn, and the Inhabitants thereof languifh, or poffibly, as it fared with God's own chofen People the Jews, to let them be no more a Nation.

Were they only the common and more ordinary Sins of this kind, fuch as Adultery, Fornication, &c. that we have caufe to complain of, thefe would miferably expofe us to the terrible Indignation of the Almighty, and the dire Effects of it. But to our Sorrow and Shame it muft be confefs'd, that yet more grievous Abominations are found amongft us, fuch as our Country had only heard of in former Ages, but which make too fad a noife in this, to the Terror and Aftonifhment of all the Faithful in the Land. *Shall not the Lord vifit for thefe things ? Shall not his Soul be avenged on fuch a Nation as this ?*

Some Endeavours, bleffed be God, have been ufed for preventing his impending Judgments, by a Profecution and Punifhment of Offenders in this kind. But, alas! unlefs others will take warning by thefe Proceedings, and will be reclaimed from their horrid Wickednefs, there will ftill be too juft reafon to look upon our felves as in dangerous Circumftances. God's Hand already lies heavy upon us. A long and expenfive War has very much exhaufted our Stores; a decay of Trade has fadly leffened our Incomes ; Parties and Divifions have fet us at odds, and filled our Minds with Jealoufies and Animo-

Animosities; the daily encrease of our Wants have multiplied Thievery, Violence, Extortion, and other Instances of Injustice; our Losses by Sea, and Disappointments by Land, call loudly upon us to attend to our Condition, to amend our Ways and our Doings, to humble our selves before God, and to sue to him for Mercy and Pardon, whereby to try if he will be intreated to *hear from Heaven, and forgive our Sins, and heal our Land.*

And to make us the more sensible of our Duty in this respect, I thought it might be useful to publish this Serious and Pious Discourse in our own Language, to caution Persons against the Sins here condemned, and excite and teach them how to get rid of them. And how were it possible for any to indulge themselves in these scandalous Immoralities, if they did well confider with themselves, how heinous a Sin *Uncleanness* is, and what are the terrible Effects of it, how it defiles the Body, disturbs the Mind, ruines Mens Estates and Reputation here, and is the ready way to Everlasting Destruction hereafter?

How wretched and deplorable the State of *Sodom* and *Gomorrah*, and the Cities about them was, when they *suffered the vengeance of Eternal Fire*, as St. *Jude* speaks, *ver.* 7th, none can doubt. As neither can it be question'd whether their filthy and unnatural Lusts were the Occasion of so severe a Destruction. *They gave themselves up to vile Affections, to work those things which are unseemly,* to the grossest and most enormous

enormous Lewdnesses ; and though God bare with them for a time, he would not do it always, but at length allotted them that recompence of their Wickednefs which it fo loudly called for. For, * *The Lord rained upon Sodom and Gomorrah* * Gen. 19. *Brimftone and Fire from the Lord out of Heaven.* 24, 25. *And he overthrew thofe Cities, and all the Plain, and all the Inhabitants of the Cities, and that which grew upon the Ground*, to fuch a degree, that they have ever fince remained (*a*) lamentable Examples of the Divine Juftice, for the Terror of all fucceeding Generations. And can we hope to efcape better than they, if their intolerable Wickednefs be found amongft us? Our Bleffed Saviour has taught us, That the Cafe of finful Chriftians will be far worfe than theirs at the Day of Judgment, St. *Matth.* xi. 20, *&c.* And I know not how any can promife themfelves it fhall not be fo in the mean time too. I am fure that if this Vice, rarely heard of in thefe Parts till of late Years, be not rooted out from amongft us, it will forebode fome heavy Vengeance to befall us, and God only knows how foon. *If we will not hearken* and reform, *but will walk thus contrary to the Lord, he will walk contrary to us in fury, and will chaftife us yet feven times more for our Sins.*

This Crime, as one juftly defcribes it, is in it felf monftrous and unnatural, in its Practice filthy, and odious to extremity ; its Guilt is crying, and its Confequences ruinous. It de-

(*a*) Jofeph. 'Ιυδ. ἁλωC. l. 4. c. 27. Tacit. Hift. l. 5. p. 427. Ed. Lipf. Solin. Polyhift. c. 48.

ftroys

ftroys Conjugal Affection, perverts Natural Inclination, and tends to extinguish the hope of Posterity.

Another heinous Inftance of Uncleanneſs, is *Adultery*; a complicated Wickedneſs, contrary to the expreſs Prohibition of Almighty God, in the VIIth Commandment, to the Doctrine of the Prophets, and to that of our Bleſſed Saviour and his Apoſtles in the New Teſtament, contrary to the Faith ſolemnly given at Marriage, contrary to the Intent of that holy Ordinance, contrary to Natural Juſtice, by the Damage done to the injur'd Party, and eſpecially to the Husband, by a Spurious Iſſue, whereby himſelf and his Children are wrong'd, poſſibly his whole Eſtate, or at leaſt a conſiderable, perhaps the greateſt part of it, is ſwallowed up by a Stranger; and which is notoriouſly deſtructive of that mutual Affection Husband and Wife ought to have for, and that Comfort and Satisfaction they were deſigned to take in each other.

The very Heathens had ſuch an abhorrence of this Sin, that they annexed divers ſevere Penalties to it. Sometimes (*a*) they allowed whomſoever that ſhould take any in the Fact, to kill them; and (*b*) the Woman, if not killed, was to be expoſed to the utmoſt Shame. Sometimes (*c*) the Husband might put the

---

(*a*) Heraclid. de Polit. apud. Ælian. var. Hiſt. p. 441.
(*b*) Ib. p. 447. (*c*) A Gell. l. 10. c. 23.

Wife

Wife fo taken to Death, or (*d*) might punifh
the Man in fuch a manner as effectually to
prevent their coming together again, and
(*e*) might moſt grievouſly torment him.

Among the Ancient Jews, (*f*) *Adultery*
was puniſhed with Death, and by God's own
Appointment. And though in time they came
not to have it in their power (*g*) to inflict
Death upon Offenders againſt their Law,
(*a*) they however decreed, and accordingly
made uſe of, other ſevere Methods of handling
Tranſgreſſors in this kind ; whereby both to
teſtifie their Deteſtation of this Vice, and to affright Perſons from daring to venture upon it.

And amongſt Chriſtians, it has been reckoned
fo heinouſly offenſive to Almighty God, that
Divines have thought one fingle deliberate Act
of it, equal in Guilt to a Habit of ſome leſſer
Sins. And our Author, in his Book of
the Caufes of Corruption (*b*), couples this Sin
with Apoſtacy from Chriſtianity, and affirms
one fingle Act of it to put a Man out of a
State of Salvation. *Tertullian* (*c*) repreſents it
as worſe than denying the Faith in times of

(*d*) Plaut: Mil. Gloriof. Act. 5. (*e*) Juv. Sat. 10.
v. 315, 316. (*f*) Levit. 20. 10. (*g*) St. Jo. 18. 31.
(*a*) Buxt. Synag. Jud. c. 47. (*b*) Il y a certains Pechez
fi atroces, comme l'Adultére, l'Apoſtaſie, dans les quels il
n'arrive gueres à un homme de tomber plus d'un fois, à
moins qu'il ne foit tout-a-fait mechant ; mais icy un ſeul de
ces pechez eſt incompatible avec l'eſtat de regeneration.
Par. 1. Sour. 4. p. 164. (*c*) Nemo volens negare com-
pellitur, nemo nolens fornicatur : nulla ad libidinem vis eſt,
niſi ipſa —— Quis magis negavit, qui Chriſtum vexatus, an
qui delectatus amiſit ? Tert. de Pudic. c. 22.

Perfecution, becaufe not extenuated by thofe
Fears and Penalties that occafion fuch a Denial.
And according to the Meafures of the Primitive Difcipline, (d) the Holy Communion was
denied to Adulters for Seven Years together,
(e) fometimes much longer; and fometimes
(f) they were never to be received into Communion, not even at the Point of Death.

And as to their Worldly Concerns, it is ordinarily feen, (a) that Adulterers fuffer no fmall
Inconvenience by their Lewd and Vicious
manner of Life, but meet with all the feveral
Mifchiefs, and more than, I fhall have occafion
to mention under the next Head. So that the
Wifeman had abundant reafon upon this account for his Affertion, *Prov.* vi. 32, 33. that
Whofoever committeth Adultery with a Woman,
lacketh Underftanding; he that doth it deftroyeth
his own Soul. A Wound and Difhonour fhall he
get, and his Reproach fhall not be wiped away.

Fornication likewife is a Sin, not only abominable in the Sight of God, but hated alfo
and abhorred by all wife and good Men; and
that proves of very pernicious confequence in
this prefent Life. It is not fo injurious as this
laft named, and has not therefore altogether

(d) Albafp. Obfervat. l. 2. c. 17, 18. & Concil. Ancyr.
Can. 20. (e) Greg. Nyff. Ep. ad Letoium. (f) B. Cypr.
Ep. 55. ad Antonian.
(a) Οἱ δ᾽ ἀπὸ Ἐπικύρε ὁ διὰ τῦτο ὁ μοιχεύεσιν, ὅτε ἀσάχει θ,
τῳ μοιχεύειν, ἀλλὰ διὰ τὸ νενομικέναι τέλΘ τ᾽ ἡδελὼ, πολλὰ
δ᾽ ἀπαγία κωλυτικὰ τ᾽ ἡδονῆς τὸ ἄξασαι μιᾶ τῇ τῦ μοιχείαν
ἡδονῇ, &c. Orig. con. Celf. l. 7. p. 374.

fo many Difficulties and Dangers attending it;
but yet it opens a Door for fo many dreadful
Evils, as may well deterr all from it, who are
not willing to run blindfold upon their own
Deftruction. It is frequently known to fubject
Perfons to divers acute Pains and loathfom
Difeafes, to waft their Spirits, impair their
Vitals, corrupt their Flefh, rot their Bones ;
to deform themfelves, confume their Eftates,
and *bring them to a morfel of Bread* ; is a great
Reproach and Difgrace to them, caufes many
defperate Quarrels, and upon thefe and other-
like accounts becomes a means of fhortening
their Days, and often-times of tranfmitting
Poverty, and Shame, and an unhealthy Conftitution to their Pofterity. It makes Men
foft and effeminate, and is full of Cares and
Fears, and attended with Uneafinefs and Dif-
content, Jealoufy and Diftruft, impatient Defires, and yet perplexing Delays and Difap-
pointments ; and the End of it is ordinarily
(*a*) Grief and Repentance. It puts its Vaffals
upon the vileft and moft fhamelefs Contrivances
and Attempts, for compaffing their Defign,
and fatisfying their Luft. It keeps them (*b*) in
perfect Slavery, and tempts them to live more
like Beafts than Men. It renders them a Peft
and Plague to their Neighbours, a Shame and

(*a*) Demofthenes Laidi, Ego, inquit, pœnitere tanti non
emo. Aul. Gel. l. 1. c. 8.   (*b*) Ὁ ᾗ πόρνῷ ἁμαρτίας
ἀδοξότερῷ δᾶλῷ· βόρβορον ᾗ ἀν]λεῖν παρ᾽ αὐτῆς τεταςμένῷ,
μολυζμῶ συνάγς σωφρν, ᾗ ἀκάθαρτον λειτυργεῖ ἐργασίαν.
Greg. Nyff. Orat. cont. Fornicarios.

Affliction

Affliction to their Relations, and irreconcileable Enemies to their own Welfare, whether with respect to the Quiet of their Minds, the Ease and Health of their Bodies, or the Success of their Affairs and Concerns in the World ; all which are very often entirely ruined by it. And whatsoever good Qualities they may have otherwise, this one infamous ungovernable Appetite clouds and sadly obscures them all. It is a Sin that not only Christians have abundant reason to detest and renounce, but which divers in the Heathen World would rather die than yield to ; as others also, when overpower'd, against their own Wills and utmost Endeavours to the contrary, would not suffer themselves to survive such Abuse. Of which there are many Instances, and St. *Jerom* men-
* Cap. 26. tions several of them * in his First Book against *Jovinian*.

Polygamy (a) is another branch of the Sin here condemned, as our Author well observes, *Part* i. *p.* 11, 12. which though sometimes practised among the *Jews*, is by no means lawful amongst Christians. Our Saviour declares it to be Adultery, for a Man to put away his Wife, and marry another, St. *Luke* xvi. 18. And it cannot be more consistent with the Doctrine and Laws of the Gospel, with the Na-

(a) Τῷ γὸ ἀνθρώπῳ μία δέδο) ʔῇ τῷ Θῶ βοηθός, ἢ τῇ γυναικὶ μία ἐφήρμοσεν κεφαλή. Id. ad Letoinca.

ture

ture and Ends of Matrimony, with the mutual
Obligation then folemnly entred into, or with
the Husband's Relation to his Wife, with whom
he is pronounced * *one Flefh*, to take another * Ephef.
without putting her away. All fuch Contracts 5. 31.
therefore are no better than meer Delufions,
whereby to deceive and quiet an uneafie Confcience, and do not prevent the Guilt of the
Converfation confequent upon them. They
are but another Species of Adultery, and are
to be look'd upon and conftantly avoided as
fuch. There is a remarkable Note of the
learned Dr. *Whitby* to this purpofe, in his Com-
mentary upon 1 *Cor.* vii. 4. *The Wife hath not*
power over her own Body, but the Husband;
and likewife alfo the Husband hath not power
of his own Body, but the Wife. " Here (faith
" the Doctor) is a plain Argument againft
" *Polygamy*; for if the Man hath not power
" over his own Body, he cannot give the
" power of it to another, and fo cannot marry
" another; nor could the Wife, exclufively
" to him, have the power of his Body, if he
" could give it to another." In fhort, † God † Gen. 2.
at firft inftituted Marriage between one Man 22. *&*
and one Woman; and whatfoever Abufes had St. Matth.
crept in afterwards in this refpect our Saviour 19. 4.
took care to rectifie, and reftored it to its
original Inftitution, fo to remain to the
World's end. And there is no going contrary
to this, without offering apparent violence to
God's own Appointment, and the Ends and
Obligations of the former Marriage, and con-

fequently (*a*) not without incurring the dreadful Guilt of Adultery.

Near of kin to Polygamy, is *Concubinage* *, and equally unlawful amongſt Chriſtians. Our Saviour gives no manner of Countenance to it in his Goſpel. And his Apoſtle St. *Paul* forbids Uncleanneſs in ſuch a manner, as to make *Marriage* and *Touching a Woman* equivalent Phraſes, and to teach, That (*b*) *out of Marriage all is Sinful.* As our Author has fully ſhewn, *Part* I. *Sect.* I. *Ch.* 5.

Inceſt is another egregious Violation of the Laws of Chaſtity, and heinouſly provoking in the Sight of God. It was this coſt *Amnon* his Life, 2 *Sam.* xiii. 22; and will be ſure to bring down a far greater Deſtruction upon all that take not care to refrain from it. The Ignorant (*c*) *Perſians* might more eaſily allow themſelves in it; but Chriſtians ſhould be mindful that they are utterly inexcuſable, if they have but an Inclination to, and Deſire of it in their Heart.

And again, *Self-Pollution* is another Unnatural and Dangerous Species of *Uncleanneſs.*

(*a*) Divina Lex ita Duos in Matrimonium, quod eſt in corpus unum, pari jure conjungit, ut adulter habeatur, quiſquis compagem corporis in diverſa diſtraxerit. Lact. Inſtit. l. 6. c. 23.

* Concubina eſt mulier quæ conſuetudinis, non matrimonii causâ retinetur, &c. Calv. Lexic. Jurid.

(*b*) Quiſquis affectus illos frœnare non poteſt, cohibeat eos intra præſcriptum legitimi Tori, &c. Lact. Inſtit. c. 23.

(*c*) Πᾶϲζαι μὲν ϰ̀ ἐϰ ἄτοπον ἡγῦν), ϑυϰϊεῖ μίγνυϰ. Diog. Laert. l. 9. in Vitâ Pyrrhonis.

This

This we see remarkably punifh'd in *Onan*, by a particular Stroke from Almighty God. For it is not to be thought that his Guilt lay totally in not raifing up Seed to his deceafed Brother *Er*, though that was a very confiderable Aggravation of it ; but the way he took to prevent it, would have been highly culpable at any other time. As it was, it proved fo intolerable a Provocation, that Almighty God could not bear with it, and therefore immediately cut him off by reafon of it : *Gen.* xxxviii. 10. *The thing which he did difpleafed the Lord, wherefore he flew him alfo.*

Nor, laftly, is the Duty of Chaftity violated only by Lafcivious and Impure Actions, but by *Filthy and Obfcene Difcourfe*, which is not only a certain token of a corrupt Heart, but often-times proves an inducement to farther degrees of Wickednefs, and is what no good Chriftian can poffibly allow himfelf in : And again, by *Luftful Thoughts and Defires*, which our Bleffed Lord declares to be a leffer Inftance of *Adultery*, and which are certainly very highly offenfive to Almighty God, and no lefs dangerous to all who are chargeable with them ; St. *Matth.* v. 28. *Whofoever looketh upon a Woman to luft after her, hath committed adultery with her Already in his heart.*

There are fome other Inftances alfo of Wantonnefs and Impurity, which all Chriftians are concerned to beware of ; as the *Reader* will

fee

fee by the following Excellent *Difcourfe* (*a*), to which I referr him for them.

All I defign farther, is only to offer fome few other Arguments, in order to the Cure of this dangerous and fhameful Vice.

And here I might begin with prefling Perfons to reflect upon the many Mifchiefs already noted as naturally confequent upon *Uncleannefs*, even in this World, with refpect to their Souls, Bodies, Reputation, Eftates, and even their own Lives, and their Pofterity after them. Which if ferioufly and attentively confider'd, will readily appear of that pernicious Influence, that every one muft prefently fee, the gratifying a Brutifh Affection can never be worth all this Mifery. And here let not Perfons delude themfelves. They may poffibly think to manage their Lewdnefs fo, as to have the Pleafure they defire, without incurring the evil Confequents that fo frequently attend it. But if ever they be fo hardy as to make the Attempt, they will be in great danger of finding themfelves grofly miftaken, and that thefe vain Hopes will fail them, and they will then fee their Folly when 'tis too late. For when once Men allow themfelves in any Lewd, Intemperate Courfe, daily Experience fhews how it captivates their Underftandings, and gets the Afcendant over their Wills, and carries them much farther than they ever intended, or had any apprehenfion of. When they have

---

(*a*) *Efpecially* Part I. Sect. 1. chap. 7.

begun

bégun to give way to their vicious Inclinations, thefe are apt to grow upon them, and become more and more impetuous, and never to give over, till they have got the maftery over them; and then no one knows whither they will carry them. All their Refolutions of Prudence and Management are apt to fail them, and they quickly find, to their coft, how much wifer, and fafer, and better upon all accompts it had been to have rejeꞓed the firft Temptation to their Wickednefs. For at beft, this Vice ufually carries Perfons on, by degrees, till they are got beyond Recovery; but fometimes it is quicker in its Operation, and ruines them, and expofes their Vanity and Folly in a very little time. This our Bleffed Saviour gives us a lively Reprefentation of, in the Parable of the *Prodigal Son,* who having received his Portion from his Father, and probably a large one, went at a good diftance, where his Father might have no knowledge of his Doings, and foon fpent all, (*a*) ζῶν ἀσώτως, in Riotous Living, in great (*b*) Profufenefs, (*c*) Luft, and (*d*) Intemperance. But then the Effeꞓ hereof was, that in a little time he brought himfelf into fo diftreffed a Condition, that he was forced to undertake one of the meaneft of Employments, to feed Swine; and,

---

(*a*) St. Luke 15. 13. (*b*) Ἐςὶ ᵹ κ̀ ἡ ἀσωτία κ̀ ἡ ἀνελδ-Θεία πεὶ χρήματα ὑαϾολαὶ κ̀ ἐλλείψεις. Ariſtot. ad Nicom. l. 4. c. 1. (*c*) Τὲς ᵹ ἀκεϱεῖς κ̀ εἰς ἀκολασίαν δαπανηρὲς ἀσώτɤς κϱλɤ̃μɛν. Ibid. (*d*) Ἀσώτως, intemperanter. Mald. in loc. Ἀσώτως, prodigaliter, intemperanter, libidinoſè, laſcivè. Corn. à Lap.

which

which was worse, to want bare Neceſſaries for a Subſiſtence, and even (*e*) to wiſh that he might *fill his Belly with the Husks that the Swine did eat; and yet no Man did give unto him.* This was the ſad Effect of his Exceſs; and they that imitate him in his Vices, muſt expect the like uncomfortable Attendants upon them. Which one Conſideration, one would think, were a ſufficient Caution againſt a Luſtful Courſe of Life, to all who are deſirous of their own Welfare and Happineſs in this World.

But this is incomparably the leſſer part of what I have to urge againſt this Vice. For if we conſider ourſelves as Chriſtians ſolemnly dedicated to God at Baptiſm, and who muſt be Judged by Him at the Laſt Day, theſe Meditations will plead much more ſtrongly for an utter Abhorrence of it, and a conſtant Care never to come within the Verges of it; and particularly upon theſe following Accounts.

1. All *Uncleanneſs* is a palpable Violation of our Baptiſmal Covenant, wherein we ſolemnly obliged ourſelves to renounce the Fleſh, (that is to ſay, all Senſuality and Voluptuouſneſs) aſwell as the World and the Devil. For there is no living up to this Profeſſion and Obligation, without being continually upon our guard againſt all thoſe ſinful Luſts which we have thus renounced. And indeed, what an Affront

(*e*) Ibid. v. 16.

is it to our Lord, and what vile Treachery
and breach of Covenant, when Perfons have
thus given up their Names to Chriſt, and
promiſed to obey his holy Laws, and, in particular, to abſtain from all Impurity, if they
ſhall yet draw back; and profeſſing to know
God, ſhall in Works deny him, living in Wantonneſs and Unlawful Pleaſures, like the Gentiles who knew him not, or rather in ſuch
deteſtable Lewdneſſes as the wiſer amongſt theſe
would have abominated? We cannot doubt
but that we are all ſtrictly engaged to * _cleanſe_ * 2 Cor.
ourſelves from all Filthineſs both of Fleſh 7. 1.
and Spirit, and to perfect Holineſs in the Fear
of God. And what a monſtrous Incongruity
muſt it be, for ſuch to indulge themſelves in
any Carnal and Senſual Immoralities, in direct
oppoſition to the Vow ſo ſolemnly made
againſt them! This muſt neceſſarily argue a
great Stupidity and Regardleſneſs of their Duty;
which were ſufficiently blameable in any, but
in Chriſtians who pretend to tread in their
Saviour's Steps, and to obey all his Commandments, is moſt exceedingly provoking.

2. _Uncleanneſs_ is a frequent Occaſion of
many other Sins. From what hath been ſaid,
it evidently appears to be heinouſly offenſive
in itſelf, without any of thoſe aggravating
Circumſtances that often-times attend it, and
inhance its Guilt. But it muſt needs ſeem
much more ſo, when taken in conjunction
with thoſe other Sins which often-times flow

from

from it, and are the unhappy Confequents of it : fuch as Profufenefs, Lying, Falfe Oaths, Quarrels, and Slaughter ; fome of which it makes ufe of for compaffing its Defigns, others for concealing them, and others upon the difcovery of them. The Luftful Perfon breaks through all Impediments that lie in his way, to obftruct the Accomplifhment of what he aims at. And tho' never fo many Sins muft be committed before he can bring his Ends about, he will very hardly fuffer himfelf to be withheld by the fear of them. He will feek to deceive, will Proteft, and Swear, and Vow, what he does not believe to be true, or never intends to perform ; will Quarrel and Fight, and fo venture the taking away another's Life, or lofing his own. The like Methods he will be ready to flie to afterwards for hiding his Wickednefs, fticking at no fort of indirect Means whereby to keep his Shame from being known. And if however he find himfelf miftaken, and his Sin is brought to light, and himfelf either reproached with it, or call'd in queftion about it, with what Lyes and Perjuries, what Subornation and Falfe-Witnefs will he endeavour to juftifie himfelf ? Befides that this Sin frequently tempts to the Murdering of Children thus brought into the World ; and then again to the Practice of all the forement= ion'd Iniquities, in order to the concealment of this. And, oh ! how egregioufly heinous, how dreadfully dangerous, how exceedingly unbecoming the Chriftian Profeffion, and how

intolerably

intolerably provoking in the Sight of God, muſt ſuch a Maſs of Wickedneſs be. A Sin that is big with ſo many others, and moſt of them of ſo flagitious a nature, calls upon all to be very watchful that they be not betrayed into it. I grant, all that commit this Sin, do not fall into all thoſe others likewiſe : But ſince too many do, and none that indulge themſelves in this, are ſure they ſhall not, common Prudence would direct by all means to refrain from it. When *David* committed his Adultery with *Bathſheba*, it is not to be imagined that he had any Deſign upon *Uriah's* Life; and yet the taking away of this, prov'd to be the Event of it. So *Herod's* Familiarity with his Siſter-in-Law *Herodias*, was the original Cauſe of St. *John Baptiſt's* being Beheaded. And whoſoever once begins with this Sin, may certainly depend upon it, that he knows not when or where he ſhall end.

3. Another peculiar Aggravation of this Sin, above all others I know of, is, that moſt of the Inſtances of it are ſuch wherein the Sinner cannot be wicked alone. Other Iniquities Men may commit by themſelves ; but here, for the moſt part, two muſt inevitably concurr, and muſt be Partners of each other's Guilt, and muſt expect to ſuffer for it accordingly. St. *Paul* charges *Timothy, Not to partake of other Men's Sins, but to keep himſelf pure,* 1 Tim. v. 22. But in no caſe is ſuch a Caution more needful, than in this before us ; there being
no

no readier or fairer way to contract a share in another's Guilt, than by engaging them in the Lusts of Uncleanness. *Gregory Nyssen* (*a*) observes of Rapine, Envy, Slander, and Murder, That they do not so affect the Doer, as him against whom they are levelled, or on whom they are acted. So that a Covetous Man may get what is another's, without losing his own; and a Bloodthirsty Man may kill another, without hurting his own Body: but he that defiles another by Fornication, cannot possibly be undefiled himself. I add, That he cannot commit this Sin, without having both his own and the other's Crime to answer for; and therefore not without involving two Souls at one and the same time in the same Guilt and Ruine. And by consequence, he is a deadly Enemy both to himself and his Accomplice, and, under a pretence of Kindness, exposes both to dreadful and intolerable Evils both in this World, and in that which is to come.

Nor does he always stop here, but many times contrives Ways to draw in others besides, either in order to the gaining the Consent of the Accomplice, or helping to Opportunities for his Wickedness, or perhaps afterwards for assisting in the making away with the Issue of it, or at least in the concealment of such Murder. In all which Cases, he not only betrays all Persons so employed into a

---

(*a*) De Fornicat. fugiend.

great

great meaſure of Guilt, but thereby likewiſe miſerably encreaſes his own. And if this one Sin alone, without any ſuch Aggravation, had been enough to ruine him beyond Recovery; how ſad muſt his Caſe be, when he reflects, how much worſe he has made it by this means, and how many others alſo he has brought into the like Ruine with himſelf? Certainly a Sin of thus deſtructive a nature, gives fair Warning to all that will in the leaſt conſider it, to flie from it with greater Averſion, than from a Lion or a Tyger, or whatſoever the moſt rapacious Beaſt of Prey.

4. *Uncleanneſs* has this peculiar Charge, againſt it, That the Apoſtle St. *Paul* declares it to be in an eſpecial manner againſt our own Bodies. *Flee Fornication,* ſays the Apoſtle, 1 *Cor.* vi. 18. *Every Sin that a Man doth is without the Body; But he that committeth Fornication ſinneth againſt his own Body.* As much as to ſay, Other Sins pollute the Heart and the Soul; but all Sins of Impurity pollute the Body likewiſe. Other Sins are committed againſt God, or our Neighbour; but theſe againſt one's Self. They foul the Fleſh, and contaminate the Body, which ſhould be kept in Chaſtity and Purity, and, as the Apoſtle ſpeaks, *ver.* 19. as *a Temple of the Holy-Ghoſt.* And how deplorable the State of ſuch who yet indulge themſelves in it will be, the ſame Apoſtle acquaints us, 1 *Cor.* iii. 17. *If any Man defile the Temple of God, him will God deſtroy.*

The

The Wife-Man also assures us of him that *goeth after a strange Woman*, That he does it to his own Destruction : *As an Ox goeth to the Slaughter, as a Fool to the Correction of the Stocks, or as a Bird hasteth to the Snare, and knoweth not that it is for its Life.* Often-times this. Vice not only involves in it multitudes of other Evils, but exposes to Temporal Destruction and Death. But the greatest Infelicity and infinitely the worst it is or can be liable to, is that Eternal Death which follows upon it in the other World. *Him will God destroy* for ever and ever. And this Confideration therefore I have referved for the last place.

5. This Vice leads to inevitable Destruction of both Body and Soul in Hell. It is the chief of those *Lusts of the Flesh* which the Scriptures so severely condemn, and so constantly dissuade from. Under what Character it went in the Old Testament, may be collected not only from the *VIIth Commandment*, and such other Prohibitions as those, *Deut.* xxiii. 17. *There shall be no Whore of the Daughters of Ifrael, nor a Sodomite of the Sons of Ifrael :* And *Levit.* xviii. 20. *Thou shalt not lie carnally with thy Neighbour's Wife, to defile thy self with her ;* but likewife from such Denunciations as that, *cap.* xx. 10. *The Man that committeth Adultery with another Man's Wife, even he that committeth Adultery with his Neighbour's Wife, the Adulterer and the Adulteress shall surely be put to death :* From such Expressions as those of the Wife-
Man

Man, *Prov.* v. 3, 4, 5. *The Lips of a Strange Woman drop as an Honeycomb, and her Mouth is smoother than Oil. But her End is bitter as Wormwood, sharp as a two-edged Sword. Her Feet go down to Death; her Steps take hold on Hell.* And *chap.* vi. 24, 25, 26. *To keep thee from the Evil Woman, and the Flattery of the Tongue of a Strange Woman. Lust not after her Beauty in thine Heart; neither let her take thee with her Eyelids. For by means of a whorish Woman, a Man is brought to a piece of Bread, and the Adulteress will hunt for the precious Life.* Chap. xxii. 14. *The Mouth of a Strange Woman is a deep Pit; he that is abhorred of the Lord shall fall therein.* And again, chap. xxiii. 27, 28. *A Whore is a deep Ditch; and a Strange Woman is a narrow Pit. She also lieth in wait for a Prey, and encreaseth the Transgressors among Men* And *Eccles.* vij. 26. *I find more bitter than Death, the Woman whose Heart is Snares and Nets, and her Hands as Bands: whoso pleaseth God shall escape from her, but the Sinner shall be taken by her.* And again, from such Expostulations and Reprehensions as those of the Prophets; *How shall I pardon thee for this? thy Children have forsaken me, and sworn by them that are no Gods: when I had fed them to the full, then they committed Adultery, and assembled by troops in the Harlots Houses. Shall I not visit for these things? saith the Lord; and shall not my Soul be avenged on such a Nation as this?* Jer. v. 7, 9. And *chap.* vii. 9, 10. *Will ye Steal, Murder, and commit Adultery,* &c. *And*

come

come and stand before me in this House, which is called by my Name, and say we are delivered to do all these Abominations ? And Hof. iv. 1, 2, 3. *Hear the Word of the Lord, ye Children of Israel ; for the Lord hath a Controversy with the Inhabitants of the Land, because there is no Truth, nor Mercy, nor Knowledge of God in the Land. By Swearing, and Lying, and Killing, and Stealing, and committing Adultery, they break out, and Blood toucheth Blood. Therefore shall the Land mourn, and every one that dwelleth therein shall languish, with the Beasts of the Field, and the Fowls of Heaven ; yea, the Fishes of the Sea also shall be taken away.* Where *Adultery* is manifeftly one of thofe crying Sins, for which thefe heavy Judgments were to be brought upon the Land. And from this and the foremention'd Texts, together with others of the like nature, it is plain, that the Sin of *Uncleannefs* was abundantly condemned, and caution'd againft, amongft the Jews.

What Notion that faithful Servant of God, *Job*, had of it of old, we learn from himfelf, *Job* xxxi. 1. *I made a Covenant with mine Eyes : Why then should I think upon a Maid ?* And a little after, *ver.* 9, 10, 11, 12. *If mine Heart hath been deceived by a Woman, or if I have laid wait at my Neighbour's door ; then let my Wife grind unto another, and let others bowe down upon her. For this is an heinous Crime ; yea, it is an Iniquity to be punished by the Judges.* Nor was any thing more common in the Old Teftament, than for the Prophets to exclaim

againft

againſt Idolatry, as Spiritual Whoredom; which we may be ſure they would never have done, if that Carnal Whoredom, whereto they compared, it had not been look'd upon as a Crime of more than ordinary both Guilt and Danger; a Sin wherewith the Almighty will be highly incens'd, and for which He will not therefore fail to avenge himſelf proportionably upon the obſtinate, impenitent Offenders.

And in the New Teſtament our Bleſſed Saviour reckons *Adultery* and *Fornication* amongſt thoſe Evils, which *proceed from within, and defile a Man,* St. *Matth.* xv. 19, 20. *And know ye not,* ſays his Apoſtle St. *Paul,* 1 *Cor.* vi. 9, 10. *that the Unrighteous ſhall not inherit the Kingdom of God? Be not deceived; neither Fornicators —— nor Adulterers, nor Effeminate, nor Abuſers of themſelves with Mankind —— ſhall inherit the Kingdom of God.* And again, *Gal.* v. 19. *The Works of the Fleſh are manifeſt, which are theſe, Adultery, Fornication, Uncleanneſs, Laſciviouſneſs, &c.* Of which, ſays the Apoſtle, *ver.* 21. *I tell you before, as I have alſo told you in times paſt, that they which do ſuch things ſhall not inherit the Kingdom of God.* And again he ſpeaks of it as a Truth all were fully ſatisfied of, That the Luſtful and Unclean muſt never hope to reign with God, and our Bleſſed Saviour and Redeemer : *Epheſ.* v. 5. *This ye know, that no Whoremonger nor Unclean Perſon hath any Inheritance in the Kingdom of God and of Chriſt.* And again once more, *Heb.* xiii. 4. *Whoremongers and Adulterers God will judge :*

judge : He will pafs a fevere Sentence upon fuch grofs Offenders, and will never admit them to taft of the Heavenly Felicity.

But this is not all. Poffibly they might efteem it no great Punifhment to be kept out of Heaven, where they can never think to enjoy any of thofe brutifh Satisfactions, which take up their Thoughts, and employ their Minds at prefent. And therefore they would do well ferioufly to attend to that other part *St. Mat. of their Sentence, which will be * to *depart 25.41. into Everlafting Fire, prepared for the Devil and his Angels.* This will be the doleful Fate of all impenitent Sinners, and of thefe therefore amongft the reft. As will be yet more apparent, if it be remembred that, *Rev.* xxi. 8. the *Abominable,* Ἐβδελυγμῥνοι, thofe that allow ‖ St. Mat. themfelves in the groffer Acts of filthy Un-5. 32. & cleannefs, and *Whoremongers,* Πέρνοι, which 19. 19. includes both ‖ Adulterers and Fornicators, are *compared with* 1 Cor. 6. recorded amongft thofe who fhall be con-10. & demned to the difmal fiery Lake, *the Lake that Gal. 5. burns with Fire and Brimftone.* 19.

The Sum is, That this Vice of *Uncleannefs* is an egregioufly Wicked and Deftructive Sin; a Sin that very often is attended with dreadful Confequents in this World, and brings Ruine and Mifery to Perfons Bodies and Souls, Relations and Pofterity ; and has feveral peculiar Aggravations that very much inhance its Guilt, and fo make it far the more intolerable in relation to a Future State. It is not only a manifeft Breach of our Baptifmal Vow, as all other

W'ilful

wilful Sin is, but it is what in a particular manner is committed againſt our own Bodies, and beſides is a common Occaſion of bringing others in to partake of the like Wickedneſs. In moſt Inſtances there muſt be a Partner concern'd in it, and many times ſeveral others are prevail'd upon to be ſome way Abettors to it. And ſo it is highly inſtrumental, in order to both the preſent, and future, temporal and eternal Ruine of Mankind.

And now can there poſſibly be imagin'd any ſuch Pleaſure in it, as may countervail all theſe terribly pernicious Effects of it? Are all the Cares and Troubles, and all the Shame and Diſgrace the Luſtful Perſon brings upon himſelf here, the Pains and Diſeaſes he contracts, the needleſs and extravagant Expences he runs himſelf into, the Poverty, the Streights and Wants whereto he is hereby reduced; are all theſe nothing, in compariſon of the Satisfaction he enjoys in his Lewd and Diſſolute manner of Life? Or rather, on the other hand, are they not ſuch unaccountable Inſtances of Folly, as all Wiſe and Conſiderate Men are ſtartled at, and have ſuch an Averſion to, that nothing in the World can prevail with them to order their Lives accordingly? But then, in relation to another Life, the Miſchief is infinitely greater, Nor can the moſt ſenſeleſs Lunatick upon Earth act more inconſiſtently, than they do who abandon themſelves to this Vice; and ſo for the gratification of a preſent unreaſonable brutiſh Appetite, are ſure to be intolerably, unconceivably, infinitely miſerable to all Eternity.

b Yet

Yet this is the certain State of all who live and die in this Sin. They for the moſt part render themſelves very unhappy and wretched in this World; and in the World to come can hope for nothing better than Indignation and Wrath, Tribulation and Anguiſh, Pains and Tortures, and Blackneſs of Darkneſs, with the Devil and his Angels, for evermore.

Wherefore the Reſult of theſe awakening Conſiderations ſhould be, an unfeigned Love and Practice of the Virtue treated of in the latter Part of the following *Diſcourſe*; that all who read them, be invited to hate the Garment ſpotted and defiled of the Fleſh, and to *cleanſe * 2 Cor. themſelves* (as St. *Paul* exhorts) * *from all Fil-* 7: 1. *thineſs both of Fleſh and Spirit, perfecting Holineſs in the Fear of God.* The Apoſtle St. *Peter* tells us, all *Fleſhly Luſts war againſt the Soul,* 1 S. Pet. ii. 11. and thereby informs us of the Lovelineſs and Excellency, the Safety and Advantage of Chaſtity, which being diametrically oppoſite to thoſe of Luſt, muſt have a directly contrary tendency, and muſt naturally conduce to the Welfare and Happineſs of all that have attained to it. It prevents the forementioned dreadful Evils, preſerves us from living like Beaſts in this World, and prepares us for the Enjoyment of Eternal Happineſs in the other. And it is therefore well worth all the Care, and Watchfulneſs, and Mortification, and Prayer, and Faſting we can uſe for acquiring it where it is wanting, or preſerving it where it is.

See what a high Eſteem the Patriarch *Joſeph* had of this Virtue, and how reſolved he was,

not

not to part with it on any terms! Whom, when a Captive in *Egypt*, neither his wanton Miftrefs, with all her own Charms, and moft earneft Solicitations, nor all the additional Motives that either Hope or Fear might fuggeft, could invite to defile himfelf with her. She offered herfelf firft, without putting him to the trouble of trying her; and this when he was in the Heat and Vigour of Youth, and fo the lefs likely to reject her Motion. And it was not a common Proftitute who thus accofted him, but a Woman of Credit and Reputation, as may be concluded from her Husband's readinefs to believe her groundlefs Accufation of innocent *Jofeph*, and to lay all the blame upon him. She was much his Superior in Quality, his Miftrefs, the Wife of *Potiphar*, an Officer of Character and Intereft in *Pharaoh's* Court, and a Captain of his Guards. And whether Beautiful or not we cannot know, fince the Scripture mentions nothing of it; yet confidering her Condition, It is reafonable to fuppofe her fet off with all the outward Ornaments that Art or Nature could afford for rendring her Amiable and Inviting. It is poffible alfo fhe might have tried other Methods of Enticing, as *Reuben* is made, (*a*) in the Teftament of the Twelve Patriarchs, to fay fhe did. But it is much rather to be depended upon, that her Intereft in her Husband might have been a likely means of advancing *Jofeph* to a higher

---

(*a*) Καὶ γὸ πολλὰ ἐποίησεν ἡ Αἰγυπλία, κ̀ μέγυς παρεκάλεσε, κ̀ φάρμακα αὐτῶ προσήνεγκε. Grab. Spicileg. Patr. Sect. I. p. 149.

Station, had he condefcended to comply with her. And no lefs, on the other hand, might it be prefumed that his Denial would prove, as in Fact it did, very much to his Difadvantage, and, for ought he knew, would terminate in his utter Ruine. Efpecially confidering the Diftance he was at from his Native Country and Relations, being fold a Slave into *Egypt*, and fo without that Countenance and Affiftance he might otherwife have expected upon any caufelefs Accufation. Befides, this was not a fingle Attempt, but often and eagerly repeated, to try if he could any way be wrought upon, to hearken at one time, to what he had rejected at others. And, laftly, to compleat all her Stratagems, fhe had at length found out a convenient Opportunity, when they were both alone, and no body in the Houfe to detect them, if he fhould comply, nor, on the other hand, to difprove her falfe Accufations upon his Refufal. Perhaps, never did more, and more inviting Circumftances conourr to fet off a Temptation to the beft advantage. And yet fuch an Apprehenfion had the religious Patriarch of this Sin, and he knew it to be fo difpleafing to Almighty God, and fo dangerous to himfelf, that he remained immoveable as a Rock, under all the Solicitations he met with, refolutely repelling the Temptrefs with this fhort but unanfwerable Expoftulation; *How can I do this great Wickednefs, and fin againft God?* Gen. xxxix. 9. And ver. 12. as *She caught him by his Garment, faying, Lie with me*; rather than yield to her unreafonable and luftful Defire, *he he left his Garment in her Hand, and fled, and got him out.* A noble Example of a Soul that was above the transitory Pleasures and Enjoyments of this present World, or whatever might defeat his Hopes and Expectations in the other! And no less convincing a Token is it of the clear Sense and Persuasion he had, that this was a grievous and a crying Sin, a Sin of a deep Dye, and whereby he should have been sure greatly to provoke Almighty God, and to bring down a severe Vengeance upon himself, if he had not kept upon his Guard against it.

What an intolerable Shame is it then for Christians, who have had Life and Immortality brought to light by the Gospel, have had their Duty, and the indispensable Obligation they are under to live in Purity and Holiness, fully displayed before them, and whom their Saviour has Redeemed with his own most Inestimable Blood : What an intolerable Shame, I say, is it for such not to retain a like invincible Reverence for *Chastity?* This is no more than our Lord requires of all his Disciples, no more than we all make Profession of, no more than we have solemnly vow'd and covenanted to perform ; and without which we can never hope to be Sav'd.

For God's sake therefore, and for their own sakes, both Souls and Bodies, let all who name the Name of CHRIST be mindful to depart from all Iniquity, and in particular from all Impurity. *Without Holiness, there is no seeing God,* Heb. xii. 14. And this none can have any pretence to, who leads an immoral and vicious Life. And all such therefore are very nearly

b 3   con-

concerned to bethink themselves, and to reform whatsoever is amiss in their Conversation ; and if they have indulged themselves in any sort of Uncleanness, a true Love, either of God or themselves, would direct them to recover themselves out of it with all the speed that may be.

It is related of the Philosopher *Democritus*, (*a*) That he put out his own Eyes, to avoid the Temptations of this Vice. This indeed is not required of Christians, but only to arm ourselves against those Temptations that either by the Sight, or any other way present themselves to our Minds ; that so whatsoever impure Inclinations arise at any time in our Hearts, may be immediately stifled, and may not be suffered to infect us, and draw us aside to the Satisfying of them. And if Persons will not do thus much to Save themselves, will not deny themselves, and mortifie the Flesh, and be continually upon their Watch, constantly and indefatigably begging also of God to assist their weak Endeavours, and preserve them in Chastity all their days, they must blame themselves only, if they be unhappy at present, and abundantly more so hereafter, to all Eternity.

(*a*) Tertul. Apol. c. 46. & Petav. de Rat. Temp. l. 3. b. 8.

The

The Author's
PREFACE.

Uncleanness *being a Shameful Sin, and of which it is trouble-some to discourse, I was for a long time unsatisfied, before I could bring myself to resolve upon the Publication of this Work. I observ'd it very difficult to treat of a Subject of such a Nature, with all the Exactness that is necessary. And I doubt not but others besides me have been with-held from it by the same Consideration, and that this is the principal Reason why so little has been written against this Vice.*

And yet perhaps there is no part of Christian Morality, whereupon there is more need of Writing than this. Uncleanness is one of those Vices that reign most generally. It cannot be denied, that there are amongst Chri-

stians

ſtians a great Number of Perſons, who abandon themſelves to the greateſt Exceſſes of this
Sin, and to whom, what St. Paul *affirmed* of
the Heathens, may *fitly be applied*, *That
being paſt feeling, they have given themſelves up to all ſorts of Pollution,* Epheſ.
iv. 19. *But howſoever there are very great
and very frequent Scandals given this way,
there is good reaſon to ſuppoſe that the
Number of Offenders* is much greater than
it appears; inaſmuch as they who commit this
Sin, ſtudy all they can to conceal it, and
often-times order the Matter ſo as no Man
can make the leaſt diſcovery of them. In
ſhort, There are Multitudes in the World,
who, though free from the Crimes of Impurity, are yet poſſeſſed by the diſorderly
Paſſions of the Fleſh, and defile themſelves
diverſe Ways, by Actions and Deſires contrary to Chaſtity. Whence it appears, that
this Sin is very common, and that it is high
time to oppoſe it.

But if a Man enquire, how it comes to
paſs, that this Vice reigns ſo in all Places:
It muſt be owned, that one of the chief
Cauſes of this Evil, is the ſcarcity of
Inſtructions

The PREFACE.

Instructions and Assistance in relation to it. It is certain, that did Persons rightly understand the Heinousness of this Sin, and the Reasons there are for refraining from it, if they would seriously call to mind those admirable Precepts of Purity, and the powerful Motives to Chastity which are offered by the Gospel, if they would make use of those so effectual Means, which the Gospel affords for conquering the Desires of the Flesh, and living Continently and Holily, Uncleanness would be much rarer than it is. But Christians are not ordinarily sufficiently informed of this Matter. In Sermons, it is treated of only in General. And there are few Books relating to it, whereby to supply the want of Oral Instructions ; insomuch that whilst there is plenty of wicked Books to promote Impurity, and the Number of them is every day encreasing, there is hardly any Tract to be met with for reclaiming Persons from so dangerous a Passion. This has been my long Observation, and has made me conclude, a Discourse against Uncleanness must needs be highly useful. I have also taken some Pains this way for divers Years; for the Edification of the
Church

The PREFACE.

Church where I serve ; yet I have never resolved till now to publish my Thoughts upon this Subject.

One thing I must beg leave to advertise those who shall read this Treatise, and which I beseech them to have always before their Eyes ; and that is, That the Case is by no means the same with the Matter I am treating of, and other Points of Morality. For in handling other Topicks, a Man may safely say whatever he thinks any way advantageous to his Design, and has nothing to hinder him from rallying together whatever he apprehends necessary, and proposing his Arguments in their utmost extent and force, making them as plain as possible, and answering all Difficulties relating to them. But in arguing against Uncleanness, the same Liberty is not to be taken, but a Man is extremely confined, and is obliged to express himself with Circumspection and Caution, for fear of intrenching upon Modesty. For which Cause, I have not been able to press my Reasonings so home as were to have been wished, nor to enforce my Proofs with that degree of Evidence they might other-

otherwise have had. Some Points should have been more enlarged upon, and some Objections more particularly confidered; but this would have neceffitated me to touch upon some things which Decency forbids. There are alfo divers things which I am obliged to exprefs only in general Terms, others which I dare but juft hint, and others again that I am forced totally to fupprefs. However, I make it my endeavour to fupply this Defect, inevitable in a Work of this nature, by the Principles I lay down; and I intreat my Readers alfo to help it on their part by their Attention and Reflections.

And whereas this Book may come into the hands of divers who are guilty of the Sin here condemned, I earneftly befeech and conjure fuch to confider ferioufly what I advance; and that whilft they are reading it, they will duly reflect upon their own Cafe, and will difengage themfelves from the Snares of Uncleannefs whilft they may. I beg thofe alfo who have not incurred this Guilt, and more particularly the Younger fort of them, may make a good Ufe of what they

meet

meet with here, and that it may be a Means of securing them against a Sin whose Consequences are so fatal, and which involves those that indulge themselves in it in the utmost Misfortunes.

THE

THE TABLE.

PART I.

Of UNCLEANNESS.

Chap. III.

The TABLE.

PART II.

Of CHASTITY.

The TABLE.

Hieronymus adverſus *Jovinianum,* lib. I.

Periclitamur Reſponſionis verecundiâ ; & quaſi inter duos ſcopulos, & quaſdam neceſſitatis & pudicitiæ Συμπληγαδες, hinc atque inde vel pudoris vel cauſæ naufragium ſuſti- nemus. Si ad propoſita reſpondeamus, pudore ſuffundimur. Si pudor imperârit ſilentium, quaſi de loco videmur cedere, & adverſario feriendi cauſam dare. Melius eſt tamen, clauſis, quod dicitur, oculis, Andabatarum more pugnare, quàm directa ſpicula clypeo non repellere Veritatis.

E R-

ERRATA

PAge xxii. Line 2. read *others* ; p. 16. l. 1. r. *The* ; p. 18. l. 35. for *will* r. *would* ; p. 24. l. 12. r. *Superscription* ; p. 47. l. 37. r. *that* ; p. 71. l. 32. r. *Ascendent* ; p. 84. l. 7. r. *of his* ; p. 96. l. 25. r. *Effects* ; p. 129. l. 7. dele *where* ; p. 153. l. 21. for *themselves* r. *him* ; p. 154. l. 2. for *I say*, r. *I answer* ; l. 15. r. *spiritual* ; p. 177. l. 37. r. *Objects* ; p. 189. l. 23. r. *any one* ; p. 190. l. 10. after *governs* add (,) a Comma ; p. 220. l. 10. r. *that* ; p. 249. l. 24 & 25. dele *to* ; p. 253. l. ult. r. ἀγωνιζόμεθα ; p. 261. l. 38. r. *Sicknesses* ; p. 264. l. 13. r. *Assistance* ; p. 270. l. 13. dele *as*.

CH

A

A
DISCOURSE
CONCERNING
UNCLEANNESS
And in behalf of
CHASTITY.

PART I.
Of UNCLEANNESS.

SECT. I.

That Uncleanness is a Sin.

IT being necessary in the beginning of this Treatise to shew that Uncleanness is a Sin, I shall therefore apply my self in the first place to prove this concerning Uncleanness in general, in the second place with respect to Adultery, and thirdly with regard to those other

B

Species

Species of it which may at any time be committed, in Deed, in Word, or in Thought. And because there are two different Ways to discover,
whether any thing be sinful; the one, when it is
condemn'd by the Light of Nature and Reason;
the other, when it is forbidden by those Laws
which Almighty God has delivered to Mankind
in his written Word: I shall make it appear from
each of these, that Uncleanness is so, and therefore utterly unlawful. And to this end it will be
requisite to enquire first, what Nature and Right
Reason teach as to this Point, and then what is
the Doctrine of Scripture concerning it.

CHAP. I.

Considerations from Nature.

THough the Proofs that may be alledged from
the holy Scriptures are enough to perswade
all such as own the Truth of the Christian Religion, and are abundantly more cogent and convincing, than any that can be brought from the
Dictates of Nature, it will however be most proper to begin with these latter, whereby to make it
evident that what Revelation teaches concerning
Uncleanness, has an exact Agreement with Right
Reason. And here divers Reflections readily present themselves, which to all that shall calmly
and impartially consider them, will appear highly
just, admirably well suiting with the Nature of
Man, and manifestly tending to the Good of Society.

I. This therefore I lay down as a Principle,
That Mankind ought to have some Rule in their
Search

Search after, and Ufage of whatfoever is pleafing to Flefh and Senfe, and that we are not always to attend to our own Paffions, and follow their Motions. For every one muft neceffarily acknowledge, either that we ought all to be left entirely to our own Management, or elfe that we muft have fome Rules given us for the better Government of our Lives. If it be pretended that we are to be left to our felves, this is to degrade us into the Rank of Beafts, which, for want of Reafon to direct them better, blindly and impetuoufly purfue their own natural Inftinct. And this were in truth a meer brutifh Notion, unworthy of a Rational Creature, and which would go a great way towards abolifhing all that is wont to be ftiled either Vice or Virtue. Even the Nature of Man fhews that he ought to regulate his Defires, and that all things are not permitted and allowed him. His own Reafon and Judgment will enable him to difcover what is for his own Advantage, and to diftinguifh what he is to do, and what to refrain from. Befides that he has it in his Power to keep under his Paffions, his Conftitution being fuch, that they cannot carry him afide without his own Concurrence, but he finds it in his own Choice, either to follow, or refift them ; and that by confequence he is bound to make a right ufe of his difcerning Faculties, and the Power that God has given him. Nor can any deliver themfelves up to the Government of their Paffions, without infinite Mifchief to themfelves, and occafioning all forts of Diforder in the World, and producing much greater Confufion amongft Men than is to be feen in the very Brutes, which being determined by a fecret Inftinct, are hereby contained within their certain Bounds, and never arrive at the Exceffes of thofe Perfons, who inordinately abufe their Reafon and Phancy, to fearch

and

and find out means of ſatisfying their unreaſonable Paſſions, and are continually under the ſole Conduct of their own extravagant Humour. But this is more eſpecially to be feared, in reſpect to the Luſt of Uncleanneſs, as being a Paſſion that is too often obſerved, to hurry People on to the fouleſt Extravagances. Whence it clearly follows, that we are not left entirely to our own Liberty, but that Care muſt be taken to govern and regulate our Deſires, and keep them within their proper Limits.

And if you would know what are the proper Limits and Rules to be obſerved in this Caſe, do but ſeriouſly conſider a while with your ſelves, and you will preſently be convinced, that there is no more effectual Remedy to be preſcribed than Marriage. No other ſure Direction can be given beſides this, nor any ſo proper means of ordering things aright, and preventing the terrible Effects of Incontinence. Take away this one Barrier, and let Allowance be given to Impurity, and immediately there will be an end of all Rule and Order. Nothing would be able to put a ſtop to the Licentiouſneſs and Extravagances that would hereby break in upon us, but all other Bounds that might be fixed would forthwith be broken down. Wherefore the true and only Means of regulating Mankind, and maintaining an innocent Converſation amongſt them, is to reſtrain them by Marriage, and leave them ſubject in other reſpects to the Laws of Chaſtity: As will farther appear by what follows.

II. My ſecond Argument ſhall be taken from the Advantages and Excellence of Marriage. On which whenſoever we ſeriouſly and attentively fix our Meditations, we cannot ſufficiently admire the Wiſdom of our great Creator, in the Proviſion he has thus made for the Preſervation of

Man-

Mankind. And accordingly it might administer occasion for divers Reflections, That Almighty God, who could have peopled the World, by only commanding Men to be, as he did our first Parent *Adam*, would choose rather to have them propagated by the ordinary way of Generation; and to that end created them at the beginning both Male and Female, and ordained a strict Union between them. But it not being to my purpose to enter at present upon these several Considerations, I shall content my self only to observe, That this was a sensible Demonstration, that the Almighty would take this Method, to lay a sure Foundation of Society, and the Happiness of Mankind. It is plain he design'd hereby to establish a most intimate Union of Parents betwixt themselves, and with their Children; and that the Ordinance of Marriage is the best way to promote the Happiness of Families, and by consequence of larger Societies. This State was requisite for the Good of Mankind, for their mutual Comfort and Satisfaction, for the Education of Children, and for the Preservation of Order and Quiet in the World. Moreover the Laws of Marriage, at least very often, prevent their having Children as long as they live, and in too great Numbers, each of which would be a great Obstruction to their good Education. Neither, were it not for this, would People be so concern'd, as they now ordinarily shew themselves to be, for the Good of the Publick and for Posterity. It ought also to be consider'd, That seeing Men are endued with Reason, and have a Sense of Virtue, it is therefore of great Importance to them to choose such a State of Life as may repress the Violence of a most dangerous Passion, and which has most mischievous Consequences attending it; which State can be no other than that

of

of Matrimony. All theſe Conſiderations, together with ſeveral other that might be added to them, make it very clear, that Marriage is an Inſtitution moſt beneficial to Mankind, and every way worthy of the immenſe Goodneſs, and infinite Wiſdom of God. And that it is an Ordinance every way ſuitable to the Nature of Man, and of abſolute Neceſſity, appears from this, That it has been every where received, and its Neceſſity has been ſo much the more freely own'd, and its Laws ſo much the more carefully obey'd, by how much the better inſtructed, and the more civilized any People have been.

But now Uncleanneſs has a neceſſary Tendency to ſubvert this ſo happy Inſtitution, and ſo ſingularly advantageous to Mankind. Inſomuch that if this Vice were once look'd upon as an indifferent matter, many Perſons would not marry at all, becauſe of ſome Troubles and Inconveniences that are incident to the Married State ; and even the greateſt Part of thoſe that ſhould marry, would neither be able to live in Unity, Satisfaction, and Peace, nor would love their Children, nor take that Care of them, which is incumbent upon all Parents. So that whereſoever Luſt prevails to the Contempt of Marriage, (which, as I have already obſerved, is a moſt neceſſary Ordinance, in order to the Welfare of Mankind, and is the Foundation of all Societies) ſeeing it hereby diſſolves the Bonds and Relations, that are wont to unite Perſons moſt firmly to each other, it is manifeſtly wicked and unlawful, and would be a means of introducing all ſorts of Crimes, and Miſchiefs into the World. In ſhort, as there is no Harm in keeping to the Laws of Marriage, and obſerving them exactly, this being only to live conformably to Reaſon and Virtue ; ſo, on the other hand, the Evils ariſing from the Abolition of these Laws, and the Allowance of inordinate Lusts would be unavoidable and endless.

III. Uncleanness is contrary to the most inviolable Laws of Justice, and that Order which must be preserved in Society. For if there be any one Principle of natural Justice that is certain and indisputable, it is this, That every one should be allowed a Subsistence; and especially that Children are to be provided for and brought up. To doubt of this is to shew our selves unnatural and worse than Beasts. Children we all know are born in a very feeble Condition, and have for a long time such need of Support, that were they left to themselves, they must all be lost. And hence it is most highly necessary, that there should be some others to take care of them. But of whom can this be required? Nature it self teaches that there are none under such Obligation to it, as those who brought them into the World. The Milk wherewith Mothers are naturally furnished, testifies them to be in an especial manner determin'd by the Law of the Creator, to suckle their little ones. Nor are the Fathers less concerned to take care of them. Neither can the Mothers make due Provision for their Maintenance and Education, without the Father's Assistance.

But then to the end that both Fathers and Mothers may apply themselves to nourish and bring up their Children, it is requisite they should know them, and that their Birth should be such as they may securely depend upon; besides the divers weighty Reasons there are, why this should likewise be known in the Society whereinto they are born. Parents ought too after this to have a natural Tenderness and Affection to their Children, whereby to incline them to the greater care of them. This Love is a principal, and original

Cause,

Caufe, not only of all the Good that Fathers do
to their Children, but alfo of innumerable other
matters, moft beneficial to Society, in which Men
now engage, but which they would never engage
in, if a paternal Kindnefs did not put them upon
it. Again, it is moft proper for Fathers and Mothers to live together, that they may jointly take
care of their Children, and may have them near
at hand upon all occafions. Moreover they fhould
have Time and Means for nourifhing and breed-
ing them up; upon which account it would be
very inconvenient to have them in too great
number. All this is perfectly agreeable to Reafon
and Juftice; but withal I muft add, That all this
can never be effected any other way than by Marriage.

The Permiffion of Uncleannefs would fubvert
thefe natural, and neceffary Laws. Fathers would
frequently not know their own Offspring; and
would have no means of being affured that any
of them were really their own. And both Fathers and Mothers would be at a lofs as to the
Method of bringing them up; partly for want
of being Members of the fame Family, and fo
not living together with them; partly becaufe
there would be too many for them; and again
for other Reafons eafily difcernible. Uncleannefs
has a confiderable Influence upon Paternal Affection, and if it doth not wholly extinguifh it, it
however greatly weakens it; and tempts both Parents, but more efpecially the Fathers, to abandon their Children, and fo as much as in them
lies to become their Murderers. And fo the Confequence would be, that their Children being
neglected and ill educated, would not only become unhappy during their whole Lives, but
would caufe a thoufand Diforders to the Publick.
If any one defire to be fatisfied, that thefe would
be

be the natural Effects of Uncleanness, he need only recollect how it far'd among the Heathens, with whom this Vice was fo cuftomary. In fome places their Infants were expofed, as foon as born, and vaft Numbers of them perifhed. In fome places Parents looked upon themfelves as having a Right of putting them to death. And others fold them ; which was one Caufe of the prodigious Multitudes of Slaves, that were in thofe times. All thefe horrible Enormities, which Chriftian Religion has extirpated out of the World, would immediately return, if Impurity were again taken for an indifferent matter.

I know not what can be replied to thefe Affertions, unlefs it be, That in truth thefe Diforders would be found, if Men entirely abandoned themfelves to Senfuality ; but that no fuch Mifchiefs are to be feared, fo long as they contain themfelves within certain Rules. But here I demand again ; What Rules and Bounds fhould they have fet them ? And how could thefe forementioned Inconveniences be prevented, otherwife than by the Help of Marriage ? Poffibly it may be faid, Children might be nourifhed and brought up, though not born in Marriage, provided thofe, who brought them into the World, would agree together to take care of them. Whereto I anfwer firft, Howfoever fome might do this, it will be impoffible to expect that all fhould ; as is eafy to infer from what has been already faid. I fay further, That thefe People could never be fo well affured of the Condition and Birth of their Children ; nor would find themfelves under fuch powerful Obligations to love them, as in Marriage. And yet once more ; Either it is pretended that thofe Fathers and Mothers, who fhould have enter'd into Compact, to take care of their Children, might be again difcharged of their Obliga-

                                                    tion,

tion, to the intent they might place their Care upon others, or it is not pretended. If it be admitted that they ought to be difcharged, this were to open a Paffage for all thofe fame Mifchiefs, which I have been juft now mentioning, to break in upon us. If it be faid, they may not be releafed, and that they muft remain faithful to each other, I affirm that they have hereby in a manner fubjected themfelves to the Laws of Marriage. And fo thofe who have recourfe to this kind of Evafion, confirm, inftead of confuting, the Truth I have been maintaining, returning to the Inftitution of Matrimony before they are aware of it; and without confidering where they are, they acknowledge the Reafonablenefs and Neceffity of it.

IV. If it be a true and natural Principle, that Parents are to love their Children, and take care of them, is is no whit lefs reafonable for Children to love and honour thofe from whom they have received their Life, to obey them, to comfort them, and to affift them in time of Age, of Sicknefs, or of Want. Thefe have always been efteem'd facred and inviolable Duties. But as little as People think of it, it is very apparent, that if Uncleannefs were allow'd of, Children would not know how to anfwer their Obligation in thefe Points. An infinite Number of them would not fo much as know their own Fathers, not to fay that they would not dwell in the fame Neighbourhood with them. They would not be fenfible of the fame Motives to love and affift them. Nor would they at all take themfelves to be under the fame Obligations with thofe, who being born in Marriage, pafs generally the better part of their Lives together with their Fathers and Mothers, and are indebted to them for the chief part of whatfoever Advantages

they

they enjoy, and have frequent occasion of making Returns to them upon account of what they are thus indebted for.

V. Another Consideration which shews how Men are naturally obliged to keep to the Laws of Marriage, and to abstain from all Uncleanness, is the Proportion that is ordinarily observable between the two Sexes. Which being a powerful Argument against Polygamy, and all kind of Uncleanness, it therefore deserves to be the more particularly attended to. The Holy Scripture informs us that God created at the first one Man and one Woman. And daily Experience shews that the same Method is still continued amongst all that are born into the World. It is not one of the least surprizing Instances of Providence, that such an Equality is preserved in relation to the two Sexes, that their Number is yet alike, and there are to this Day as many Men as Women. The Fact is certain; Enquiry has been made, and it has been found that there is very little difference betwixt the Births of both Sexes; and that if at any time there have been born a few more Men than Women, or a few more Women than Men, the Disparity has proved so small as not to be worth speaking of. And he must put out his Eyes, who will not see that this Proportion and Equality is the Effect of an admirable Wisdom, and could not have been so ordered but by a particular Providence. And hence it clearly follows, That the Author of Nature has determined to provide for the Preservation of Mankind by the help of Marriage; and that Marriage is to be, not of one Husband with many Wives, nor of one Woman with many Husbands, but of One and One. And so it is easily to be observed, That Uncleanness is inconsistent with this Order of Nature, and that Proportion there is between

the

the two Sexes, and that the only allowable Courſe in this Caſe is Marriage. Nor is there any departing from this Rule, ſo plainly marked out by Nature, without introducing a thouſand dreadful Extravagances, and Mens falling into Adultery, and other more abominable Crimes not fit to be named : As is to be ſeen whereſoever Polygamy, and other Inſtances of Uncleanneſs prevail.

There is no room for pleading upon this Occaſion, That a great many Men are taken off by War ; becauſe our preſent Buſineſs is to obſerve things as they are in their own Natural State. Our Bleſſed Saviour *Jeſus Chriſt* has taught us, in the nineteenth Chapter of St. *Matthew*, that without regarding the Irregularities which the Corruptions of Men may have introduced in relation to Marriage, recourſe muſt be had to the firſt beginning of things, and the Creator's Original Inſtitution muſt be kept to : Which I am ſure is a Doctrine no Chriſtian can poſſibly diſpute ; and which beſides is exactly agreeable to Reaſon. God did not make Men to deſtroy one another. Nor can it ever be proved that Men may make new Laws to themſelves, may change that Order which God had eſtabliſhed at the beginning, and may wander from thoſe Rules which even Nature has appointed, under pretence, that through the Wickedneſs of Men, at ſome certain times, and in ſome certain places Wars have ariſen, and other Diſturbances, contrary to the Order of Nature. Many other Conſiderations might farther be added upon this Subject, were it neceſſary ; but what has been already ſaid is enough to ſatisfy any reaſonable Man.

VI. It is a good Proof of any Duty's being conſonant to the Law of Nature, if it can be ſhewn that Mankind have in all Ages given their Judgment in favour of it. But now if it be asked,

asked, What Sentiments the World has ever had concerning this Sin of Uncleanness, thefe two Particulars can no way be denied.

Firft, That even amongft the Pagans this Vice could not pafs without a Note of Infamy and Difgrace. It is ordinarily taken for granted, that they looked upon Fornication as of an indifferent nature, and that it was accordingly allow'd amongft them. But this cannot be affirmed of all without diftinction, as if there were none of them who had not this Notion of it. There is no doubt to be made but many of them were of this Opinion, as appears from the Writings of feveral of their own Authors. And who knows not that their Practice was accordingly, and that thefe Idolatrous People were extreamly lafcivious, and addicted to the gratifying their Lufts? And it is no great matter of Surprize that they were fo, confidering the ftate of Ignorance and Corruption in which they lived, upon all other accounts. Yet it is not true that Uncleannefs was generally reputed indifferent amongft them ; it being very unjuft to fix the Opinions of fome licentious Poets upon them, as the common Sentiment of them all. There is no Difficulty at all in proving from the Teftimony of their own Writers, that not only Adultery, but fimple Fornication too, went under the Character of a wicked Practice, and no way reconcileable to Honour and Virtue. This is evident from the Sayings of divers of their wifer Authors, from the Laws that from time to time were made amongft them in favour of Marriage, from what fome of them have written of Modefty and Decency of Behaviour, from the Praifes they gave to thefe Virtues, from divers very remarkable Examples of Chaftity and Continence which occur in their Hiftories, from the ill Opinion they fhew'd themfelves to have of the Incontinent,

from

from the Care such took to conceal their Miscarriages of this nature, and from several other Considerations. They accounted it a great Mark of Reproach for unmarried Persons to be thus familiar with each other. So that I cannot see how it can be said that the Generality of the Heathens imagin'd Fornication to be naturally so very indifferent, as many have supposed concerning them. Almighty God, who wou'd not suffer the Principles of Religion and Virtue to be utterly extinguished amongst these poor ignorant People, preserved some Notion of Chastity in them, as well as of divers other Duties.

The *Second* thing which I desire to be consider'd in behalf of what I have asserted, is, the Sense of Shame and Modesty that so naturally appears in all who are not become more like Brutes than Men, and the Reservedness whereto it invites them. I grant Education has a great Influence upon Persons, and makes them more or less circumspect as to the manner of their Conversation, and some have attained to such a Measure of Assurance, that Bashfulness and Modesty make very faint Impressions upon them, and indeed are almost entirely banished from amongst them. But then, there are possibly no Men in the World, who have not some small Remainders of Shame and Modesty left in them. Yet granting any such can be found, it will by no means follow from hence that Modesty and Chastity are only an empty Name, and that no regard is to be had to them. There are some People and Countries, where Robbery passes with Impunity, where Fathers expose, abandon, and sell their Children, where Man's Flesh is fed upon, and where no notice is taken of those several Laws of Justice, which other Nations esteem inviolable, and whereon depends the Happiness and Peace of all Civil Society.

ciety. Is this a Reason therefore to conclude that these Laws are surely arbitrary, and not rather of perpetual Obligation? It is no less than the utmost height of Folly, to judge of the nature of things, and particularly to conclude what is Just and Unjust, by the Notions of the most brutish of all Mankind; and so pretend to govern the World by the Sentiments of the lesser Part, and who make the vilest Figure in it, and have in a manner divested themselves of their Reason and Humanity. And common Prudence therefore would direct on the contrary, in this as well as all other Cases, to prefer the general Consent of such as strictly follow the Dictates of their Reason. Now it is always to be observed, that the more cultivated any People are, and the more improved in their Understanding, they feel themselves under the more indissoluble Obligation, from the Laws of Decency and an inoffensive Conversation.

And no wonder therefore that we see the Apostles of our Lord in their Writings combating Uncleanness with this same Argument taken from the known Necessity of a modest and reserv'd Deportment. St. *Paul* affirms, *Ephes.* 5. 12. that *It is a shame to speak of those things which the Heathens did in secret.* And *Chap.* 4. 19. that *Being past feeling, hardened in their Wickedness, and so not sensible of the Evil of their doings, they had given themselves over unto Lasciviousness, to work all Uncleanness with Greediness.* This *Feeling* therefore or Sense, which the Apostle here speaks of, can be none other, than the Sense of Modesty and Shame, which many among the Gentiles had almost totally lost.

I conclude then from the Reasons hitherto proposed, That if we consult only the Light of Nature and Right Reason, this alone will supply us with considerable Arguments against Uncleanness, the

the Evil of which Vice I proceed next to ſhew from the Holy Scriptures. And I ſhall begin with thoſe Proofs of it which we meet with in the Old Teſtament; and afterwards ſhall deſcend to thoſe which we cannot but obſerve in the New.

CHAP. II.

Proofs taken from the Old Teſtament.

1. THE firſt Proof that the Books of the Old Teſtament afford to our purpoſe, is the Inſtitution of Marriage. And though I have already obſerved it, I muſt in this place again take notice that the ſacred Writings teach this Eſtate to have been eſtabliſhed by God †, at the firſt beginning of the World. And being thus of Divine Inſtitution, it ought to be accounted ſo much the more inviolable and ſacred. And that it was inſtituted immediately upon the Creation, is a very good Evidence that the Almighty did not deſign Mankind to be preſerved, and the World to be peopled any other way than by Marriage. In ſaying that *the Man ſhould cleave to his Wife, and they two ſhould be one Fleſh,* he lets us ſee it was by no means his Intention that Perſons ſhould go aſtray from this Law, and abandon themſelves to Senſuality and Incontinence. No, his Deſign was to confine them to a certain Order, and certain Rules. It is alſo to be remember'd that Marriage was inſtituted before the Fall; and if it were needful in the ſtate of Innocency, it is much more ſo now that Man's corrupt and ſinful Nature is ſo ſadly prone to Senſuality and all kind of Wickedneſs; and whoſe Condition now more
eſpe-

† Gen. 2. 24.

especially calls for Reftraint and Government. I add, that God has enacted divers particular Statutes, for rendring this firft Inftitution yet more inviolable ; Marriage being one of thofe things, about which God gave the *Jews* the greateft number of Injunctions. And by confequence whatfoever is contrary to the Inftitution of Matrimony, is unlawful.

It may perhaps be objected that Polygamy and Divorce were common among the *Jews,* which fhews they were not ftrictly tied to the Laws of Marriage, as is pretended. But to this our Bleffed Saviour returns anfwer, † That thefe Irregularities were tolerated amongft that People, not because Almighty God approved of them, but only by reafon of *the Hardnefs of their Hearts.* As to Divorce he declares, that as it was ufed amongft them, it was contrary to God's firft Inftitution, and *at the beginning it was not fo,* and neither fhould it be for the future, but things fhould be refetled amongft his Difciples, in their own Original Eftate, wherein they ought to be, and as God had of old appointed them at the time of the Creation. Thus you fee that Jefus Chrift has not given new Laws concerning Marriage, but thofe which the Gofpel impofes are precifely the fame with thofe that had been before ordained from the beginning of the World.

† St. Mat. 19. 8, 9.

2. But this is not all : For there are divers Paffages in the Books of *Mofes,* where Uncleannefs is plainly condemned. God commands, *Deut.* 23. 17. that there be *no Whore of the Houfe of Ifrael, nor a Whoremonger of the Sons of Ifrael.* It is true the chief Defign of this Law was to prevent their having any Proftitutes among them, as there had been amongft the Idolatrous Nations. Neverthelefs it may fairly be concluded from hence, that Uncleannefs in general is forbidden, and that

C

For-

Fornication is undoubtedly a Sin; becaufe if this were allowed of, it will be hard to give a good Reafon, why Proftitution fhould be a Crime. It is certain likewife that God gave this Law becaufe of the Danger the *Ifraelites* were in of being tempted to commit Idolatry, by means of Uncleannefs, left they fhould follow the Example of the Idolatrous Nations, with whom Proftitution was wont to accompany the Service of their Idols. But this was not the only Reafon of the Law. And that God condemned Impurity not only when joined with Proftitution and Idolatry, but becaufe it is evil in its Nature, appears, befides what has been already faid to prove it, becaufe he forbids it, out of the Cafe of Proftitution, and where there is no Danger of Idolatry. As will be fhewn more fully in the Sequel of this Difcourfe.

3. Levit. 21. 9. *The Daughter of any Prieft, if fhe profane her felf by playing the whore, fhe profaneth her Father, fhe fhall be burnt with fire.* This Law particularly relates to the Prieft's Daughters, in as much as other Women were not obnoxious to the fame Penalty. And there are thefe two Reafons why it does fo. The one, becaufe God requires a fingular Degree of Purity in the Minifters of Religion, and that whatfoever relates to them fhould be holy. The other, becaufe God would fecure the Family of the Priefts, and the Places of Divine Service, from any fuch Abominations as were too ufual in the Idol-Temples, and in the Families of the Idolatrous Priefts. But ftill this Law fuppofes that Fornication is a Sin. For not to infift upon it, that it is not conceivable that God will have threatned the Penalty of Death for what had no where been forbidden, and which was of an indifferent nature, the Terms of the Law, and the Reafon God affigns of it, deferve

to

to be serioufly attended to. God commands the
Prieft's Daughter that fhall be convict of Uncleanneſs, in whatſoever manner fhe fhall have
committed it, and though fhe have never been
chargeable with either Proftitution, or Idolatry, to
be put to death. And the Reaſon he gives of this
Law is, becauſe *this Daughter is both defiled her felf,
and has diſhonoured her Father ;* which implies that
Fornication is both a Defilement, a thing un-
feemly and wicked in its felf, and by Confequence that this is not one of thoſe poſitive
Laws, which are founded only on the good Pleaſure of God.

4. Which Doctrine is farther confirm'd by God's
not only condemning Incontinence in the Priefts
Daughters, but in all other Women too. He de-
crees, *Deut.* 22. 19. That if a Man accuſed a Woman whom he had eſpouſed, of having misbeha-
ved her felf before her Marriage, he fhould be
obliged in caſe he did it wrongfully, to pay a
Sum of Money to her Father. And pray obſerve
the Reaſon of this Appointment, *Becauſe he has
brought an evil Report upon a Virgin of Iſrael,* as much
as to ſay, he has diſgrac'd her by charging her
with ſo infamous a Fault. Where it is manifeftly ſuppoſed, that Uncleanneſs, without Proftitution and Idolatry, is a matter of Infamy and
Guilt. But if the Husband could make good his
Charge againſt her, the Woman was forthwith
ftoned at her own Father's Door. No doubt God
Almighty order'd this Puniſhment to be inflicted;
becauſe of the Injury hereby done to the Huſ-
band. But then it is to be noted, That had fhe
in reality done no Evil, and her ſimple Fornication were no Sin, the Husband would have had
no juft Cauſe of Complaint againſt her, becauſe
fhe had then done nothing but what fhe lawfully
might do. And if this were the Caſe, it is not to

be

be conceived, that God would have subjected her to so severe a Punishment. And it cannot therefore be questioned but the Women against whom this Law was made, were guilty of Sin. The Terms of the Law are very express, *v.* 20. *She shall be stoned because she hath wrought Folly in Israel, to play the whore in her Father's house;* and so are an undeniable Condemnation of simple Fornication. For here is not a word of Uncleanness as accompanied with Prostitution or Idolatry, or as it is committed by a Person already betrothed, but only of a Woman not yet betrothed, and in her Father's House, who has fallen into Sin there, and possibly but into one Act of it. The Sin thus committed, you see, is called Fornication, and Folly, and is said to be shameful, and not fit to be seen in *Israel.* Which shews that this Law and all others which God has enacted against Incontinence, suppose the Baseness and Sinfulness of it. It is clear that God would have all who are unmarried to live chastly, and that all who did otherwise acted contrary to that Virtue and Holiness, which he had required of the People of *Israel.* And yet there is one Circumstance more to be observed, That Offenders against this Law were to be *stoned at their Father's Door.* Which being some sort of Punishment to their Fathers, would lay an Obligation upon them to attend the more carefully to the Conduct of their Children : Which is one of those Arguments I might have taken occasion to enlarge upon, but that my present Design will not admit of it.

5. In the same Chapter, *v.* 28, 29. God commands that whosoever should have abused *a Damsel that was a Virgin,* should pay a Sum of Money to her Father, and should be made to marry her, *whom he had humbled,* defiled, and disgraced. Which could not be, unless Impurity were disgraceful

graceful and opprobrious. And here it is especially to be noted, That that Man should never be at liberty to put away the Woman whom he had thus disgraced.

6. There are several particular Laws in the Books of *Moses* relating to Uncleanness, and which were intended to keep the *Jews* at a distance, not only from this Sin, but from all Approaches to it ; and so to dispose them to Purity and Chastity. By which Laws we are taught that it is not only the grosser Act that defiles, but there are divers Tendencies to it that in some degree produce the same effect. *Moses* speaks of divers Species of Pollution, all which the *Jews* were commanded to beware of, and for which several sorts of Purifications were prescribed. But seeing these Laws are such as I cannot well recite in this place, and cannot therefore make my Observations upon, I only point at them in two Words, though I might draw very forcible Arguments from them to prove that God's Design in them was to oblige the *Jews* to live in Purity.

7. Lastly, It is past doubt that the Sin we are now treating of always passed amongst the *Jews* for unlawful ; as might be evinced from many historical Occurrences in the Old Testament, too long to be here recited, but which fully prove that they constantly affixed a Note of Infamy upon it. This appears also by the Writings of *Josephus* and *Philo*, both which speak so honourably of *Moses*'s Law, and particularly with regard to Chastity and Continence. I might also alledge to this purpose divers Passages of the *Rabbi's*, and divers Laws and Customs of that Nation, obliging the younger sort to Chastity; and particularly directing the young Women to be retired, and live in great Purity. But this would be too tedious a Task. And I think it enough to have alledged

the

the Principal of thofe Proofs which the Old Teftament furnifhes us with upon this Subject.

If now we pafs on to the New Teftament, this
will give yet more Light to the Caufe in hand.
Both the Gofpels and the Epiftles contain fuch
clear Inftructions, and fo many and fuch exprefs
Laws againft Uncleannefs, that it is impoffible for
fuch who believe thefe facred Writings, and read
them with any manner of Attention, to retain
the leaft Doubt of it. I fhall firft mention fome
general Confiderations, before I proceed to thofe
others which are more particular.

C H A P. III.

Some General Observations from the New Testament.

I Shall firft propofe fome General Confiderations arifing from the Chriftian Doctrine and
Religion, to let you fee with what fingular Care
and Diligence all ought to watch againft this
Sin.

1. Now it is certain the Gofpel does not lefs infift upon this Point than the Law; and feeing
Chriftians have received a far greater meafure of
Light and Grace than the *Jews,* they are to be fo
much the more cautious of all Defilement of this
nature. Wherefore having already feen that the
Law of *Mofes* formally condemns all Uncleannefs,
and as well in Single as Married Perfons, and enjoyns Chaftity to all forts of People, there is no
pretending that the contrary Liberty is not prohi-
bited to all Chriftians. It is much lefs excufable
in us: For notwithftanding God required an unfeigned

feigned Holiness of the *Jews*, and permitted them
no Lusts of the Flesh, there were some Irregularities however tolerated amongst them. But *Jesus*
Christ † has declared, as has already been noted, †S. Matt.
that it should not be so in the Christian Church, 19. 8, 9.
and that his Disciples should hold themselves obliged, inviolably to observe the strictest Laws of
Chastity, and more particularly those which had
been enacted in respect to Marriage, immediately
upon the Creation of the World. And here the
Reader may please to observe after what manner
our Blessed Lord explains that Commandment,
Thou shalt not commit Adultery, St. *Matth*. 5. 27, 28.
and how much farther he carries the Doctrine of
Chastity than had been usual with the Jewish Do-
ctors. Whereby he plainly gives us to understand,
that his Purpose was to oblige his Followers to a
singular degree of Chastity, and that if the contrary Practices were forbidden under the Jewish
Law, they are now much more so under the
Gospel.

2. This first Consideration will appear of the
more force, if we take notice in the next place,
that the Gospel condemns whatever tends to promote Sensuality and the Gratification of the Flesh,
and ties the Heart too close to the World and its
Enjoyments. This is the true Spirit of the Gospel,
and the principal Aim of the Christian Religion.
The great and prime Lesson of our Saviour is † *to* †S. Matt.
*deny our selves and * all worldly Lusts*. And as ever 16. 24.
any would advance in Piety and the Love of God, *Tit. 2.12.
they must be sure to mortify their Carnal Inclinations, to keep under their Bodies, and get the
Mastery over their unreasonable and unruly Pas-
sions. It is St. *John's* Assertion, that † *If any Man* 1 Ep. 2.15.
love the World, the Love of the Father is not in him.
And among those things which incline the Heart
to the World, and obstruct the Love of God, this

Apostle

* *v.* 16. Apoftle names in the firft place * *the Luft of the Flefh* ; becaufe this Paffion is moft common, and moft violent, and Men are wont to be fondeft of Corporal Pleafures. The Motions of this Paffion are fo powerful in thofe who have not duly labour'd to fubdue it, its Enticements are fo bewitching, its Returns fo frequent, that thofe who indulge it quickly become its Slaves, and it banifhes the Love of God from their Hearts, together with the Defire of Spiritual and Heavenly things. This is the Reafon that they who are addicted to fenfual Pleafures, are not in a condition to tafte of thofe Spiritual Joys which Religion and Piety fet before them ; or to delight themfelves with the Love of God, and Communion with him. For this Caufe the Gofpel fo effectually recommends Temperance, and requires to be modeft in the Defire and Ufe of lawful things, and enjoins Abftinence, Fafting, and Mortification. Which is much more than fimply forbidding the Sins of Impurity. All thefe Doctrines aim at rendring us Chaft and Pure, to prevent our giving up our felves to the Love of the Creatures, and becoming Slaves to Pleafure. And they are of abfolute neceffity, to keep us from being feduced by the Flefh, and to beget the Love of God in us, and put us upon feeking after the Joys of Heaven. This is the Foundation, and the Epitomy of all Chriftian Morality. And he that has throughly learned thefe Principles, will eafily perceive, that if there be any Duty neceffary in Religion, it is Chaftity ; and if there be any Paffion againft which Chriftians are diligently to guard themfelves, it is Uncleannefs.

3. And this brings me to a Third General Confideration, and which is uncontestable. It is that the Purity to which Chriftians are called by the Gofpel is fo extenfive, as to reach even to their

Words,

Words, to their Looks, and to their Thoughts.
They are to *flee all Appearance of Evil*, and whatfoever may expofe them to it ; are to reprefs the
firft Motions of Luft, and to mortify their own
Inclinations even in relation to things in their
own Nature Allowable and Indifferent.   All thofe
Duties are undoubtedly eftablifhed, by the Declarations of our Lord and his Apoftles.   And can
any now in the leaft queftion what Character Uncleannefs deferves ?   Is it poffible that Fornication
can be thought no Sin in a Chriftian, when an obfcene Word is fo, when a bare Caft of the Eye attended with a luftful Defire is by no means to be ex-
cufed, when it is a Sin to cherifh and encourage
impure Thoughts in the Mind, when there may
be Sin in the Ufe of Lawful things ?   Had People rightly underftood thefe Maxims, had they
well confidered the Spirit of the Gofpel, and the
Genius of the Chriftian Religion, there would
have been no need to infift upon thefe Truths,
or to be put to the trouble of proving Uncleannefs to be a Sin.   But the Generality live in a
fhameful and ftupid Ignorance in this refpect ;
and have no tolerable Notion of Holinefs and
Chriftian Perfection.   And fo there is no reafon
to be furprifed at their having fuch loofe Sentiments concerning Uncleannefs.

4. When the Gofpel enjoins Chaftity, it enjoins it to all forts of Perfons, and in all Condi-
tions.   As may be obferved throughout the New
Teftament.   St. *James* fays the true Religion, and
which alone renders us acceptable in the fight of
God, † *is to keep our felves pure and unfpotted from the* † S. Ja. 1.
World.   And St. *Paul,* fpeaking of the Luft of Un- 27.
cleannefs, exprefly affirms * this to be *the Will of* * 1 Theff.
God, even our Sanctification, that ye fhould abftain 4. 3. 4.
from Fornication, and that every one of us fhould know
how to poffefs his Veffel in Sanctification and Honour.
                                                 Which

Which Words plainly teach Chaftity to be a General Duty. All Men have their own Body, and
all ought to keep it pure, and confequently Chaftity ought to be the ftudy of all whether Married, or Unmarried. Which is a fufficient Proof
that Uncleannefs is forbidden to fuch as are not
yet engaged in Marriage. St. *Paul* fays they
ought to preferve their Body in Purity and Holinefs. And after this it is very abfurd to pretend
that Uncleannefs never becomes a Crime till it ar-
rives at Adultery, or an entire abandoning onefelf
to all Pollution.

But what we have yet farther to add will fet
this Truth in its full Light, and will make it abundantly evident, that St. *Paul* defign'd nothing
lefs than to condemn all Impurity of whatfoever
kind.

CHAP. IV.

*Some General Reflexions upon thofe Paffages
of the New Teftament, which refpect Uncleannefs.*

NOW we fhould pafs on to fome more Particular Confiderations, and exprefs and for-
mal Proofs; but that it will be proper before we
mention the Paffages to be hereafter infifted upon,
to make fome reflexion in the firft place, upon
the Terms wherein this Sin is defcribed; fecondly, upon the Apoftles manner of fpeaking of it;
and then, thirdly, upon the Reafons they had to
exprefs themfelves in this manner.

I. And

I. And first it is to be observed that the Apostles not only condemn Impurity in general, but distinguish also the several sorts of this Sin, as Adultery, Fornication or Whoring, and other Sins not necessary to be mentioned here. This Distinction is to be seen throughout the New Testament; as *Heb.* 13. 4. *Whoremongers and Adulterers God will judge;* and 1 *Cor.* 6. 9. *Neither Fornicators, nor Adulterers, nor the Abominable shall inherit the Kingdom of God.* St. *Paul* in this latter Passage specifies several different Sins; and proposes Adultery and Fornication, as two distinct Species of Impurity. He puts a difference between Fornicators and Adulterers, as well as between these and the Abominable, Idolaters, Drunkards, and other grievous Sinners.

The signification of the Word Adultery is what every body knows. None but can tell that it imports a Violation of the Marriage Covenant. And those called Fornicators or Whoremongers, are such as defile themselves in an Unmarried State.

And it is to be remember'd, the Apostles did not invent new Terms, or new Names, for Vices or Virtues, but made use of those which were in common use, and whose Meaning all could understand. For instance, when they spake of Drunkenness, or Covetousness, no body that heard them but immediately knew what they intended. In like manner common Usage had taught all, whether Jews or Gentiles, what Fornication and Whoring meant. The Pagan Authors had delivered themselves in the same Terms the Apostles did. It is true they had made use of them in different Senses; † sometimes for either Impurity at large, or for Adultery, and again at other times

---

† Πορνεία, Scortatio, μοιχεία.

for

for Impurity committed out of Marriage, and even simple Fornication *. And who then can doubt whether the Apostles condemned this Species of Uncleanness, especially when they distinguish it from Adultery? However, this will be made yet more clear by a particular Enquiry into divers Passages, which can bear no other Sense than this.

II. Let us consider therefore what the Apostles say of Uncleanness. And there are two very particular Instances relating to it in the New Testament that call for our Attention. The former is that the holy Writers treat oftener of this than of any other Sin. Let any Man examine all the places in the New Testament, where mention is made of Vices and Sins, and he will find there is not any one other Crime so many times named as Uncleanness. The other Particular to be remarked, and which is peculiar to this Sin, is, that the Apostles ordinarily name it first, and in their Catalogues of Vices set it in the Front of all the rest. This is a clear Case. † One need only run over the New Testament to be convinced of it. And the Reader will see it made out in the Remainder of this Chapter. Whence it appears very clearly, that Uncleanness is one of the principal Sins that the Apostles set themselves to oppose ; and that all Christians are under a particular Obligation to renounce it.

III. The Apostles having shewn such an Aversion to this Sin, it may justly be concluded that they had very good and substantial Reasons for their so doing ; which it will not be amiss to relate in this place.

---

* _In this Sense_ Lucian _us'd the Word,_ Μεμοιχευἱῶς. _Fabulos._ Dial. 31. Καὶ ὑπό τινῷ μεμοιχευϰῶς ὀινθείς αὐτἱω, &c.

† _See_ S. Mat. 7. 21. Rom. 1. 26, &c. 1 Cor. 5. 11. & 6. 10. Gal. 5. 19. Coloss. 3. 5, &c.

1. The firſt is the Strength of this Paſſion, and the Inclination Mankind have to whatſoever is pleaſing to Fleſh and Senſe. This Inclination was one of the firſt and moſt fatal Effects, of that Change, and Corruption which our firſt Parent *Adam's* Sin occaſioned in his Poſterity ; and ſo makes it neceſſary to be the more carefully upon our Guard, againſt the Sin I am now diſcourſing of.

2. This Sin reigned amongſt the Heathens ; who lived in Pollution, and all ſorts of Diſſoluteneſs, and a Habit of indulging their own unruly Deſires, and by this means gave occaſion to the Apoſtles to repreſent them, as a People who had proſtituted themſelves to all Laſciviouſneſs. And this in truth is the Character the Apoſtles chiefly give of them. † *God,* ſays St. *Paul, gave them up* † Rom. 1. *to their own vile Affections, and to Uncleanneſs through* 24. 26. *the Luſts of their own Hearts.* And a little after, * *they were filled with all Unrighteouſneſs, Fornication,* * *v.* 29. *and Wickedneſs.* He ſays at another time, † *that* † Eph. 4. *being paſt Feeling, they gave themſelves over to commit* 19. *all Uncleanneſs with greedineſs.* Thus St. *Peter* teſtifies of thoſe Idolaters, that they were ſo commonly uſed to live in Uncleanneſs, *' *that they* 1 S. Pet. were ſurprized at the Chriſtians Refuſal to *run* 4. 3. *with them into the ſame Exceſs of Riot,* or Diſſoluteneſs. This being the Caſe with theſe Pagans, the Apoſtles who wrote either to ſuch of them as were newly converted to Chriſtianity, or to the *Jews* who lived amongſt them, found it neceſſary to ſet themſelves particularly againſt Impurity.

3. There was a third Reaſon for them to ſpeak often with great Freedom againſt this Sin ; a peculiar Reaſon, and which related to thoſe Times in which the Apoſtles lived ; and it was the Cauſe they had to fear left the Practice of it ſhould be

a

a means of drawing the Chriſtians aſide into Idolatry and Apoſtacy. And ſince this gives a great light to the whole matter in hand, and helps to the underſtanding of a great many Texts in the Holy Scripture, where Uncleanneſs is ſpoken of, I ſhall beg leave ſomewhat to enlarge upon it.

We muſt know then that this Vice was not only very common amongſt the Heathens, as is ſhewn in the preceding Article; but moreover was made in ſome ſort a part of their Religion, and the Worſhip they paid to their falſe Deities. And no wonder, conſidering what impure Objects they had for their Adoration. Such as *Jupiter*, and *Venus* or *Aſtarte*, the Goddeſs of Luſt. Impurity was annexed to the Worſhip of Idols; and it was a natural Conſequent of the Feaſts, Sacrifices, and Revellings, which they kept in honour of their ſuppos'd Deities. Till at length it came to paſs, that this Wickedneſs was committed in the Places dedicated to the Service of their Idols, and theſe Places were filled with infamous Perſons. Which Cuſtom obtained in ſo many diſtant places, and grew ſo Publick, that Proſtitution came to be a ſort of Conſecration. And this is the reaſon why the Proſtitutes were anciently called by the ſame קְדֵשָׁה † Name with thoſe that were † *Conſecrated.* Heathen Authors will furniſh us with plenty of Proofs and Examples to this purpoſe. And ſome are to be met with in the Holy Scripture. This alſo * *See* Exod. gave occaſion for * divers Laws which occur in 34. 15. the Books of *Moſes.* It is obſerved in the Hiſtory Deut. 23. of the *Iſraelites*, that Idolatry was often introdu-18, &c. ced by the aſſiſtance of Uncleanneſs. *Moſes* reports, *Numb.* 25. 1, 2. 3. that the Children of *Iſrael*, being led by the Daughters of the Idolatrous *Moabites*, to their Feaſts, and the Sacrifices of their Gods, they were ſeduced through *the Whoredom*

dom they had committed with them, and they did eat, and bowed down to their Gods. It was through this Lust that *Solomon* † fell into Idolatry. In whose Son *Rehoboam's* days the People also corrupted themselves, and forsook the Service of the true God. And it is expresly recorded of them, that at this time, * *there were Sodomites in the Land, and they did according to all the Abominations of the Nations which the Lord had cast out before them.* And the Author of the History of the *Maccabees* giving an Account how the Temple had been prophaned by *Antiochus,* tells amongst other things ‖ that *the Gentiles had filled the Temple with Riot, and Revelling, and they dallied with Harlots, within the Circuit of the holy places.*

† 1 Kings, 11. 4.

* 1 Kings, 14. 22, 23. 24.

‖ 2 Macc. 6. 4.

This Pagan Dissoluteness reigned also in the Times of the Apostles. And it was so much the more to be feared that the Converts to Christianity would be seduced by this bait, in that besides the usual Inclination Men have to Sensuality; these new Christians, either were gained from the Pagans who had lived a long time in these Abominations, before their Conversion, or from the *Jews* who lived among these Pagans. The Apostles therefore set themselves principally against this Vice, not only because it is a heinous Sin in it self, and diametrically opposite to that Holiness which the Gospel requires, but because of the Danger the Christians were in, of relapsing into Idolatry. And for this Reason it is, that * Idolatry is so frequently joined with Uncleanness, as well as with Drunkenness and Gluttony. Debauchery and Intemperance accompany'd the Heathens Worship. And the Christians being invited to the Entertainments and Rejoicings which were made at the end of the Sacrifices which had been offered to Idols, might easily fall into Idolatry, unless they set themselves to avoid these Occasions,

* 1 Cor. 6. 10.
1 S. Pet. 4. 3, &c.

fions, by living foberly and chaftly. St. *Paul*
makes this very evident, 1 *Cor.* 10. 6, 7, 8. Where
to caution the Chriftians againft affifting at the
Idolatrous Feafts, he propounds to them the Example of the *Ifraelites*, whom the *Moabitifh* Women had drawn into Idolatry. Now *thefe things*,
fays he, *were our Examples, to the intent we fhould not*
luft after evil things as they alfo lufted. Neither be ye
Idolaters, as were fome of them, as it is written, The
People fate down to eat and drink, namely in the Idol-
Temples, *and rofe up to play,* to commit Wantonnefs
and Lewdnefs.

To conclude this Point, the Hiftory of the
Primitive Church teaches, That the *Nicolaitans*,
the *Gnofticks*, and other fuch like Hereticks which
arofe at that time, were for introducing all at
once both Fornication and Idolatry. As any one
may read in the fecond Chapter of St. *John*'s Revelation ; or the fecond Chapter of the fecond
Epiftle of St. *Peter*.

This is one of the Reafons the Apoftles had to
fpeak fo often againft Uncleannefs ; but yet it is
neither the only one, nor the moft confiderable.
They condemned this Sin not only upon account
of the Danger of Idolatry , but for other Reafons too taken from the Nature of this Vice. As
is our Bufinefs next to fhew, in a more particular
Difcuffion of the principal Places of the New
Teftament, where Impurity is treated of ; and
whence it will evidently appear, that not only an
Indulging our felves in this infamous Sin is here
forbidden , but that fimple Fornication is condemned.

C H A P.

CHAP. V.

A Particular Enquiry into thofe feveral Paf-
fages, where Uncleannefs is forbidden.

THofe Words of our Bleffed Saviour, St. *Mar.*
7. 21. call for our ferious Attention. *From*
within, out of the Heart proceed Evil Thoughts, Adulte-
ries, Fornications, Murders, &c. After which he adds,
Ver. 23. All thefe evil things come from within, and de-
file the Man. In thefe Words our Lord does not
name Adultery only, but Fornication likewife,
and diftinguifhes them from one another. But
what fays he of this latter Sin? It is plain he
puts it in the Rank of things evil in their own
nature. For his Defign in this Chapter is to diftinguifh between Evil and Indifferent things, between what pollutes a Man, and what does not.
He lets us fee the Pharifees were deceived in
thinking they fhould be defiled by eating with
unwafhen Hands, according to the Tradition of
the *Jews.* He tells them this is not that which
defiles a Man, and renders him blame-worthy,
but that which comes from within the Heart,
namely Adulteries and Fornications. He fays exprefly that thefe are wicked, or evil in their own
nature, and fo render a Man impure. This Paffage fhews alfo that our Saviour reckons Uncleannefs in the fame rank with Robbery, and Murder, and other heinous Crimes, which all the
World owns to be naturally evil. So that after
this fo exprefs Declaration of our Saviour Chrift,
it cannot be doubted but Uncleannefs is a Sin, and
indeed a great Sin.

D   It

It will not be befides our purpofe in this place to enquire into that Law which we have recorded, *Acts* 15. 28, 29. in thefe Words. *It feemed good to the Holy Ghoft and to us, to lay upon you no greater burden than thefe neceffary things, that ye abftain from Meats offered to Idols, and from Blood, and from things ftrangled, and from Fornication.* For the right underftanding of which Law, it is to be obferv'd, That it related to thofe who from among the Heathens were converted to the Chriftian Religion; as appears by the whole Chapter, and more particularly by the Infcription of that Letter of the Apoftles, whereof this Decree is a Part. It was at that time a Subject of Debate, Whether thofe Pagans that took upon them the Profeffion of Chriftianity were bound to be circumcifed, and obferve the other Ceremonial Ordinances of *Mofes.* And the Apoftles being affembled to decide this Queftion, pronounce it not neceffary for the Gentiles to fubject themfelves to Circumcifion nor the Ceremonies of the Law. But yet they held it requifite to forbid them *Meats offered to Idols, Blood, things ftrangled, and Fornication.* Of all the Ceremonial Laws the Apoftles impofe none upon the Gentile Converts, except fuch as related to things offered in Sacrifice to Idols, Blood, and things ftrangled; which alfo were forbidden in the feventeenth Chapter of *Leviticus.*

The Apoftles would have the Gentiles abftain from thefe things for the fame reafon for which God had formerly forbidden them to the *Jews;* that is to fay, the more effectually to fecure them from Idolatry. The Truth is, thefe were Idolatrous and Superftitious Cuftoms of the Heathens, and Rites which accompanied their falfe Worfhip, as divers Authors have teftified very fully. It therefore concern'd the Apoftles at this time, to forbid the Chriftians to eat of fuch Food, as had

been

been offered to Idols, of Blood, and of things ftrangled, becaufe in eating of thefe they incurred the Danger of falling into Idolatry; and moreover becaufe they might hereby fcandalize either their Brethren, or perhaps the *Jews.* Touching which matter whofoever pleafes may confult the eighth Chapter of the firft Epiftle to the *Corinthians.* At the fame time the Apoftles forbad Impurity, in conjunction with thefe Meats offered to Idols, Blood, and things ftrangled; becaufe, as has been faid, it was one Confequent of the Worfhip of falfe Gods, and of the Idol Feafts.

If what I have been difcourfing be well underftood, and due Attention be given to the Defign and Spirit of this Apoftolical Canon, and the Reafons whereupon it is grounded, there will be no difficulty in apprehending how the Apoftles came to join Impurity with things indifferent in their own nature. They did it upon the account of thefe Ufages being joined to, and as it were infeparable from the Heathen Worfhip. I confefs there is a great difference between Uncleannefs and fuch Meats as the Apoftles here forbid to be eaten. Thefe Meats are not evil in themfelves; nor were the Chriftians required at that time to abftain from them, but only for fear of being betray'd into Idolatry, or of giving Scandal. In other Cafes, where was no fuch appearance of Danger, the ufe of thefe things might be permitted. So faith St. *Paul* in the eighth and tenth Chapters of the firft Epiftle to the *Corinthians,* in regard to things facrificed to Idols. But Uncleannefs is in its own Nature unlawful, it *defiles a Man,* and Chriftians are under a Neceffity of fhunning it; and not only for the Caufes mentioned in relation to the Meats here forbidden; but for other Reafons, taken from the nature of the Sin it felf, and the Turpitude of it. This is plain from

the

the foregoing Confiderations, and the Paffages I have cited, and thofe others I have yet to add.

The Apoftle St. *Paul* gives this Advice, *Rom.* 13. 13. *Let us walk honeftly as in the day time, not in Rioting and Drunkenness, not in Chambering and Wantonness,* or Uncleannefs and Lafcivioufnefs. Here the Apoftle reflects upon the Debaucheries and infamous Familiarities of the Pagans, and fpeaks of them as inconfiftent with a regular and orderly Converfation, and every way unworthy of fuch as enjoy the Light of the Gofpel.

The firft Epiftle to the *Corinthians* contains divers Paffages very exprefs to this purpofe ; particularly in its fifth, fixth, and feventh Chapters.

In the fifth Chapter St. *Paul* very earneftly exhorts not only to fly Uncleannefs, but thofe too that were guilty of it. He would have People feparate from thefe, and caft them out of the Church. From whence it is eafy to judge, in what Deteftation Impurity is to be had amongft Chriftians. *I wrote to you,* fays he, *in an Epiftle,* and *Now have I written unto you, not to company with Fornicators,* ver. 9. 11. He would have them excommunicated ; and puts them in the Front of thofe Sinners, that ought not to be fuffered in the Church. So it follows, *If any Man that is called a Brother be a Fornicator, or an Idolater,* &c. *with fuch an one eat not,* ver. 11. and ver. 13. *Put away from among your felves that wicked Perfon.*

In the fixth Chapter he infifts farther upon the fame Subject, but after fomewhat a more particular manner. Here he makes it the peculiar Matter of his Difcourfe ; he argues concerning it, and fets himfelf purpofely to prove that Uncleannefs is highly criminal in a Chriftian ; he offers Variety of Reafons, and feveral Confiderations, fo as he is not wont to do when treating of other Vices. This courfe he takes, becaufe he found it

necefneceſſary to convince the *Corinthians* of the Dreadfulneſs of this Sin.

He tells them, *ver.* 10. that *Neither Fornicators, nor Idolaters, nor Adulterers, nor the Effeminate, nor Abuſers of themſelves with Mankind,* &c. *ſhall inherit the Kingdom of God.* In which Declaration he includes all ſorts of Unclean Perſons, whether Adulterers or Fornicators, or thoſe that defile themſelves in any other manner, and ſubjects them all to the ſame Condemnation with thoſe that committed the fouleſt Crimes, of being excluded from the Kingdom of God. Then he repreſents to theſe *Corinthians,* ver. 11. how God had extended his Favour to divers of them, in recovering them from their Pollutions, and waſhing them with the Blood of *Jeſus Chriſt,* and the Power of the Holy Ghoſt, by calling them to the Chriſtian Religion; and hereby teaches them that they were indiſpenſably engaged to avoid all Uncleanneſs, and that this Sin is incompetible with a Profeſſion of Chriſtianity.

But then foraſmuch as ſome might be apt to object, That the Uſe of thoſe things which are neceſſary for the Body is allow'd us; for Inſtance, that there is no Sin in eating whatſoever ſort of Meat; and that the Caſe is the ſame as to Uncleanneſs. To this St. *Paul* makes two Replies.

1. He ſays, *ver.* 12. Though a thing be permitted, there is no need that it ſhould be always put in practice. *All things are lawful for me, but all things are not expedient. All things are lawful for me, but I will not be brought under the power of any thing.* Which Words import not, that all things are allowed without diſtinction; but that it is not always requiſite to do what is allowed; and that Men ought not to abuſe that Liberty, which is granted them of uſing indifferent things; leſt ſo they be inſlaved to theſe things, this being directly contrary to Piety. This is the Caſe of the Senſualiſts and

Licen-

Licentious, who make themselves Slaves to the Flesh, and have their *Belly for their God,* as St. *Paul* speaks, *Phil.* 3. 19. The Apostle adds, *ver.* 13. *Meats are for the Belly, and the Belly for Meats, but God shall destroy both it and them.* And these Words explain the foregoing, and teach us that when St. *Paul* had said, *All things are lawful for me,* he did not mean this in general of every thing, but only of all Meats. And this he said, because those that would entice Christians to Impurity, made it their Business to persuade them, that the Use of all sorts of Meats, not excluding such as had been sacrificed to Idols, was permitted them. Wherefore he tells them the Use of Meats was permitted and necessary, that God had created them for the Sustenance of Man, and that Man was of such a Constitution, as to have constant need of them for his Support. Whereby the Apostle intimates that no Meat is by nature polluted and unlawful, and that it is allowed to use any sort of it ; only with this Reserve, to which himself here directs, that we do it with Discretion, and so as that it may never become an Occasion of our either sinning against our selves, or scandalizing our Neighbour. But withal he at the same time adds, that *God will one day destroy both the Meats and the Belly,* as much as to say, The Use of these things shall be abolished at the Resurrection ; and hereby gives us to understand, that the Use of Meats relating only to this animal and corporal Life, and being therefore to continue only for a time, it is highly unbecoming Christians, who profess to have more elevated Affections, and to aspire after a Spiritual, Heavenly, and Immortal Life, to set their Minds upon what is pleasing to the Flesh.

   This is what St. *Paul* discourses of Meats ; and it is his first Answer to those who pretend an Allowance

lowance of all things relating to the Body. But
he proceeds farther, and gives quite a different account of Uncleanness, from what he does of
Meats. *The Body,* says he, *is not for Fornication, but
for the Lord, and the Lord for the Body.* The Import
of which Words is, that the Body was not given
us to be employ'd to any infamous purpose, and
that Christians are by no means to take the same
Liberty here, that they may in Meats. St. *Paul*
could not more clearly instruct us, that the Case
is not the same with Uncleanness, and with the
Use of Meats, and that it ought not to be ranked
amongst things Indifferent and purely Natural, or
perhaps necessary, as Eating and Drinking are.
*The Body is made for Meats, but it is not made for Un-
cleanness ;* on the contrary, it is made for the
Lord, and is to be employ'd only to holy Purposes, and which are according to the Will of
God. He adds, *And the Lord is for the Body ; and
God hath both raised up the Lord, and will also raise up
us by his own Power ;* that is to say, Our Bodies belong to God as well as our Souls ; he has consecrated them to himself by the Redemption wrought
for them ; and he will raise them up at the last
Day, to the end he may be glorify'd both in our
Bodies and in our Souls. This Right then which
the Lord has over us, and particularly over our
Bodies, and the Glory whereto he has ordained
us, lay an indissoluble Obligation upon us, to
keep our Bodies undefiled, shunning all sort of
Pollution, whereby to prepare them for a happy
Resurrection, and an Admission into the Kingdom
of Heaven.

However, left any should pretend that Uncleanness is no hindrance but that our Bodies may
still belong to the Lord, and may be raised in his
due time, and enter into his Glory ; the Apostle
shews the Impossibility of this, and that the Sin

of

of Uncleanness deprives Men of Communion
with *Jesus Christ*, ver. 15. *Know ye not that your Bodies are the Members of Jesus Christ?* He supposes
our whole selves to belong to Christ, and more
particularly that our Bodies are to be employ'd in
his Service, and the promoting our own Happiness; as all Christians are bound to confess. And
the Thought hereof ought to breed in every one
of us a Detestation of Uncleanness. The next
Words are, *Shall I then take away the Members of
Christ, and make them the Members of an Harlot?*
And these Words imply two things. *First*, That
it is a most unworthy Act to take away a Member of Christ; it is to offer him the utmost Affront; it is to force from him what is truly his
own, and what he has purchased with no less a
Price than his own Blood. And this Affront is
so much the more outrageous, in that the Offender thus quits his Blessed Redeemer, to join himself to an infamous Person. The very Thought
of such an Exchange is enough to strike a Man
with Horror; and this St. *Paul* testifies in the following Words, *God forbid!* This is the most deplorable state a Man can bring himself into, inasmuch as whosoever is not a Member of *Jesus
Christ*, must unavoidably perish. In the second
place St. *Paul* notes that this is the certain Effect
of Uncleanness, that this is a Sin which breaks off
Communion with Christ, and renders such as are
guilty of it the Members of an Harlot. And this Doctrine he confirms in the Verse next following.

*What, know ye not, that he which is joined to an
Harlot, is one Body with her? For it is written, they
two shall be one Flesh.* Here the Apostle refers
to what God had said upon the Creation of
the Man and the Woman; he saith, *They two
shall be one Flesh.* These Words properly relate
to Marriage; nevertheless St. *Paul* applies them

to

to Uncleanneſs, inaſmuch as though the Union of Unclean Perſons is Unlawful, and God has no where intimated the leaſt Approbation of it, it is however in reality ſuch an Union as of two makes one Fleſh. And by Conſequence whoſoever falls into this Sin, becomes one Body with, and a Member of, a Harlot. Which is exceedingly unworthy of a Chriſtian, and inconſiſtent with our Union to our Bleſſed Lord. As St. *Paul* maintains, by what he ſubjoins in the next Verſe. Ver. 17. *But he that is joined to the Lord is one Spirit with him.* The Meaning of which Aſſertion is, That thoſe who are joined to Chriſt by a true Faith, are animated by his Spirit, have the ſame Will, the ſame Purpoſes, the ſame Deſigns with with him, and ſo are utterly eſtranged from all Thoughts of forſaking him to follow the Deſires of the Fleſh, and to join themſelves to diſſolute and unclean Perſons.

To this purpoſe he proceeds, *ver.* 18. *Flee Fornication. Every Sin that a Man doth is without the Body ; but he that committeth Fornication ſinneth againſt his own Body.* Whereby St. *Paul* does not intend only, that Unclean Perſons hurt their own Bodies, and bring divers Miſchiefs upon themſelves ; for there are ſeveral other Sins which hurt the Body likewiſe ; but he doubtleſs ſays it for theſe two Reaſons. *Firſt,* becauſe this Sin is directly oppoſite to our Union with Chriſt, ſeeing it cannot be committed without making us one Body with the Harlot. The Body ceaſes thenceforwards to be a Member of *Jeſus Chriſt*, as the Apoſtle has already taught, and by Conſequence they that indulge themſelves in this Sin, are great Enemies to themſelves, and ſin againſt their own Body. *Secondly,* St. *Paul* ſays this becauſe Uncleanneſs being of a ſhameful and infamous nature, it pollutes and diſhonours our Bodies, and our Perſons, fons, beyond other Sins. Which Obfervation of the Apoftle is explained by what he affirms of the Heathens, *Rom.* 1. 24. that *being given up to Uncleanefs., they difhonoured their own Bodies between themfelves.*

St. *Paul* urges another Confideration, *ver.* 19. *What, know ye not that your Body is the Temple of the Holy Ghoft which is in you, which ye have of God?* And this is a very powerful Confideration for diffuading from Uncleanefs, being taken from the Glory whereto God has raifed us even in regard to our Bodies. They are the Temples of the Holy Spirit, becaufe the Holy Spirit dwells in us, and pours forth his Benefits upon us, fanctifies us, and confecrates us to the Service of God. Wherefore our Bodies partaking of this Honour, we are bound to preferve them in Purity, and to employ them to holy Purpofes. For if the Places dedicated to the Worfhip of God, may not be prophaned by any Pollution, but muft be kept pure and undefiled, how great ought the Holinefs of our Bodies to be, feeing God has condefcended to make them the Temples of his Holy Spirit? This Reflexion of St. *Paul* lets us fee plainly, that whenever any give themfelves over to Uncleannefs, they ceafe to be the Temples of the Holy Spirit, juft as the Apoftle had faid before, that they ceafe to be the Members of *Jefus Chrift.* Which fhews this Sin to be the Occafion that the Holy Spirit of God withdraws from the Heart of fuch as are guilty of it, becaufe this Spirit cannot dwell with Pollution.

Finally, St. *Paul* concludes his Difcourfe concerning the Sin I am treating of, with this Advice, *ver.* 19, 20. *Ye are not your own, for ye are bought with a Price : therefore glorify God in your Body, and in your Spirit, which are Gods.* Which the Apoftle might fpeak with the greater Earneftnefs, to

con-

convince us that it is in no wise permitted us to order our selves according to our own Desires, and to follow the Motions and Inclinations of the Flesh ; but that we are to pay an absolute Submission to the Will of him whose we are. As we are Christians, whom our Lord has purchased with his own most precious Blood, he has an absolute Dominion over us ; our Bodies, our Souls, our whole selves are entirely his, and may not be put to any other Use than what is agreeable to his most holy Will.

I cannot forbear repeating it, that this Chapter calls for an especial Attention ; and that St. *Paul* does not only exhort the *Corinthians* to fly Uncleanness, but proves by several Arguments, how unbecoming Christians this Sin is ; he proposes his Reasons with great Earnestness and Vehemence ; he insists upon it ; and makes use of the most powerful Dissuasives from it. And after all this can it possibly be made a Question, Whether Uncleanness be sinful, and absolutely forbidden ?

I know not how what I have said can possibly be answered, nor to what Evasions our Libertines can have recourse, for eluding the force of these Passages. It may perhaps be pretended that St. *Paul* does not condemn simple Fornication, but only the utmost Excess of Impurity, or that Crime which is committed with profligate and prostitute Persons. Nor do I deny but he might have that Crime in his view, in this Chapter ; yet whosoever shall seriously attend to all that has been said, and shall weigh all the Reasons and the Proofs that have been alledged, will easily observe that this is not all the Apostle condemns, and that the Arguments he produces are levelled against all manner of Uncleanness. However to set this matter in its due Light, and to stop the Mouths of such as would

try

try to elude the Proofs brought from this Chapter, I proceed to make it indisputably evident, That all sort of Uncleanness, that simple Fornication, in a word, that all that is without Marriage is forbidden to Christians.

To prove this we need only pass on to the Seventh Chapter of this same Epistle. St. *Paul* having spoken of Impurity in the preceding Chapter, examines in this into certain Questions relating to Marriage. Whence I might offer divers Considerations; but I shall content my self to touch only the Chief of them. Now what we read here is so clear and express, that nothing can be imagined plainer or more decisive. In the beginning of the Chapter St. *Paul* designing to answer those Questions about Marriage and Celibacy, of which the Church of *Corinth* had desired his Resolution, tells them *it is good for a Man not to touch a Woman*, hereby recommending the state of Celibacy as preferable to that of Matrimony. He describes the state of Celibacy in these Words, *Not to touch a Woman*, which is a plain Proof that all who are Unmarried are to live in perfect Continence, and abstain from all impure Conversation, of whatsoever nature. And to the same purpose, *ver.* 34. he declares the state of an unmarried Woman to be this, that she *careth for the things of the Lord, that she may be holy both in Body and in Spirit.*

Again the Apostle says, *ver.* 2. *Nevertheless because of,* or to avoid, *Fornication, let every Man have his own Wife, and let every Woman have her own Husband.* It is as clear as the Day that St. *Paul* calls all that is committed out of Marriage, after whatever manner, by the Name of Fornication. Nor could he have more expresly signify'd what he means by Fornication, and how far the Importance of this Word is to be extended. *To avoid For-*

Fornication, let every one have his own Wife, &c.. This shews clearly both the Sin spoken of, and the Obligation Christians are under to avoid it ; that the Apostle imposes upon unmarried Persons of either Sex a Necessity of living in Chastity ; and that out of Marriage all is sinful.

St. *Paul* after this having mentioned the Duties of Married Persons, returns *ver.* 8, 9. to speak again of the Unmarried, *I say therefore to the Unmarried and Widows, it is good for them if they abide even as I. But if they cannot contain themselves, let them marry, for it is better to marry than to burn.* Which Words need no Comment upon them. Either they have no Sense at all, or they signify a Necessity of living in an exact and perfect Continence, or else of Marrying ; and that there is no Medium between these two Estates. If Uncleanness. were not a Sin, in a Word, if any thing had been permitted besides Marriage, the Apostle could not have spoken in this manner, without laying a Snare for People's Consciences ; neither would he have said that Marriage was the only means of avoiding Uncleanness, the only Remedy against Incontinence. Hence therefore I conclude, that St. *Paul* condemns not only the last Excesses of Uncleanness, and that unbounded Liberty some may take this way, but even simple Fornication ; and this so plainly, that I persuade my self none can have any Scruple remaining concerning it. Let us pass to St. *Paul's* other Epistles.

Gal. 5. 19. The Apostle undertaking to explain what it is to live after the Flesh, says, *The Works of the Flesh are manifest*, or easy to be known. Then he proceeds to enumerate the principal Sins of the Flesh, and names first *Adultery, Fornication, Uncleanness, Lasciviousness.* He names these Sins before others, as being most manifest, and most easily discernible. And he does not name Adultery alone,

alone, but joins with it Fornication, together
with Uncleanness and Lasciviousness, which comprehends all the Species of Impurity. He joins
with this Sin, *Witchcraft, Murder*, and other Crimes.
And he expresly protests, that *they which do such
things shall not inherit the Kingdom of God.* By which
Passage it appears, that if there be any one Sin
that excludes from Heaven, Impurity does it.

The same Apostle treating of the Duties of the
Christian Life, in the fourth and fifth Chapters of
the Epistle to the *Ephesians*, insists chiefly upon the
Renunciation of Uncleanness. He professes that
Christians may not live as the Pagans did, who
were overwhelmed with thick Darkness, and so
fell into terrible Exorbitances. And to set forth
their excessive Corruption, in its due Colours, he
offers at no other Proof but the Impurity of their
Lives. *The Gentiles*, says he, *being past feeling, have
given themselves over unto Lasciviousness, to commit all
Uncleanness with greediness.* He exhorts the Christians
to be by no means like them ; and recommends
Chastity to them, not only in their Actions, but
in their Discourse ; *Let no corrupt Communication
proceed out of your Mouth.*

In the fifth Chapter he continues his Exhortation to a holy Life ; and generally what he presses
is with relation to Impurity. Ver. 3. 4. *But Fornication, and all Uncleanness, let it not be once named
among you, as becometh Saints. Neither Filthiness, nor
foolish Talking, which are not convenient.* And to
add the more weight to this his Exhortation, he
subjoins *ver.* 5. *For this ye know, that no Whoremonger, nor unclean Person, hath any Inheritance in the
Kingdom of Christ, and of God.* And not content
with having denounced this so dreadful a Punishment to the Impure, and lest any should not be
duly sensible of the great Evil of the Sin to which
he threatens it, he repeats his Denunciation in
                                                    these

thefe Words; *Let no Man deceive you with vain Words; for becaufe of thefe things cometh the Wrath of God upon the Children of Difobedience.* And again he cautions and preffes them carefully to avoid this Sin, and all fuch Perfons as would invite them to it. Ver. 7. *Be not ye therefore Partakers with them;* and again, *ver.* 11. 12. *Have no Fellowfhip with the unfruitful Works of Darknefs, but rather reprove them; for it is a fhame even to fpeak of thofe things which are done of them in fecret.* The Tendency and Defign of which whole Difcourfe is to infpire the Chriftians with an Abhorrence of Impurity.

It is obfervable likewife that he purfues the fame Defign, in the third Chapter of the Epiftle to the *Coloffians.* According to his ufual Method, he begins his Exhortation with a particular refpect to Chaftity, *ver.* 5. *Mortify therefore your Members which are upon the Earth, Fornication, Uncleannefs, inordinate Affections, evil Concupifcence.* And his manner of fpeaking concerning Impurity is very remarkable. He diftinguifhes this Sin from others, and makes it an Article by it felf; he infifts upon it more largely than upon the reft; he enforces his Exhortation with both Menaces and Motives, *ver.* 6, 7. After which refuming his Difcourfe, he treats of other Sins; but then he but lightly touches upon them in a word or two. Ver. 8. *Put off all thefe, Anger, Wrath, Malice, Blafphemy,* &c. Which is a farther Confirmation, that of all forts of Sins, there is none the Apoftle feems more avowedly to condemn than that of Uncleannefs.

In the fourth Chapter of the firft Epiftle to the *Theffalonians,* fee how he begins his Recommendation of Holinefs. Ver. 2, 3, 4, 5. *Ye know what Commandments we gave you by the Lord Jefus For this is the Will of God, even your Sanctification, that ye fhould abftain from Fornication; that every one of you*
fhould

should know how to possess his Vessel (that is, his Body) *in Sanctification and Honour ; not in the Lust of Concupiscence, even as the Gentiles which know not God.* Upon which Words divers Reflexions naturally arise. For instance, St. *Paul* says, the Will of God, and one of the principal Commands of *Jesus Christ*, is, That we live chastly : Hereby testifying that without Chastity, there is no Holiness or Obedience to the Divine Will ; and consequently no Hope of Salvation. He says that it is *the Will of God that we abstain from Uncleanness,* that is, that we perfectly renounce it, and in no wise suffer our selves to be betray'd into it. And again he more fully explains himself, by declaring that *every one of us* ought to possess, or preserve his Body in Holiness and Purity ; as if he should have said, That all sorts of Persons without exception ought to be very watchful over their own Bodies to preserve them from all manner of Pollution, and to live in Continence and Chastity. And he proves all Christians to be under this Obligation, by declaring it unlawful for them to follow the inordinate Desires of the Flesh, as the Gentiles do who know not God.

Nor may we omit what is affirmed in the thirteenth Chapter of the Epistle to the *Hebrews,* ver. 4. *Marriage is honourable in all, and the Bed undefiled ; but Whoremongers and Adulterers God will judge.* We need only read these Words to convince us, that Marriage is a Holy and Honourable State, provided that we live chastly in it ; but withal that God will punish all unclean Persons; as well those that violate the Sanctity of Marriage by Adultery, as those who live incontinently out of Marriage. The Opposition St. *Paul* makes between Adultery and Fornication on the one hand, and Marriage on the other, shews plainly that except in the Case of chast and pure Marriage, all

is

is faulty; and, as Marriage is an honourable State, so Uncleanness is juft matter of Reproach and In-famy. The Apoftle would not have put Fornica-tion in the fame Clafs with Adultery, if it were of an indifferent nature; nor would have threa-ten'd thofe that fall into it with the Judgment of God, as he does the Adulterers.

I might have cited a great number of Texts out of the New Teftament, and by enquiring in-to the other Epiftles, particularly the fecond Epi-ftle of St. *Peter*, Chap. 2. and the Epiftle of St. *Jude*, might have fhewn that Impurity was the principal Character, which the Apoftles gave to the falfe Chriftians, and falfe Teachers of thofe Times. But I will not enlarge upon this Subject. What I have faid is enough to let every one fee who does not wilfully fhut his Eyes, that Un-cleannefs is condemn'd through the whole New Teftament; and more particularly that Fornica-tion is a Sin. This Nature teaches, and the Old Law confirms; but the Gofpel gives fuch abun-dant Evidence to the Truth of it, that there is no being certain of any thing in Religion, if not of this.

C H A P. VI.

Of Adultery.

AFter what has been difcourfed of Unclean-nefs and Fornication, there will be no need of treating at large of Adultery. The Confide-rations which have been offered againft Unclean-nefs in general, are yet of greater Force when ap-ply'd to this Vice. But however there are other

E   par-

particular Reasons besides these, which plainly discover the Enormity of it.

I. A very little Attention will suffice to inform us, that it violates the most sacred Laws, and in particular those of Marriage, which are so serviceable, and so necessary to the Good of Mankind. These Laws of Marriage have in all Ages been looked upon as inviolable, and are especially to be so esteemed by all who are instructed in the Doctrines of Religion, and are satisfy'd that God is the Author of Marriage. It was God who in the Beginning created one Man and one Woman, and said, *They two should be one Flesh.* Here is the first Institution of Marriage; and our Blessed Lord cites it in his Gospel, St. *Matth.* 19. 4. to prove the Unlawfulness of those Divorces, which had obtained among the *Jews.* Whence it is easy to judge what Opinion each one ought to have of Adultery. For upon Supposition that Divorcing is contrary to the Law of Marriage, Adultery is yet more opposite to it. If our Lord Christ says, that those who put away their Wives without any just Cause, to marry others, or that marry them who have in this manner been put away, are guilty of Sin; What must be said of those who being under the Bonds of Marriage, yet abandon themselves to Uncleanness? Those Engagements which are inviolable even from the nature of Marriage, become much more so amongst Christians, by the Faith mutually given at the Entrance upon this State, and the solemn Promises then made, in the Presence of God, and by all that is most sacred. So that the Violaters of these Engagements and Promises, in breaking their Conjugal Faith, are justly chargeable with the utmost Perfidiousness, and undoubted Perjury.

What

What I here fay relates equally to all whether
Men or Women. Nor fhall I ftand to enquire in
this place, whether the Crime is greater, on the
Husband's fide, or on the Wife's. In fome refpects the Fault of the Woman is the worfe, and
in others that of the Husband exceeds it. But be
this as it will, it is certain that in regard to the
Divine Inftitution, and the Nature, and End of
Marriage, and to Right Reafon, the Engagements
are Equal on both fides, and both Husband and
Wife are under the fame Obligation of Fidelity to
each other. This appears from what our Saviour
difcourfes concerning Divorce, St. *Mar.* 10. 11.
*Whofoever fhall unjuftly put away his Wife, and marry
another, committeth Adultery againft her.* St. *Paul*
fays exprefly, 1 *Cor.* 7. 3, 4, 5. *The Husband hath
not power over his own Body,* or is not Mafter of it,
*but the Wife ; and the Wife hath not power over her
own Body, but the Husband.* Whereto he alfo fub-
joins divers other Confiderations †, which put it †*See v. 10,*
beyond all Difpute or Contradiction, that the En- 11. *&c.*
gagements are reciprocal, and the Right equal on
both fides. This he fuppofes throughout the
whole Chapter, as every one muft fee that reads
it with any manner of Attention. Befides, that
I may juft mention it by the bye, the Words now
cited are an inconteftable Argument againft Polygamy ; as well as thofe at *ver.* 2. *Let every Man
have his own Wife, and every Woman her own Huf-
band.* Indeed his whole Difcourfe reftrains Marriage to Two Perfons. And fo the Apoftle teaches
it to be as little in the power of the Husband to
have many Wives, as it is in the Power of the
Wife to have many Husbands.

If we reflect moreover upon what has been argued, to fhew the Advantage of Marriage to Society, and the Welfare of Families, we fhall foon
be convinced, that thefe Effects fo highly bene-

ficial to Mankind, are not to be expected any longer than its mutual Obligations are inviolably obferved. Adultery deftroys the Foundation of that Peace and Quiet of Families which is defign'd by it, that Union and Happinefs of the Married Perfons, and the good Education of their Children ; and inftead hereof introduces Trouble, Divifion, Jealoufy, Hatred, and other Mifchiefs innumerable. We have likewife feen that Fathers are under a natural Obligation to take care of, bring up, and love their Children, and that to this purpofe it is required they fhould know them, that they may look after them, and live with them. And this Confideration fhould fatisfy us, that Adultery is inevitably attended with divers other Crimes, and moft heinous Inftances of Injuftice, and that the Confequents of it are very terrible. It hinders Parents Care of their Children, and occafions their leaving them expofed to the wide World, brings ftrange Children into Families, and robs the right Heirs of the Portion of Goods that God and Nature had allotted them. I will not enlarge upon thefe Confiderations, nor mention fome others that might be added, for fear of being tedious, and becaufe they fo readily occur of themfelves, and every one is fo fenfible of them, that there is none but muft own Adultery to be a moft heinous, notorious Crime.

II. Yet I muft obferve in the Second Place, that the Obfervations which may be made againft Adultery, are fo natural, and fo convincing, that they have always been taken notice of. It has been acknowledged in all Ages, that this Sin is deftructive of Juftice, Order, and the Good of Society. And the Law whereby it ftands condemned, is not fuch as thofe which are made for fome one particular Country ; but it is of general Obligation, and as ancient as the World it felf.

It

It has been confented to at all Times, and in all Places; and there have been very few Laws befides, that have obtained a like Univerfal Approbation. Whenever we read the Hiftories, and Statute-Books, the Opinions, and Cuftoms, of the different Nations of the World, we cannot but take notice how Adultery has been conftantly condemn'd. Uncleannefs was too commonly practifed among the Heathens; yet not fo generally, but that Marriage was ever refpected by them, and Adultery looked upon as an abominable Wickednefs, and which they thought not undeferving to be punifhed with Death. This all who have been any whit converfant in Hiftory and Antiquity cannot but be fenfible of.

Nor do only particular Authors give this Reprefentation of it; as *Ariftotle*, who determines †that Adultery, whether it be in Man or Woman, *ought to be put in the Rank of the fouleft and moft infamous Enormities*; but we have alfo the Concurrence of Legiflators, and of whole Countries. The *Egyptians*, the *Lacedemonians*, the *Greeks*, the *Romans*, the *Goths*, the ancient *Germans*, have forbidden Adultery under the fevereft Penalties, and almoft all under Pain of Death. And even at this day it efcapes not better amongft the *Africans* and *Americans*.

It is alfo to be noted, that it was not only forbidden, but the Practice of it was very rarely known amongft thefe People; and * *Plutarch* and other Authors give fuch an Account of it, as may well put us Chriftians to the blufh. And if per-

---

† Polit. l. 7.

* Plutarch *fays, in his* Laconick Apothegms, *that Adultery was heretofore looked upon at* Lacedemon, *as impoffible and incredible; and gives this Reafon of his Affertion, That needlefs Ornaments, and Perfumes, Superfluity and Luxury were banifhed that City.*

haps

haps it be pretended that whilst these Heathens refrained from Adultery, they did it not from any Sense they had of its Guilt, but only for fear of the Punishment to which they should thereby expose themselves; and that it was thought unlawful only because it had been so severely forbidden; I do not deny this, and must own that Impunity is the Cause of its becoming so usual as it is in our Days. Yet I must affirm that it was not barely a Fear of the Laws that made this to be reckon'd a Crime; for they who made these Laws, and settled these Penalties, did it not from a Sense of Fear, but for Reasons taken from the Nature of the Thing itself. Now the if Pagans had this Notion of Adultery, much more ought Christians to have it in Detestation. And we may assure ourselves, these Idolatrous Nations will one day rise up in Judgment against those, who living in the Church of Christ, give themselves up to this horrible Wickedness, and will not be with-held from it by the Light of the Gospel, and the Dread of Eternal Vengeance.

III. And now to come to the Holy Scriptures, and to begin with the Times preceding the *Mosaick* Law; it is plain, Adultery was then accounted amongst the Blackest of Crimes. *Job* says, Chap. 31. 11. *It is an heinous Crime, yea it is an iniquity to be punished by the Judges.* And *Joseph* before the Days of *Job*, testifies what an Abhorrence he had of it, by the Answer he gave to *Potiphar's* Wife, when she would have enticed him to it. Gen. 39. 9. *How can I do this great Wickedness, and sin against God?* And if we look still backwarder, we shall find in the twelfth and twentieth Chapters of *Genesis*, how *Pharaoh* King of *Egypt*, and *Abimelech* King of *Gerar*, having taken *Sarah* to themselves, and intending to marry her, not knowing that she was already Wife to *Abraham*, both

both returned her to him immediately, when once they understood her Relation to him ; taxing him withal, for not having let them know it sooner, *Why didst thou not tell us she was thy Wife, and hast brought upon us and upon our People a great Sin ?* The like Account is also to be met with in the twenty sixth Chapter of *Genesis.* And it is an ancient Tradition of the *Jews,* That amongst the Laws delivered by God to *Noah* after the Flood, and in him to all Mankind, one was against the Abuse of Marriage by this grievous Sin.

If we pass on to the Law of *Moses,* this will afford us divers Observations very pertinent to the Matter in hand.

1. God expresly forbids Adultery in the Decalogue. In this Law which contains the most inviolable Rules of Justice, and which the Almighty published on Mount *Sinai,* with Thunder and Lightenings, one Commandment is, *Thou shalt not commit Adultery.* And this Crime Is put in the Divine Law in the same rank with Idolatry, Murder, and Theft.

2. Amongst the Laws which God afterwards delivered by *Moses* for the Explication of the Decalogue, there are several relating to Marriage and Adultery, which were particularly design'd to prevent the Commission of this Sin.

3. God who is a just Judge, and assigns to each Sin a Penalty proportion'd to the Heinousness of its Guilt, has decreed Adulterers, whether Men or Women, to be put to death. *Levit.* 20. 10. and *Deut.* 22. 22, *The Adulterer and the Adulteress shall be put to death.*

4. But this is not all. For seeing this Sin may be committed secretly, God thought fit to order a Method for the Discovery of it ; so that a Woman suspected could not escape Death, if really guilty ; I mean *the Waters of* † *Jealousy.* If the

† Numb. Man 5. 11, &c.

Man had entertain'd a Suspicion of his Wife, he was to bring her to the Priest, before whom she was to stand with her Head uncovered, and with the Offering of Memorial in her Hand, and to drink of the bitter Water, which he was to give her to that end; saying to her at the same time, *If no Man hath lien with thee, and if thou hast not gone aside by Uncleanness to another instead of thy Husband, be thou free from this bitter Water that causeth the Curse ; but if thou art guilty,* (then he caused an Oath to be administred to the Woman, full of Imprecations against her self) *the Lord make thee a Curse and an Oath among thy People, when the Lord doth make thy Thigh to rot, and thy Belly to swell.* Whereto she was to answer, *Amen, Amen.* There were Ceremonies to be observed in her taking these Waters; and the Effect they produc'd, if the Woman was faulty, was, that she would immediately swell and die.

5. Another Law shewing the Heinousness of Adultery, and how inviolable and sacred the Rights of Marriage are, as likewise in what Purity all ought to live even before they enter upon that State, is that which orders such as should fall into Uncleanness, after they are once espoused, to be treated as Adulteresses. *Deut.* 22. 23, 24 ; That they with the Partners in their Sin should be punished with Death, and the People should stone them.

It would be too tedious an Undertaking, to recite here all the Laws, the Threatnings, the Reprehensions, and the Examples to this purpose that are to be met with in the Old Testament. I shall only take notice, that Adultery is one of those Sins the Prophets so severely reprove the *Jews* for. They commonly join it with Idolatry, and say their City *Jerusalem* and their People should be destroy'd because of the Adulteries that were committed in the midst of them. In the Censures
which

which *Jeremiah* paſſed upon the *Jews*, he inſiſted upon their Idolatries, their Perjuries, their Murders, and particularly their Adulteries, as a Proof of their abominable Hypocriſy, and a Preſage of their Deſtruction. Jer. 7. 9. *Will ye ſteal, murder, and commit Adultery, and ſwear falſly?* &c. And in the twenty ninth Chapter of the ſame Prophet, he foretels both King and People ſhould be carried Captives to *Babylon, Becauſe they had committed Villany in Iſrael, and had committed Adultery with their Neighbours Wives,* ver. 23. The like Reproofs and Menaces are alſo to be met with in the fifth Chapter of this Prophet. *Jeremiah,* and in the reſt of the Prophets.

IV. As to the New Teſtament, I ſhall not give a particular Account of what Paſſages are to be found there concerning Adultery, becauſe I have already mention'd moſt of them in the Chapter immediately foregoing. We ſee this Sin condemned moſt expreſly and by Name, St. *Mar.* vii. 21. 1 *Cor.* vi. 10. *Gal.* v. 19. and above all *Heb.* xiii. 4. *God ſhall judge the Whoremongers and Adulterers.* St. *Paul*'s manner of Speech concerning the Laws and Rights of Marriage in the firſt Epiſtle to the *Corinthians,* Ch. vii. is likewiſe very full to our purpoſe.

And hereto alſo agrees the Notion which the Ancient Primitive Chriſtians had of Adultery. By whom this Sin was looked upon as of a moſt provoking nature ; and they therefore proceeded with the utmoſt Severity againſt ſuch as were found guilty of it. It was one of thoſe three egregious Crimes, againſt which the Eccleſiaſtical Diſcipline was exerciſed in its utmoſt Rigour ; the other two being Idolatry and Murder. Whence Offenders in this kind were uſed to be kept under Excommunication for many Years together ; and there was a Time, when they were not to be re-

ſtor'd

stor'd to the Peace of the Church, till at the Point of Death. St. *Cyprian* testifies † that there were some Churches where Absolution was never granted them. And though perhaps this might be an over-rigorous Course with them, nevertheless we see by it, what a mighty Abhorrence the first Christians had of Adultery. And accordingly the Practice of it was very rarely to be heard of amongst them. They could then boldly plead for themselves against their Pagan Adversaries, * That *they committed neither Murder nor Adultery, and indeed had not known there were any such Crimes committed in the World, had they not observed how customary they were amongst these same Pagans.* And even the better and juster sort of the Pagans themselves, could not but own the Purity of the Christians both Religion and Manners, and bear testimony to them, That *they engaged themselves by a solemn Oath, neither to be guilty of Adultery, nor any other Crime.* As is plainly to be seen in that noted Letter ‖ which the younger *Pliny* wrote to the Emperor *Trajan*.

However after some time the Case began to alter. The Dread of this Crime abated; the Discipline relaxed; and those Abominations which the Gospel had given a great check to, not only gained at length an Admittance; but became frequent amongst its Professors; and is still unhappily too prevalent with them, to the great Dishonour of our most holy Religion.

Wherefore having thus seen what the Gospel of our Lord, what *Moses*'s Law, what Nature, and

---

† *Ep. ad Anton.* Et quidem apud Antecessores nostros qui d'm de Episcopis istinc in Provinciâ nostrâ, dandam Pacem Moechis non putaverunt, & in totum Poenitentiae locum contra Adulteria clauserunt.

* *Min. Fel. Octav.*

‖ *Plin. l.* 10. *Ep.* 97.

what

what the very Heathens have taught concerning
Adultery, I ask what Sentiment we ought all to
have of this Sin and those that commit it ? And
whether a Man muft not have renounced all Religion and even Natural Juftice, before he can
deliver himfelf up to a Crime fo infamous as
this ?

Thus I have fhewn that Uncleannefs is a Sin,
whether it proceed to the groffer Act of Adultery,
or terminate only in Fornication. I fhall not in
this place infift upon thofe other Crimes into
which Uncleannefs is apt to draw Perfons, fuch
as Inceft, and thofe terrible Enormities which Modefty forbids to name ; and which Almighty God
has formerly thought fit to punifh with Fire from
Heaven. Thefe are fuch monftrous Impieties, as
one can hardly tell how to mention. And all the
Reflection I fhall make upon them, is that of
St. *Paul* upon a like Occafion, *Rom.* i. which yet
ought to ftrike all thofe with a Fit of Trembling,
who fuffer themfelves to be enflaved to the infamous Lufts of Impurity ; namely, that when People are poffeffed with thefe Paffions, there is nothing fo foul as they will not be ready to venture
upon ; they lofe all Senfe of Shame, and involve
themfelves in all manner of Licentioufnefs. God
in his juft Judgment gives up all fuch as thus forfake Him, to the Defires of their own Hearts, till
they arrive at the moft intolerable Abominations.
And their Senfuality is too apt to entice them to
fuch Enormities as Human Nature recoils at, and
feems fcarce capable of yielding to. Of which
yet we have too plain Examples in the *Sodomites*
and the ancient *Canaanites*. And we have all
therefore very good reafon, ferioufly and with a
hearty Concern for our own Welfare, to confider
thefe Examples and thofe dreadful Exceffes, whereinto Senfuality cafts People headlong, when once
they

they give themselves up to it. And this Consideration ought to have a powerful Influence upon us, to keep us within the Bounds of our Duty, and to engage us to be continually upon our Guard against all Uncleanness, as a most dangerous Lust, and most earnestly to be avoided.

C H A P. VII.

Of the other Species of Uncleanness.

ADultery and Fornication are not all the Sins into which People are betray'd by Uncleanness; but there are other Species of it besides these two. There are a great Number of Persons, who are no way chargeable with these gross Sins, whose horrid Guilt I have been hitherto relating, who yet cannot clear themselves from the Charge of being Sensual, Impure, and Slaves to the inordinate Motions of the Flesh. And forasmuch as the greater Part of these are not apprehensive of the dangerous Condition they are in; nay, oftentimes on the contrary, take themselves to be innocent, or at least not to have incurred any considerable Guilt, it is but fit they should be disabused, and made more sensible how the Case is with them. This therefore is what I am next to apply my self to; and I beseech all that shall read what I here offer to their Consideration, seriously to attend to it, and impartially to examine and try themselves by it.

I say then, there are other Species of Impurity besides those hitherto treated of. And these may properly be reduced to three Heads, impure Actions, impure Words, and impure Thoughts.

I. There

I. There are many Actions contrary to Modesty and Chastity ; some whereof by the Violence of the Passion, and the full Consent of the Will, or by reason of the Malignity and Infamy of the Action, almost equal the Crime to which they tend. For some unchast Persons are hurried on by their Lust, to try in every thing to gratify their brutal Passion, as far as they can contrive to do it without committing the Fact. But here I must be very wary, and leave to my Readers the Trouble of considering with themselves what I may not say, and applying to all the Actions of Impurity, what I may but just touch upon very briefly, and only in general Terms. Amongst these, Actions contrary to Purity are to be reckoned all those Deeds, and whatsoever Instances of Behaviour, that are uncivil and too free ; such as immodest Touches, and lascivious Gestures. Hitherto also is to be reduced Indecency and Immodesty of Apparel, as well as too familiar Converse betwixt those of different Sexes. Under each of which Articles there are divers Particulars to be treated of, but that I shall have a more proper Occasion of doing it, when they shall hereafter fall in our way.

Now forasmuch as I cannot well repeat all those Actions which are hurtful to Purity, and yet my Readers may be doubtful of some of them, and may question whether this or that be unlawful, I shall lay down this one general Rule in this place, whereby these Doubts may be easily resolved: Let natural Chastity and Modesty be first consulted ; because provided a Habit of Wickedness has not quite extinguish'd in us the Sense of Modesty which is natural to us as Men, we shall readily discern, whether an Action be unchast, or no. Next this Principle is to be attended to ; That a Christian is bound to shun whatever sensualizes the Soul,

Soul, whatever tends only to satisfy the Passions, and whatever is wont to excite them either in our selves or others. And again, Enquiry should be made what is necessary, or at least is expresly allow'd. I say then, that whensoever we are ashamed of what we do, and dare not venture upon it in the sight of others; when it is only the Effect of a disorderly Passion, and aims only at indulging Sensuality, and kindling impure Desires either in our own or others Hearts; and which moreover it is neither necessary nor expresly allow'd; we should be sure to abstain from it.

If this Rule be thought not to be clear enough, and each one has yet his Scruples remaining, and cannot well satisfy himself, whether an Action be contrary to Purity, or be not; behold another Direction which leaves no Difficulty remaining. In all doubtful Cases, and when the Conscience is yet unsatisfy'd, the safer side is constantly to be chosen, which is not to yield to our Passion. There is never any Danger in taking this Course, though there be a great deal on the other hand, or rather though it be always sinful to do † what one doubts of, and cannot satisfy himself whether it be permitted, or whether it be forbidden.

Moreover, it is easy to discern that impure Actions are forbidden for two Reasons: *First,* Be-

---

† *This must be understood of things perfectly in our own Power, and where no Command of our Superiours intervenes. For where Authority has commanded our Obedience, this Command must over-rule our Doubts. As the Judicious Bishop Sanderson has clearly shewn, in his fourth Sermon ad Clerum, Sect. 27, 28, 29, 30, 31. And the present Lord Archbishop of York, in the second Part of his Discourse of Conscience. And Dr. Calamy, Of a Scrupulous Conscience, p. 35, &c. Nor indeed will it hold in all Cases, not over-ruled by any Command of Authority. As is solidly argued in the foresaid second Part of the Discourse of Conscience, p. 16, &c.*

cause they are a likely Means of carrying Men on
to the grosser Crime. People don't ordinarily arrive at the Heighth of Wickedness all at once, but
by certain Steps and Degrees. They begin with
what they think lawful; they accustom themselves to violate the Rules of Chastity in such Instances as they persuade themselves can have no
great hurt in them. But then from these lesser
Offences, they proceed to others, whose Wickedness they cannot but be sensible of; and so at
length they fall into the more horrid Crime.
But in the second place, though we should never
come thus far, and our unchast Actions should never
push us on to the utmost Licentiousness, they however defile the Soul; they increase the Inclination
to Uncleanness, and withdraw from God. As a
very little Observation will inform those who allow themselves in these sort of Liberties.

To impure Actions may be subjoin'd such Looks
as are contrary to Chastity, inasmuch as a Man
may be guilty also of Sin in this respect, whether
in beholding such Objects, or in reading such
Books, as may be apt to beget unlawful Desires.
It is an undoubted Truth, that impure Passions are
chiefly raised and enflamed by the Sight; and that
it is impossible to continue chast, without a diligent Care to govern the Eyes, and to turn them
away from whatsoever might seduce the Heart.
Let but any one enquire into the Objects and Writings I am speaking of, and the Impressions they
are apt to make upon the Mind, and this will presently convince him of the Evil and Danger of
suffering his Eyes to dwell upon them. These Objects pollute the Imagination, filling it with lustful Thoughts; and it is only through the Temptation of Sensuality, that any can fix their Eyes
upon them, or take any manner of Pleasure in
them. The Holy Scriptures sufficiently caution
against

against these undue Liberties. It was by the Sight that *David* was enticed to commit Iniquity. And *Job* who lived at a time when Moral Chastity was less known than it has been since, had yet learned that the principal Duty of Chastity was to regulate the Sight; as he declares, *Chap.* xxxi, 1. *I made a Covenant with mine Eyes; why should I then look upon a Maid?* And no Christian can deny the Necessity of this Duty, after what our Blessed Lord has said, St. *Matth.* v. 28. *Whosoever looketh upon a Woman to lust after her, hath committed Adultery with her already in his Heart.* Agreeably hereto the Character also St. *Peter* gives of those carnal Christians, against whom he wrote, was that *they had Eyes full of Idolatry,* 2 St. *Peter* ii. 14. The Sum is, That it is an infallible Sign of an unchast Person, to delight in fixing the Sight upon such Objects as promote Impurity. As I shall have occasion to observe again in the Sequel of this Discourse; and especially with regard to lascivious Books.

This likewise I must add, That if it be sinful to behold tempting Objects, it must be no less so to present such Objects to others. Upon which account those are highly to blame, who cloath not themselves with Shamefac'dness and Sobriety, and do not cover themselves as Christian Modesty requires. They hereby become an Occasion of the Fall and Offence of others, and expose themselves to that dreadful Vengeance, which our Saviour *Christ* pronounces against those *by whom the Offence cometh.* For the same Reason unchast Pictures, obscene and lascivious Draughts and Representations, are to be utterly banished from among Christians, as just matter of Infamy and Danger. Which shews to what a dismal Ebb Christianity is now come; of which there needs no clearer Evidence than the Dissoluteness in Habits and Pictures that is so commonly to be observed. The Pagans
had

had impure Paintings and Reprefentations ; and it was an Effect of their Depravation, and an unhappy Fruit of their Religion, whofe Worfhip, and whofe Gods in a fort authoriz'd and encourag'd it.   And this was one Caufe why the Primitive Chriftians had fuch an Averfion to all Painting and Sculpture, which yet are inoffenfive Arts, provided they be not abufed to bad purpofes. The Dread they had of Idolatry infpired them with this Opinion ; and they were much confirmed in it, by the Immodefty and Lafcivioufnefs of feveral Pictures and Statues they had met with amongft the Heathens.   Like to which none were ever feen in Chriftians Houfes, during the firft Ages of the Church ; howfoever it is a fad Truth, that they are now grown fo common, and the Abufe in this refpect fo fhameful, that a great part of the Profeffors of our moft holy Religion fcarce feem to differ from thofe Idolaters.

II. The Second Species of Impurity is that of Words.   And with what a degree of Guilt thefe are chargeable, may eafily be known, if we but a little reflect upon the Caufe from whence they proceed, and the Effect they produce.

As to the former of thefe, our Bleffed Saviour has taught us, that *out of the abundance of the Heart the Mouth fpeaketh,* St. *Matth.* xii. 34.   Which though fpoken in general Terms is fitly applicable to immodeft Words ; which cannot come from other than an impure Heart, and a Perfon almoft entirely void of Shame.   As it is Impurity to Think and Do things contrary to Chaftity, fo it is no lefs to Speak them. Inordinate Thoughts and Actions without doubt are criminal, though a Man may contain his Thoughts within his own Breaft, may conceal his Actions, and may be very referved in his Difcourfe ; but if he come to that pafs, as to give a free vent to his Thoughts, and

F   to

to hold immodeſt Diſcourſe, and talk lewdly and
diſſolutely, this ſhews him to have a very corrupt
Heart, and betrays a Stock of Impudence as well
as of Impurity.

On the other ſide, impure and laſcivious Diſcourſe is apt to produce moſt miſchievous Effects,
both in the Speaker and the Hearers, and is a
great Temptation to the fouler Crime. The Liberty of Speech too many allow themſelves, and
the Cuſtom they indulge themſelves in, of ſaying, and hearkening to what is contrary to Purity and Chaſtity, is very deſtructive of Modeſty
and Virtue. There is no paſſing thoſe Limits
which Modeſty and Decency preſcribe, but Perſons quickly grow to be no longer upon the Reſerve, and take daily more and more Liberty, and
the Abhorrence they had of Uncleanneſs wears
off, their Vice becomes familiar to them, and they
accuſtom themſelves to look upon it, without any
Veil or Covering.

Unclean Diſcourſe is ſo evidently deſtructive of
Virtue and Natural Modeſty, that the very Heathens could ſay, A Virtuous Man ought never to
ſpeak what is uneaſy to chaſt and modeſt Ears;
that an Obſcene Word is contrary to Virtue, and
diſreputable to the Speaker; and that Diſſolute
Diſcourſe is to be abhor'd, as well as the Actions
themſelves *. But Chriſtians have more expreſs
Rules and Precepts for their Direction herein.
† *Eph. 4. 29.* † *Let no corrupt Communication proceed out of your
Mouth, but that which is good to the uſe of Edifying,
that it may miniſter Grace unto the Hearers.* ‖ *But*
‖ *Eph. 5. 3, 4.* *Fornication, and all Uncleanneſs, let it not be once named
amongſt you, as becometh Saints; neither Filthineſs, nor
fooliſh Talking, nor Jeſting, which are not convenient,
or becoming your Profeſſion.* See here an abſo-

---

* Plutarch. *Of Hearing the Poets.*

Inte

lute Prohibition, but withal in very general Terms, to let us know how referved, and how circumfpect Chriftians ought to be, that they fpeak nothing which does not well confift with Modefty and Decency. But efpecially it is to be obferv'd, how the Apoftle condemns, not only all grofs Obfcenity, and fuch filthy lafcivious Expreffions, as one of any meafure of Virtue would be afham'd to utter ; but in general all Difcourfe that borders upon Impurity, and any way implies it. He forbids even all light and vain Talk, all Buffoonery, and Scurrility, as not becoming Chriftians, and which fuit not with the Holinefs of their Profeffion.

So that were but People well convinced, and duly mindful of thefe Doctrines, this muft neceffarily work a Reformation in their Difcourfe and Converfation, and make them much more obfervant and cautious how they fpeak, that they never utter an unchaft Expreffion, or that tends to Impurity. It would caufe them to abftain from many things, which according to the Liberty that is ufually taken are now looked upon as innocent. For Example ; They would not then be fo ready to entertain each other with wanton Songs, and foft and effeminate Airs, and Language, upon the Subject of Love, which corrupt the Hearts of Youth more than Perfons are aware of ; though few are wont to take notice of it.

III. The Third Species of Impurity is of the Thoughts. And it is no difficult matter to fhew that impure Thoughts are finful. Whofoever confults St. *Matthew*'s Gofpel, muft needs fee how expreffly our Bleffed Saviour affirms, || that *Whofoever* || Ch. 5. 28. *looketh on a Woman to luft after her, commits Adultery with her in his Heart,* and by confequence becomes culpable in the fight of God by thefe Thoughts and Defires. So our Saviour at another time

F 2   teaches,

† St. Mar. teaches, † that thofe *Evil Defires which proceed from*
7. 23.   *within, out of the Heart, defile the Man.* And his
* 2 Cor. 7. Apoftle St. *Paul* exhorts * to *Purify our felves from*
1.
† Colof. 3. *all Filthinefs both of Flefh and Spirit ;* and to † *Re-*
5.   *nounce not only the Sin of Uncleannefs, but all unclean*
Defires. In a word, this is the Purport and Intent
of all thofe Precepts which require to govern our
Defires, and fubdue our Carnal Inclinations.
Though befides thefe there are two other Confi-
fiderations which clearly prove it our Duty, to attend to and regulate our Thoughts, as well as our
Words and Actions.

One is, That the Thoughts are the Source and
Original from whence our other Sins take their
Rife. Now it is an uncontefted Principle, that
whatever caufes Sin, is to be avoided. And feeing irregular Defires are the Spring of finful Actions, lafcivious Glances, and unchaft Words ; it is
therefore every one's Duty watchfully to refift
thefe Thoughts and Defires, and to ufe our utmoft Diligence for preventing as much as in us
lies, their thrufting themfelves into our Minds.

The other Confideration is, That fuppofing
thefe inward Motions and Inclinations of our
Heart, do not carry us on to the Crime it felf,
and pafs no farther than the bare Defire, they will
not yet fail to pollute the Soul, and breed in us
contrary Difpofitions to what our Religion requires of us. A Man is not properly defiled by
any thing that does not come from within the
Heart. But the Defires and Motions of the Soul
may be finful, though they reft there only, and
never put the Body upon Action. It is in the Intention, the Defire, and the Will, that Sin chiefly
has its being. Thus Covetoufnefs confifts in the
Love and Defire of Riches ; and Pride in the
Love of Glory and Honour. And in like manner Uncleannefs confifts in the Love of Senfuality
and

and carnal Pleaſures.   And as a Man may be Covetous or Proud without ever actually poſſeſſing
the Goods or the Glory he is ſo fond of, ſo he
may no leſs be Unclean without arriving at the
very Crime.   That which pollutes the Soul, and
renders it guilty and miſerable, is its Eſtrangement
from God ; and this is the infallible Effect of impure Thoughts.   Theſe extinguiſh Piety, Ferven-
cy in Prayer, and a Deſire of the heavenly Trea-
ſure ; and ſtupify and ſenſualize the Soul ; and ſo
much the more, by how much the more eaſily this
Paſſion gets the Poſſeſſion of the Heart, and employs the Phancy, and the Imagination, and ſuf-
fers not the Thoughts to dwell upon other Objects, nor leaves any reliſh of whatever other ſort
of Pleaſures.

And Oh that People would be perſuaded ſeriouſly and attentively to conſider this with themſelves !   The Generality of Men conclude themſelves innocent, ſo long as they cannot charge
themſelves with the Crimes of Uncleanneſs, thinking it enough, if they can ſay for themſelves, *I am
no Adulterer, nor Fornicator.*   But alas ! ſuch ought
to know that Perſons may be free of theſe Crimes,
and yet may be highly blameable in the Sight of
God.   Nor is this all ; for it is not impoſſible that
one who has actually committed the Crime, may
yet be really leſs culpable, than another who has
never committed it.   God forbid that I ſhould
pretend to flatter Sinners, or go about to exte-
nuate the great Guilt of any that deliver themſelves up to the Sin of Uncleanneſs ;   But neither
may I flatter others, who though they have never
been guilty of the Crime, live however in a Habit of this Paſſion ; but muſt deal plainly with
them, muſt ſhew them their Caſe as it is, and muſt
put them in mind of the Sinfulneſs and Danger of
the ſtate they are in.

F 3   Let

Let us therefore suppose a Man to have fallen into this Sin of Uncleanness, drawn into it by some violent Excess of Passion, but who immediately recovers himself after his Fall, bewails his Miscarriage, and makes the best Reparation in his Power, by a true Repentance and Holiness of Life. Let us suppose on the other hand, a Man innocent of the Crime, but who, this excepted, allows himself in all sort of Impurities, has polluted both Body and Heart by a hundred shameful Actions, by forbidden Looks, and dangerous Readings ; a Man whose Eyes are always wandring, and his Soul is wrought upon and captivated by every tempting Object, his Heart, and his Imagination full of lustful Thoughts and Conceptions ; who cherishes his Passions, and delights in them ; and in whom they are habitually settl'd and confirm'd. Now I would ask, Whether is the more impure and the more guilty of these two ? I do not in the least excuse the Crime, but it cannot possibly be denied, that the latter is in the worse Condition, howsoever he may pass for innocent amongst Men, and the other may be look'd upon as a heinous Offender.

But to make the Matter yet more plain, let us examine into it a little more narrowly. Thou sayst thou hast not committed the Crime ; but tell me, What is it has hindred thee ? It could not be the Fear of God, because this would no less have engaged thee to regulate thy Desires, and keep thy Heart pure. It must therefore have been, either the Want of a fit Opportunity, or some other Considerations, such as the Fear of Men, a Dread of Shame, and other ill Consequents the Crime might have expos'd thee too. The Truth is, thy Will has been entirely bent this way, thy Heart has been filled with filthy and shameful Desires, to which thou hast chearfully re-

refign'd thy felf. Wherefore flatter not thyfelf
upon this account ; but remember rather that impure Thoughts and Defires are Sins, and poffibly
may prove very great ones.

To proceed : There are divers Species and divers Degrees of impure Thoughts, between which
we are neceffarily to diftinguifh. And to this end
Enquiry is to be made, how, and by what Steps
a Man falls into Sin. And fo we fhall find that,
whether it be from the Activity of own Imagination, or from the Impreffion outward Objects
make upon us, there firft arife fuch Thoughts and
Inclinations in our Souls as pleafe and improve our
Paffions. Which unlefs we carefully refift upon
their firft Rife, the Favour we have for them will
be continually gaining upon us, till at length we
come to take delight in them, willingly admit
them, give our Phancy free Liberty to entertain
it felf with them, and let them fix themfelves in
our Minds. By which means they grow more
powerful, and we find our felves more and more
eafy towards them, and fo they prefently produce
Defires, it being natural to defire what we find
pleafes us. Sometimes thefe are wandring Defires, not apply'd to any particular Object. But
at othertimes they grow into a formed Defign,
and a Refolution and deliberate Choice. After
which there wants only a convenient Opportunity for confummating the Crime. Thefe are the
Steps and Degrees of our Paffions ; and by this
Method of Procedure it is that they come to get
the Afcendant over us ; and this oftentimes with
fuch Readinefs, and fo fpeedily, that we are fcarce
fenfible of it. Now each of thefe Degrees has
its Guilt, though not all equally. From our firft
beginning not to reject thefe Thoughts, but rather give them Entertainment, the Soul begins to
be defiled ; though when they grow up into De-

fires,

Defires, it is much more fo. And if in a while they obtain the full Confent of the Will, the Temptation then has 'done its bufinefs ; and though the Man fhould not dare to venture upon the Crime, either for want of Opportunity, or becaufe he is afraid to expofe himfelf, he is neverthelefs to look upon himfelf as chargeable with it before God. And it is properly with refpect to this Species of Luft, that our Saviour tells us, † *Whofoever looketh upon a Woman to luft after her, has committed Adultery with her already in his Heart.*

† St. Matt. 5. 28.

Having thus difcourfed of impure Thoughts, I think my felf concern'd, before I quit this Subject, to take notice, that there are alfo an involuntary fort of Thoughts that thruft themfelves into the Mind, and may feem contrary to Purity, whilft in reality they are not, and which do no harm to this Vertue, nor any way defile the Soul. Such are certain foolifh, whimfical, extravagant Thoughts, which at firft appearance feem lewd and deteftable, and perhaps very wicked ; which arife either from the fimple Imagination, or from fomething read, or heard, or feen ; or from a melancholick Diforder in the Temperature of the Body ; as many find by Experience. It is not unufual to be too often interrupted and tormented with thefe Thoughts, even in our moft ferious Retirements, and in the midft of our Devotions. Infomuch that fome have upon Confideration hereof, been caft into Fits of Defpair and the blackeft Melancholy ; concluding that thefe being the Devil's Temptations, themfelves muft certainly be under the Power of this Enemy to God and Man. And this fad Eftate of theirs is render'd yet more fad and dreadful, by their own Backwardnefs, their Shame, or Fear, to difcover it to any elfe, becaufe they apprehend it to be fuch as had never before been feen or heard of. Yet this is too com-

common, and the Number of thefe poor Souls is
far greater than People ordinarily imagine it to
be.

Wherefore we muft remember, that thefe fort
of Thoughts are not to be accounted amongft
thofe impure Thoughts I have been difcourfing of.
They are but what the Minds of the Beft are liable
to, and ought not therefore to put others into too
great a Concern. And even the more ftrange
and abominable they appear, the lefs reafon have
we to be affrighted at them. For there is no Sin-
fulnefs in any thing, but what has a Tendency to
Evil, and is fome way Voluntary. But the
Thoughts I am fpeaking of are not fuch Temptations as invite to the commiffion of Sin ; nor have
they at all the Affent of the Will.

On the contrary, thofe who complain of them,
are fo far from confenting to them, that they abhor them, and beg and pray to be deliver'd from
them. They may juftly be reputed an Effect of
human Frailty, and the Diforder of our Nature ;
but it is a grofs Miftake to rank them amongft
our Sins. There is more Evil in one Fit of Anger, or Unclean Defire, than in all thefe Thoughts,
how frightful and how deteftable foever they appear. And the beft way therefore to get rid of
them is to defpife them, and not trouble ourfelves
about them. Some are of Opinion that they are
to be oppofed and refifted, and fet themfelves
heartily to fhake them off, and beg pardon for
them of God, and are never at eafe becaufe of
them. But it were a much wifer Courfe, not to
be uneafy at them, nor fet our felves too refolutely to contend with them ; becaufe the more we
ftudy to prevent them, the more we fhall find
them return upon us. And all that many have
got by oppofing them, is only that they have
hereby fallen into a miferable Condition. Thefe

                                        Thoughts

Thoughts are not of that Confequence that I fhould have efteem'd them worth mentioning, but only for the fake of fuch as are wont to torment themfelves about them. And what I have faid is faid not only with relation to thofe Thoughts which are contrary to Purity, but in general, and of all others, as well as thefe, and even of thofe that arife againft the Divinity, and againft our Faith. But this I pofitively aver, That what I have faid has no relation to fuch Thoughts as proceed from a corrupt and profane Heart, and a Principle of Impurity and Libertinifm.

Thus I have done with what I defigned to propofe concerning the Sins of Fornication and Adultery, together with the other Species of Impurity.

SECTION

SECTION II.

Of the Effects of Uncleanness.

AFTER what has been said it cannot be doubted whether Uncleanness be a great Sin, and carefully to be avoided by all that call themselves Christians. But yet to make us the more sensible of the Evil of it, it will be requisite to consider its ill Effects in three respects ; namely with relation to the State whereinto Men are brought by it, with regard to the Sins that accompany it, and in reference to the Mischiefs that follow upon it. A serious Consideration of which three Articles, will give us a full Prospect of the Heinousness and the Danger of this Sin.

CHAP. I.

Of the State to which People are brought by Uncleanness.

THE Estate to which People are brought by Uncleanness is so exceedingly deplorable, that I persuade my self, had but Persons a right Notion of it, they would be much more afraid of giving way to it. And for this Cause I shall set myself in the next place to give some account of this State. But here I must premise, that what I am about to say, is not calculated for all sorts of Unclean Persons. Some being more deeply involv'd in this Sin, and others less, it must be

con-

confessed they are not all equally Partakers of the ill Consequents of it. And I must therefore beseech each one to apply what I say to his own Soul, so far only as he finds himself concern'd in it, and sees he has need of it.

Now this State to which People are reduc'd by Impurity, may be consider'd these two ways, *First*, With respect to the Purity of the Soul; and, *Secondly*, with respect to the Peace of their own Consciences.

I. And it is plain the State of one given to Uncleanness, is a State of Pollution, Sin, and Misery. True Piety requires to keep the Body and the Heart pure; but the Unclean are defiled both in Body and Soul, sometimes by the Crime it self, and sometimes by other Actions contrary to Purity. Their Sensuality by being the Occasion of abundance of inordinate Inclinations in them, hurries them on to many Instances of Lewdness for satisfying this brutish Passion. But the State of the Soul is chiefly to be consider'd, whilst it is ordinarily possest by lustful Thoughts and Desires. The unchast Person has his Mind rarely free from lascivious and shameful Imaginations and Phancies. His Heart is a continual Spring of evil Thoughts bubbling up in it every moment; so that there needs only the Presence of an Object to inflame his Desire. Let him but see or hear any thing relating to his beloved Sin, and his Lust is presently kindled by it. And not only so, but at othertimes when none of these Objects present themselves, his Memory serves to furnish him with such former Passages as had gratified his Sensuality; these he recalls to his Mind, and pleases himself with the Thoughts of them, instead of reflecting upon them, as he ought, with Sorrow of Heart and Confusion of Face.

This

This Paffion has no fooner got the Maftery over the Heart, but forthwith it purfues the Man every where, and keeps its Poffeffion of him at all times and in all places. Upon the moft ferious Occafions, and in the very Acts of Religion, he ever and anon finds himfelf tranfported with luftful Conceptions and Defires, which inceffantly follow him and take up his Thoughts. I fhall not need to fay how great a part of Mankind find their Minds flag, and languifh, and wander from their Bufinefs, and are full even of wicked Thoughts, when they fhould be praying to God, or hearkening to his Word. But it is certain that in many of them Impurity is the Caufe of this Diforder. A Soul that is not Chaft, will not know how to be Devout. To fuch an one the holy Exercifes of Prayer, Meditation, Reading, &c. appear infipid and unpleafant. A Love of Voluptuoufnefs is inconfiftent with Spiritual Delights, and thofe pious Affections, and Joys, and Raptures, which accompany a fincere Holinefs of Converfation.

It is undoubtedly a dreadful Cafe to be thus miferably deprived of the Love and Grace of God, and not allowed to enjoy any Communion with him. And it was not therefore without very good reafon that St. *Paul* faid, by Uncleannefs we ceafe to be Members of Chrift, and Temples of the Holy Ghoft. The luftful Man cuts himfelf off from Communion with our Saviour and the Bleffed Spirit, and defaces the Image of God that had been formed in himfelf, and bears that of the Unclean Spirit.

Which is a Condition unworthy not only of a Chriftian, but even of a Man. God has given to Mankind Modefty and Reafon as a Check to their Paffions; but Senfuality and Luft extinguifh both thefe Endowments, and render Men like the
brute

brute Beasts, which follow their own impetuous Inclinations, without any manner of Reserve: These sensual Passions divest them of their Judgment and Understanding; according to that of the Prophet *Hosea,* Chap. iv. 11. *Whoredom and Wine take away the Heart.* This is sadly verefied in the looser Sett of Men, who through their Lusts are become a sort of Brutes, whose Character is Folly, and who senselesly cast themselves upon a thousand Evils. Of all the Passions perhaps there is not one, that so wretchedly blinds the Eyes, as this does where it is indulged: For alas! What is it that such who are transported with an immoderate Desire and unchaste Love, will stick at? Either they don't take notice of the great number of Evils, whereto they expose themselves, or if they do, are neverthelefs refolved to venture upon them. They will attempt Impossibilities for the Gratification of their Lust, will dare to be made wretched Vagabonds, will squander away their Estates, will forfeit their Honours, will disgrace their Families, and bring upon themselves inevitable Misery, in spight of all that can be said or done to the contrary. And still so much the more lamentable is their Case, by how much the harder it is to reclaim them, when once they are throughly habituated to their Impurity. Whilst their Inclination grows daily stronger and stronger, their Disposition to Good is naturally and inevitably impair'd, and their Vice becomes so fixed that nothing can root it out. Or if any imagine that Age will wear it off, besides what I have to offer hereafter against this, I must at present observe that it is not always so; but there are Multitudes of aged Sinners, who burn with this impure Fire, and whose Age does not at all render them either the Wiser, or the more Chaste.

Next

II. Next we are to confider the Unclean Perfon's Eftate with refpect to the Peace of his own Confcience. And fo we fhall find him always Uneafy, or which is worfe, given up to a Hardnefs of Heart.

1. A Purity of Soul is neceffarily required in order to Peace of Mind ; the contrary Difpofition naturally breeds Trouble and Difquiet. That Tranquillity and Satisfaction which the innocent Soul enjoys, belongs not to them who are tranfported with fenfual and luftful Defires.

The Impure, efpecially thofe who are guilty of the Crime, are in continual Fear of Men, left their Wickednefs come to be difcovered ; they dread thofe that are privy to it, and fo have it in their power to make it known ; they diftruft all others ; and even their ownfelves. Nor is it any ftrange thing for guilty Perfons to betray themfelves, and difcover their own Crimes, either through Inconfideration, or in their Sleep, or in a Fit of Raving, or fome other way.

But fuppofing them to be in no apprehenfion from Man, but that they are able to conceal their Mifcarriages from all that are about them, they cannot hide them from their own Confciences, nor avoid being reproached by them ; but will at every turn be ftruck with a Senfe of the dreadful Condition they are in, and fear and tremble becaufe of it. It is often feen, from time to time, and even in the midft of their forbidden Pleafures, that the Delight they take in fatisfying their Lufts, is attended with Bitternefs and cruel Remorfe. The vileft Senfualift cannot forbear thinking fometimes, that he muft die and be bereaft of thefe Objects of his Paffion. It is true thefe Reflexions oftentimes pafs away like Lightning, and the Man contrives fome Method of lulling them afleep, and delivering himfelf from the Difturbance of them,

them, at least for a while ; but then it frequently happens, that they return and fill him with Confusion ; as particularly in the time of Sickness, or at the Hour of Death. Then Conscience is terribly awaken'd, the Miscarriages of Men's Lives come then into their Minds, and inexpressible Consternation takes hold of them.

2. But the Unclean Person is not always in such Perplexity, but sometimes is deliver'd up to a State of Security, and Hardness of Heart. And this Hardness is twofold. For as there are two things in Sin, the Sin itself, or the Fault committed, and the Punishment consequent upon it ; so are there two sorts of Hardness ; the one when the Sinner is not affected with a Sense of his Wickedness, the other when he regards not the Punishment of it.

1. The impure Person very often has either no Sense at all of his Sin, or at least, but a very weak and feeble one. This has happen'd to some of the grossest Offenders, whose Security, after so many Provocations, has been very wonderful. There are such whose Conscience might reasonably be expected to be to them a Hell upon Earth, considering how their Life has been little else than a continu'd Series of Incontinence, Pollution, and Uncleanness ; their Youth has been entirely sensual, their Practices since have been very shameful, and they have given themselves up to their inordinate Passions of the Flesh ; and yet they live at Ease, and in Mirth and Jollity. Now it is possible they may be much more so in Appearance, than they are in Reality, since none can look into their Hearts to see how they stand affected there. Yet it must be owned they are sometimes insensible of their Condition, and so are at Ease within themselves, and feel none of that Remorse and Dread I am speaking of. And this is especially

the

the Cafe of thofe who have long habituated themfelves to love their Sin, and defpife the Admonitions of Confcience ; till by degrees they come to
be no longer reftrained by any Scruples, or any inward Remorfe, and can fin boldly and without
Fear ; much like thofe luftful and licentious Pagans, of whom St. *Paul* fpeaks, *Who being paft feel-*
ing, had given themfelves over to Lafcivioufnefs, to
work all Uncleannefs with greedinefs, and whom God
gave up to their own vile Affections. In truth it
feemed hard that thofe to whom the Gofpel has
been preached, fhould ever arrive at fuch a height
of Infenfibility and Stupidity. Yet there are Profeffors of our Religion, who in this refpect fall
very little fhort of the Pagans. There are unhappy Chriftians, who have in a manner loft all Senfe
of Religion, and all Notions of Virtue, and are
even ready to undertake the Defence of their Impieties.

2. But that we may the better apprehend to
what a meafure of Security fome of thefe Sinners
may attain, it is farther to be obferved, That as
they are not fenfible of their Sin, fo neither are
they oftentimes of the Punifhment of it ; fuch
Punifhment I mean as befals them by reafon of it,
in this prefent Life. Sometimes one may perceive
the Judgments of God hanging over the Heads of
the Unchaft, and threatning to fall upon them ;
fometimes actually and vifibly purfuing them, in
their own Perfons, or in their Relations, or their
Affairs in the World, making them groan under
the Miferies, Sorrows, and divers Evils they have
brought upon themfelves ; and yet we may fee how
little Senfe they have of the Reafon why thefe fad
Afflictions are laid upon them, and how ready
they are to attribute their Misfortunes to any other
Caufe rather than to themfelves ; fome of them
continuing in their Security, till the Judgment of

G   God

God seizes them, and they die in their Impenitence. Which is the most deplorable, and most dangerous State a Man can fall into. For so long as the Sinner has a Sense of his Guilt, and the Vengeance justly due to him for it, there is some hope of him ; but when he is come to this degree of Obduracy, there is very little to be expected from him, for he is then upon the very Brink of Misery, and but one Step from everlasting Destruction.

But methinks I hear some plead, That it is not the Fate of all Unclean Persons to be thus harden'd in their Wickedness, but that some of them repent and are converted, that their Sins may be blotted out. And this is what I willingly own. But then, besides that there is some reason to question whether all that seem to be reclaim'd, are really and truly so, as I shall shew hereafter ; besides this I say, I answer, that all who are Unclean do not thus repent ; and every one therefore should dread the indulging himself in this Lust, left so he fall into a State of Impenitence, as he has too apparent Reason to expect he shall. His sinning Wilfully, and searching for Evasions whereby to encourage himself in his Sin, and to perswade himself he incurs no great Danger by it, is the natural and most likely Means of Security.

Yet besides this I have something more to add, which very well deserves to be consider'd, and will farther evidence how exceedingly dreadful that State is to which Persons reduce themselves by Impurity. For admitting that those who have committed this Sin, or at least who are addicted to Uncleanness, though they have not actually committed it, do rise again by Repentance, their Case however is very sad and uncomfortable upon these two Accounts.

1. The

1. The Impreffion that has been made upon them by their luftful and carnal Inclinations will for a long time after expofe them to Temptation and the Danger of returning to their former evil Courfes. Habits of Sin are not extirpated all at once, efpecially fuch as are attended with fenfual Pleafure and Delight. There is more Difficulty than Men are ordinarily aware of, in correcting a vicious Temper and Difpofition, and checking the Motions which naturally arife either in Body or Soul, after a long Cuftom of finning. It is not near fo eafy as People phancy to difengage themfelves of thofe Sins, which are almoft infeparably fix'd in their Imaginations, and gratify their Senfitive Faculties, and with the Thoughts of which they are wont to pleafe themfelves. The Reprefentation and Remembrance of thefe Lufts continues for a long time, ftill polluting the Soul, inftead of working in them a hearty Sorrow and true Repentance. What miferable Wretches then muft they be, who have fpent perhaps the greateft part of their Life in thefe impure Paffions, and have not yet got the Maftery over their Senfes, nor learn'd to mortify their Bodies by a long and fincere Repentance!

2. But this is not all. For though they fhould be able to furmount thefe Inconveniences, they muft yet expect to have their Confcience reprove them as long as they live. Though the truly penitent Sinner may affure himfelf of obtaining the Pardon of his Sins, he will always bear about him a Remembrance of them, which will exceedingly afflict him, and cover him with Confufion. And fo much the more nearly will thefe Reflections affect him, by how much the more Penitent he is. Oh, What Sorrow and Anguifh of Mind muft it caufe in him, to look back upon the time wherein he had forfaken his God, and bethink himfelf of

G 2   the

the Extravagance and Licentiousness of his younger Days, and all the Sins he has either committed himself, or has occasion'd others to commit! Not to add any thing here of his Doubts concerning the Nature and Validity of his Repentance, whether it be sincere and effectual, and such as is required in order to the Forgiveness his of past Transgressions.

The natural Result of which Considerations is, That the Estate to which Persons reduce themselves by this Sin, is very disconsolate and afflicting. And this will farther appear, if we proceed to consider the several other Sins wherewith it is accompanied.

CHAP. II.

Of the Sins which accompany Uncleanness.

THIS Consideration that Uncleanness is one of those Sins which never go alone, but have a Train of others perpetually attending them, is of great Use for proving the Heinousness of this Vice. And this I come now to treat of, chiefly with respect to those that are guilty of the Crime; but so as that all who are impure in any other manner, or have an Inclination to Impurity, may justly apply it seriously to themselves.

Now the Sins which here fall under our Consideration, as accompanying Impurity, are of two sorts. Some of which precede the Crime, and others ensue upon it.

I. It is certain, in the first place, that People do not usually fall into this Crime, without being chargeable with certain other previous Transgressions of their Duty. This is true of the generality

lity of Unclean Perfons, and there are very few Exceptions to it to be met with.

1. Uncleannefs almoft always fprings from Ignorance, Idlenefs, Irreligion, and Senfuality; thofe who pollute themfelves by this infamous Sin, or fet their Hearts upon the Lufts of the Flefh, being for the moft part, fuch as for want of a good Education and Inftruction in their Child-hood, have little Underftanding in Matters of Religion; or elfe are Profane and Libertines; or have but little Senfe of Piety and the Fear of God, and are very loofe in the whole Tenor of their Converfation, and live in the Neglect of Prayer and the other Exercifes of Devotion; or are Idle, Lazy, Senfual, and Lovers of Pleafures. Thefe are the Qualities which involve People, and efpecially in the Heat of Youth, in Uncleannefs, as fhall be fully proved, when I come to enquire into the Sources of this Sin.

2. But there are other Sins likewife which precede this whereof I am now fpeaking; fuch as impure Thoughts and Defires, immodeft Paffions and Inclinations, an unreferved and blameable Familiarity, unchaft Looks, Actions, and Difcourfe; and in a Word all that this Paffion ordinarily produces in them who are under its Influence. Whereto let it be added, That for the Satisfaction of this brutal Paffion, a thoufand unlawful Contrivances are made ufe of, Solicitations, artful Infinuations, Lyes, Proteftations, and even Oaths for the Confirmation of their Promifes, which yet they at length take liberty to violate. Sometimes they venture to commit great and grievous Crimes, for facilitating their way to the accomplifhment of their Defigns, and getting rid of fuch Perfons as might otherwife be an Obftruction to them. They will not ftick to facrifice their Wealth, their Reputation, and all that

G 3 is

is dear to them, not excepting their Religion and their Conscience, to this infamous Passion. Thus they pass through Diversity of other Sins before they arrive at what they principally aimed at. Before they come to be Fornicators or Adulterers, they are first Profane and Impious, their Bodies and their Souls are defiled and infected, and they have parted with their Chastity, and their Religion; so that the Crime is only an Addition of certain Degrees to that Impurity which they had before contracted.

What I have here said particularly affects two sorts of Persons, it being plain from hence that, 1. Many who have never yet dared to commit the Crime, are not however to look upon themselves as innocent; because they are highly culpable in giving way to those Sins which lead to the Crime, howsoever they have not yet ventured upon the Crime it self. 2. Those who have unhappily fallen into the Crime ought to be sensible that they are much more blameable than possibly they take themselves to be, and that their Sin of Uncleanness is not all they are chargeable with, but they have many others to answer for, which render them very criminal before God. Let them therefore call to mind what has preceded their Fall, let them recollect the manner of their past Behaviour, and what it was that brought them to this Crime, let them examine their Life, and their Conscience, with relation to the other Duties of Religion, and they will find themselves to have been perfect Strangers to Godliness, and that their Conversation has been little else than one continu'd Series of Indevotion and Licentiousness. If all that are guilty would weigh this well with themselves, they would have quite a different Notion of their Sin; especially if hereto they subjoin the Consideration of those other Iniquities that are the most common Effects of it. II. For

II. For the Truth is, there are divers sorts of Sins consequent upon Uncleanness.

1. Those who are guilty of it, at least a great part of them, continue in the Commiffion of the fame Crimes. The Difficulty of this Sin shews it felf chiefly in the beginning, and when the firft Step is taken, they thenceforward fin more boldly, and are lefs upon their guard againft it. On the one hand, their Paffion gets head, and their luftful Inclinations grow more prevalent; and on the other, Modefty and the Fear of God wear off. At firft they fin with fome Reluctancy, and they find for fometime a Struggle within themfelves; but when once they have paffed their known Bounds, they are little concerned for whatever they do afterwards. Having begun to enter upon a finful Familiarity, they ordinarily proceed accordingly, perfevering in their Sin as long as they are able, unlefs they meet with fome Impediment to prevent it; and yet then they only divert their Paffion to fome other Object.

2. They not only continue in this Sin, but proceed to groffer Inftances of it. From one Fault they go on to another, and according as the Number of their Sins increafes, they are proportionably greater and more enormous. Incontinence has it in its Power to caft Men headlong into the utmoft Excefs; it is a bottomlefs Gulph, that never can be filled; a Fire that kindles and burns more violently according to the Quantity of Fuel that is heaped upon it. And hence the Debauchee being tranfported by his own brutifh Paffions, fets himfelf to find out new Methods of fatisfying his Luft, and when he has found them, foon grows weary of thefe too, and is as much at a lofs for others, which yet in a while pleafe him no better than the former. It fares with him as with the Drunkard, who when Cuftom of Drinking has

G 4 ren-

render'd his Wine so familiar to him that he thinks
it not strong enough, seeks out for other Liquors,
and not long after as much despises these.   Fornication paves the way to Adultery, and sometimes
to what is more flagitious.   This gives birth to
those horrible Crimes which are not fit to be named, which brought Destruction upon *Sodom,* and
its neighbouring Cities, and provoked Almighty
God to exterminate the *Canaanites ;* as St. *Paul*
speaks *Rom.* i. 21. 24. where he tells us of the Heathens, that *having their foolish Hearts darkened, God
also gave them up to Uncleanness, through the Lusts of
their own Hearts, to dishonour their own Bodies between
themselves.*   When we reflect upon the Abominations of these Heathens, and of the ancient *Canaanites,* and read the Laws which the Almighty
saw fit to give the People of *Israel* upon this account, and which are contained in the eighteenth
Chapter of *Leviticus,* and moreover observe the
execrable Abominations that are yet committed,
not only amongst the Infidels, but amongst such
as call themselves Christians, and in Countries
that have naturally an Abhorrence of such beastly
Lusts, it is wonderful to think that Persons endu'd
with Reason, and who moreover make Profession
of Christianity, should be capable of such horrible Impieties.   However this lets us see to what
Excesses Men are carried by their Lusts, and what
are the Consequences of Impurity.

3. Besides these dreadful Instances of Incontinence, Impurity makes way for divers other Sins ;
it being ordinary to endeavour the concealing of
this Sin by the Commission of new ones of other
kinds.   Thus *David* became guilty of Murder, in
hope to prevent the Discovery of his Adultery,
by treacherously contriving the Death of his faithful Subject *Uriah.*   I cannot here take notice of
all the Courses Unclean Persons resort to, to the
end

end their Vices may never come to the Knowledge of the World, fome of them being too horrid to be mention'd. They deftroy their own Infants fometimes before, and fometimes after their Birth. Or if thefe Infants, the Fruits of their Impurity, don't lofe their Lives, they are ufually caft off; and thofe who have brought them into the World, mind not how they are difpos'd of, their only Care being to get rid of them; nor are they concern'd for what becomes either of their Bodies, or of their Souls. Which is one of the moft crying Sins they can poffibly be guilty of, a Sin whofe Enormity cannot be fufficiently expreffed; and yet with which vaft Numbers of Perfons, efpecially of the Men, load their Confciences.

4. Uncleannefs is very frequently followed by Tricking and Unfaithfulnefs. Nothing is more common with fuch as practice it, than to make ufe of Promifes and Oaths in order to effecting their lewd Defigns, and afterwards to break thefe Oaths and Promifes, and fo to become guilty of Perjury and Perfidioufnefs. I will not take occafion here to fay any thing of the crying Acts of Injuftice that are done to, and the Difturbances that happen in Families, by means of Adultery, becaufe I have already touched upon them in the foregoing Chapters.

5. The Crimes in which Unclean Perfons involve themfelves upon the Difcovery of their Wickednefs come next to be confidered; that inftead of confeffing their Guilt, they deny it, they lye, and this with the moft folemn Proteftations and Oaths. They feek to juftify themfelves by the moft indirect Means; and in thofe places where the Laws condemn and punifh Impurity, they ftudy by Trick, and Artifice, and all fort of undue Evafions to elude the Force of the Laws and the Strictnefs of Difcipline. They are ordinarily

avowed

avowed Enemies to all Ecclefiaftical Difcipline and Order ; and fet up with all their might for a Liberty to live as they pleafe ; and wherefoever they are able they will not fail to compafs fuch their Defign. And for this reafon it is that the Laws which were made againft this Vice have been abrogated in many places, or at leaft are grown into Difufe.

6. Uncleannefs, if perfifted in, gradually ftifles all Senfe of Religion and Confcience. Of which King *Salomon* was a famous Example, whofe ftrange Wives prevailed upon him to forfake his God, and ferve the Idols of the Nations round about him. And now in our own days it is ordinarily to be obferved, that Perfons facrifice their Religion to this brutifh Paffion, changing their Church or Party, purely for the gratifying their fenfual Defires. Oftentimes they grow profeffed Libertines and Abetters of Impiety, and fo add Impudence and Shamelefnefs to their Impurity, and fcoff at Religion, and undertake to defend their Crime. Becaufe they find themfelves condemn'd by the Doctrines of Religion, and that it were happy for them if they had no Judgment to undergo after this Life, they make it their bufinefs to perfwade themfelves, that they need fear nothing of this nature. They call the moft undoubted Truths into queftion, and diligently fearch for, and greedily entertain whatever may ferve to confirm them in thefe wicked Principles. They are taken with thofe fenfelefs Evafions wherewith the Atheifts and bold Wits fet themfelves to oppofe the Doctrines of Religion. Any Appearance of Difficulty, either in relation to fome Paffages of the facred Hiftory, or as to the Difference that is between Good and Evil, paffes with them for an unanfwerable Argument, and is a Reafon for their turning Atheifts, at leaft as far as they are able.

7. It

7. It is peculiarly to be noted, that Offenders in this kind do not sin alone, but involve others in the same Guilt with themselves. For whether they be the Tempters, or the Tempted, they are in either Case accountable for the Danger incurred not only by themselves, but likewise by the Partners in their Wickedness; since we are all equally obliged, as not to seduce our Neighbours, so neither to suffer our selves to be seduced by them, but on the other hand to endeavour, as much as in us lies, to reclaim them from Sin. And yet the Unchaft have another more direct and more pernicious way of promoting the Destruction of their Accomplices, by enticing them to cover their Guilt by still more villainous Attempts; such as exposing their Children, murdering them, telling Lies, and making false Declarations and false Oaths. The last of which is a Crime of so dreadful a nature, that Perjury is not only one of the greatest Sins any one can be drawn into, but those who are guilty of it, seldom fail of persisting in it to their Death; and dying in it, must be inevitably ruined to all Eternity. And let who will be Judge that has any Sense of Religion left in him, how heinous a Provocation it must be, to have been instrumental in order to the Damnation of another, it may be of many, and what a Load must lie upon the Consciences of all such, Though one of the Parties should afterwards sincerely repent of his Fault, and resolve to make all the Reparation in his Power, he may however expect to be continually tormented with cruel Regret and Remorse, and a constant Uneasiness for the Hazard of his Partner's Salvation; especially where there is just ground to fear such an one died in an impenitent state.

8. And yet once more: The Loss and Damnation of the Children born of these unlawful Mixtures
tures

tures is yet to be confider'd. For they are not only often fent abroad to perifh by War, or in foreign Countries; but befides, through want of Education, and by reafon of their unhappy Circumftances in other refpects, they generally grow very lewd, and fo ruine themfelves. The Sins of thofe alfo are to be taken notice of in this place, who are prevailed with to affift thefe impure Perfons in either the Commiffion or the Concealment of their Wickednefs; as likewife are the Vices which creep into Families, where either of the Parents live in Uncleannefs. For there Senfuality, Gluttony, Love of Pleafures, Idlenefs, Sloth, Divifions, Quarrels, Indevotion and Impiety are ufually very rampant. And as if this were not bad enough, an ill Management of the Family-Concerns, a bad Education, and as bad Example, too commonly tranfmit thefe Vices to Pofterity. The Children frequently tread in their Parents Steps, and by this means ruine themfelves, if not always, yet very commonly. To conclude, if to what is here faid, be added the Scandal thefe Wretches give, and the Mifchief they do, by their bad Lives, as well as by their loofe Difcourfe, it muft be owned that they are not only the Authors of their own Deftruction, but that divers others alfo fall and perifh together with them.

Thus I have inftanced in fome of thofe Crimes which are confequent upon Impurity. Some of them I fay, for a great deal more might be urged upon this Subject, that I have not meddled with. But from what has been faid, what Opinion fhould every one have of a Sin, that draws fo many others after it, and brings fuch inevitable Deftruction upon the Actors and Abetters of it? Thefe Reflexions fhould raife in all an utter Abhorrence of fo vile a Practice, but above all fhould effectually engage fuch as are already immerfed in it, to

think

think ferioufly with themfelves, how they may fpeedily get fafe out of it. This is a very fad and a very dangerous State, and whofoever is at any time taken in its Snares, will find a hearty Repentance neceffary in order to his Recovery out of them. I am fenfible this Sin does not hurry all that allow themfelves in it, upon all the other Iniquities I have mentioned; the Effects of it not being always the fame, but more fatal in fome than they are in others. Yet it is not to be thought that any can indulge themfelves herein, without incurring the Guilt of feveral other Sins with it. It is each one's Bufinefs now after all to examine Himfelf in relation to what is here faid, and to fee how far Himfelf may be concerned in it.

CHAP. III.

Of the Evils and Punishments confequent upon Uncleannefs.

I Come now to the Evils and Punifhments confequent upon Impurity. And thefe again, as the Sins that accompany it, are twofold. The Punifhments which God inflicts upon it in this World, and thofe that he referves for the other Life.

I. Almighty God has fometimes punifhed this Sin by extraordinary Judgments in this World, and with the moft exemplary Severity of any mention'd in the whole facred Hiftory. The Crimes of thofe who inhabited the Old World, and were deftroy'd by the Deluge, took their Rife from the luftful Inclinations of the Flefh. *Mofes* tells us, *Gen.* vi. 2. *That the Sons of God faw the Daughters of Men that they were fair, and they took them Wives of*

all

all which they chose; and this introduced into the World that terrible Corruption of Manners, and those notorious Crimes, which provoked Almighty God to deſtroy very near the whole Race of Mankind. Since the Deluge we have no more eminent Example of the Divine Vengeance upon a People, than the Overthrow of *Sodom* and *Gomorrah,* and the other Cities that were conſumed by Fire from Heaven, together with all their Inhabitants, and the whole Country round about. But it was the Licentiouſneſs and Senſuality of the People of this Country, which brought upon them theſe dreadful Effects of God's Indignation. After theſe we have it recorded of the *Iſraelites,* that they periſhed in the Wilderneſs †, to the number of Twenty and four thouſand Perſons, becauſe they had been drawn into Uncleanneſs and Idolatry, by the Daughters of *Moab;* an Example which St. *Paul* ſets before the *Corinthians* *, to affright them from theſe ſame Sins. All thoſe Examples are evident Proofs of the Deteſtation in which Almighty God has this Sin. In like manner St. *Peter* and St. *Jude* alledge them to ſhew that God did not fail to puniſh the Luſtful and Laſcivious. 2 St. *Pet.* ii. 4, *&c.* and St. *Jude* 7, 8.

† Numb. 25. 9.

* 1 Cor. 10: 6, 7, 8.

To theſe Examples of the Wrath of God againſt whole Nations, may be added thoſe Judgments which he has alſo executed upon particular Perſons. And it is obſerved of *David,* that after he fell into this Crime, many Misfortunes befel himſelf and his Family ‖, as the Prophet *Nathan* had threaten'd; namely the Death of his Child, the tragick Events that enſu'd upon his Son *Amnon's* Crime, and *Abſolom's* Conſpiracy and Rebellion. The like might alſo be noted of his Son *Solomon.* After the Love of Women had drawn him aſide, the Divine Protection viſibly departed from him, as we ſee, 1 *Kings* 11.

‖ 2 Sam. 12. 10.

Theſe

These terrible Punishments, thus related in the Holy Scriptures, shew fully how God detests Impurity; without any necessity of his repeating in these Days the like Examples of his Indignation. Yet there are ordinary Judgments which are seen to light upon the Unchast. There are vast Numbers of Persons and Families, who are unhappy, and ruin'd, whose Misery cannot be reckoned other than an Effect of God's Vengeance against this Sin, punishing it with Shame, Grief, Poverty, and all sort of Misfortunes. It is true these Evils are not the proper Punishments of this Sin; but rather to be esteemed an Effect of the Goodness of God towards Men. They are only Chastisements in order to the Reformation of Offenders, to make them sensible of their Sin, and careful to avoid the Torments of the Life to come. But they are withal most effectual Examples for teaching People not to indulge themselves in Sensuality.

Which they cannot ordinarily do, without shaming and dishonouring themselves. Though it is true this is not the Case of all, and that this Punishment reaches none whose ill Conduct is not publickly taken notice of. There are many who conceal their Guilt, and so pass amongst Men for innocent. But yet Disgrace and Shame rarely fail of being the Portion of the Dissolute.

Moreover this Sin exposes to Grief and Want; and many, though not every one, are punished in this manner, so plainly that it is not easy to reflect upon their Sufferings without being forced to confess, that there is a particular Curse of God hanging over this Crime. The Excesses of Incontinence leave behind them Sicknesses and Infirmities, which naturally cause Sorrow and Shame, and which frequently accompany them even to the Grave. There is no Sin by which a Man is
re-

reduc'd to such a State, as they are reduc'd to who
deliver themselves up to this, nor that has the like
terrible Effect upon the Body. So that even in
this Sense that of St. *Paul*, 1 *Cor.* vi. 18. may justly be applied, that *He who commits Fornication sins
against his own Body.* Almighty God who has made
all things with the greatest Wisdom, has annexed
divers Evils to the immoderate Use of bodily Pleasures; and chiefly with this Design, that Impurity should have such terrible Consequences, to
the end they may lay a Restraint upon People,
and not let them give way to a Passion that is exceeding prevalent with those it gets the Possession
of. And again, besides these great Evils, there
are likewise divers Infirmities that are the Consequents of Incontinence. Sobriety and Chastity
preserve the Health, and prolong the Life, above
all other Methods; and then it must follow by the
Rule of Contraries, that Lasciviousness and Sensuality shorten the Days, and are the Occasion of
many Diseases. The Causes of many Distem-
pers are very hardly discover'd; nor can the most
skilful Physician inform himself whence they have
arisen; which yet if the Truth were known,
would appear to be the Effect of Impurity.

In like manner the Guilty of this Vice fall very
often into Poverty and Misery, as a Curse naturally consequent upon their Sin. There is no manner of Difficulty, in shewing how the Unchast im-
poverish themselves; that they ordinarily sacrifice
all to their Passion, they contrive divers ways of
squandering away their Estates; and particularly
that a considerable Part goes for promoting their
infamous Designs, and then again for concealing
their Crime, and to prevent its taking air. They
are great Prodigals as to what their Lust demands
for its Satisfaction; and are most commonly idle,
dainty, effeminate, intemperate, proud, and Lovers

yers of good Entertainment. As Sobriety and Fasting are good Prefervatives againft Uncleannefs, this Vice on the other hand has for its Companions Drunkennefs and Gluttony. The Unclean are moreover negligent of their own Affairs, and if they have an Employment, will not be perfuaded to ftick duly to it. By which means they cannot but waft what they have, and bring themfelves and their Families into Straits; after this manner verifying the Saying of the Wifeman, *Prov.* vi. 26. *By means of a whorifh Woman a Man is brought to a piece of Bread*; and that of *Job*, xxxi. 12. *Luft is a Fire that confumeth to Deftruction, and roots out all the Increafe.* As the Son of *Syrach* alfo affirms, that *he that cleaveth to Harlots, fhall have Moths and Worms to his Heritage,* Ecclus. xix. 3.

And ftill there are more Mifchiefs to be born in the Families where this Vice reigns, that is to fay, the Breach it makes betwixt Husband and Wife, and all the Misfortunes that neceffarily follow upon fuch a Breach. The ill Conduct of either Father or Mother is enough to put all into Confufion. Nay, even the bare Sufpicion of either Party's being faulty, will caufe incurable Divifions in Families. Whence arifes alfo another Evil not to be paffed over in filence, and which deferves to be look'd upon as a particular Curfe of God; I mean, that thefe Evils, Shame, Grief, Poverty, *&c.* don't terminate only in the guilty Perfons, but their Pofterity after them feel the ill Effects of them. Their Children are flighted, and fickly, and poor, and miferable, not for their own, but their Parents fake. Thus whole Families are often ruin'd, and the Seed of the Adulterers falls almoft always into Diftrefs. I add farther, That the Children whofe Fathers or Mothers are this way addicted, are for the moft part prone to imitate them herein. Which comes to

pafs

pass partly from a natural Reason, because the Children partaking of the same Temper and Constitution with those from whom under God they receiv'd their Being, will be influenc'd likewise by the same Passions ; and partly by means of their bad Education, and the ill Examples they have constantly before their Eyes, it being impossible for them, whilst in these Circumstances, not to behold and observe many Passages which will be as a most dangerous Poyson to them. They are bred up in Idleness and Intemperance, which brings them to Poverty, and that Poverty tempts them to I know not how many other Sins. Which Considerations shew plainly how the Unchast involve their Children, no less than themselves, in Misfortunes of all kinds. And so we have seen one Part of the Evils which follow Uncleanness in this Life, and of which every Day furnishes us with Examples.

II. And if these Evils hitherto insisted upon are evident Signs of the Divine Indignation against the Unchast, how ought they to stand in awe of those other more inevitable, and more intolerable Punishments which are reserved for the other Life? The Unclean are not always punished in this World, but they will be most certainly in the other, unless they take care to prevent it by a timely and hearty Reformation. This the holy Scripture teaches as expresly as may be. St. *Paul* professes, as I have already noted, 1 *Cor.* vi. 9. 11. that *neither Fornicators, nor Adulterers, nor the Abominable, shall inherit the Kingdom of God ;* cautioning also at the same time, that we don't abuse ourselves, nor flatter ourselves in this respect. And the same Doctrine he repeats, *Gal.* v. 19, 20, 21. *I tell you before, as I have also told you in times past, that they who commit such things shall not inherit the Kingdom of God.* So *Ephes.* v. 6. *Let no Man deceive*
you

*you with vain Words ; for because of these things cometh
the Wrath of God upon the Children of Disobedience.* In
the Epistle to the *Hebrews,* Chap. xiii. 4. *God,* says
the Apostle, *will judge the Fornicators and Adulterers.*
And St. *Peter,* 2 Ep. Chap. ii. 9. declares and
proves by many Examples, that *God reserves the
Wicked,* and chiefly the Carnal and Impure, *unto
the Day of Judgment, to be punished.* But I shall
have another Occasion to enlarge upon this Judgment, and these Punishments. What is already
said suffices to shew, that Impurity exposes Men
to the Miseries of Damnation.

These are the Consequents of Uncleanness;
this is that dreadful State to which it brings Men,
and these the Sins into which it drives them, and
the Punishments to which it renders them obnoxious. And one would think them enough to
inspire all Persons with a Detestation of this Vice.
I am sure every one has reason to dread the
Thoughts of falling into that Brutishness and Hardness of Heart, of which all are in great Danger,
who at any time pass the Bounds of Modesty, and
part with their Chastity. And all should therefore seriously study, to prevent that Remorse,
which sooner or later will be the Portion of the
Lascivious, and to keep at a Distance from a Sin
that draws so many others after it, and in a Word,
casts its Slaves and Votaries into an Abyss of
Evils.

SECTION III.

Of the Causes of Uncleanness.

HERE I am to enquire whence it comes to pass that this Vice is so common. And in general it may be affirmed, that this is owing to Men's natural Inclinations, and the Passions which draw them into it. But now as Christians have Instructions and Motives for witholding them from Uncleanness, and our gracious God vouchsafes us the most efficacious Means, the most powerful Assistance, and the most proper Remedies, for enabling us to overcome our Passions, and this one in particular ; so is it just matter of Admiration, how it comes to pass that they profit no more by these Advantages, and that Uncleanness reigns so exceedingly amongst us. This therefore is what I propound to my self to examine into in this Section.

CHAP. I.

The First Cause, Ignorance.

THE first Cause of the Prevalency of this Vice is Ignorance. St. *Paul* ascribed † the Extravagances of the Heathens, and particularly the Impurity of their Lives, to the Ignorance in which they lived. And the same is no less true of too great a part of those who profess themselves Christians ; namely that they are not acquainted

† Eph. 4. 18, 19.

quainted with the Doctrines of Religion as they ought to be. And yet their Ignorance appears greater in relation to this Vice than others; and this possibly they are the least caution'd against of all Sins. To keep People at a distance from any Sin, they should be taught the Nature and the Heinousness of it, and should have set before their Eyes the Arguments and Reasons there are for disswading from it, together with the most effectual Means of guarding themselves against it. But these things have been too rarely insisted upon with relation to Uncleanness. So that People do not rightly understand wherein this Sin consists; and therefore conclude themselves innocent, if they have never been guilty of Fornication or Adultery. All those other Species of Impurity, spoken of before, pass with them for nothing, or as next to nothing; whether in their Actions, their Looks, their Desires, or their Words, and how contrary soever to Chastity. And not knowing the Evil that is in these Courses, they make no Scruple of them, and so become Slaves to this Passion, before they are aware of it.

Neither do they well know the Heinousness and Consequences of this Sin. For certainly had they a right Notion of these; did they truly lay before themselves the Estate to which Men are reduced by it, the Sins into which it betrays them, the Misfortunes it brings upon them, and what is to be done for the Cure of it, they would become much more cautious, and not dare to take such Liberty of gratifying their sensual Inclinations. The Gospel sets before us the most powerful Motives to Chastity, teaching that Almighty God has strictly commanded it, that we are continually in his Presence, and he sees and observes our Behaviour at all times and in all places, that we have taken upon us the Profession of a pure

and

and holy Religion, and have at our Baptism oblig'd our selves in the most solemn manner to live up to its Principles, that we must shortly die, and must come to Judgment for our Offences in this kind as well as all our other Iniquities, that there is an incomparable Reward, an immortal Crown of Glory to be lost by this Sin ; and not only so, but eternal, everlasting Agonies in the bottomless Pit will be the undoubted Portion of those that persist in it. We are also directed to the most effectual Assistances and Means of subduing the Temptations of the Flesh, such as Prayer, Meditation, Watchfulness, Sobriety, Fasting, and Mortification, and the Grace of the Holy Spirit of God, which he is ready to vouchsafe to all that humbly beg it of him, and which oftentimes assists us even before we have sought for it. All which weighty Considerations duly impress'd upon Men's Minds by good Instruction, would not suffer them to abandon themselves to the Excesses of Sensuality, as now they do. But whilst so great a Part of Mankind are grosly ignorant of these Doctrines, it is the less to be wonder'd that Impurity is so prevalent as Experience sadly shews it to be.

Now if it be enquir'd how People come to be so ignorant of what so nearly concerns them, these two Causes of it may chiefly be assign'd.

1. The Negligence of those who ought to teach them better ; and more especially of Parents, and those that are set over them in the Church. I shall presently consider the Case of Parents, and the Education of their Children. In the mean time my Business is to shew that those who are ordain'd in the Church for the Instruction of Christians, do not all take due care for their Information in this Point, and to set them at distance enough from Impurity. It is true they take occasion
some-

sometimes to speak against it in their Sermons, and to condemn and diffwade from the Practice of it ; but then they ordinarily do it in too loose and general Terms, and do not defcend to Particulars, as would, at least in fome Cafes be proper, to make their Auditors understand what this Sin is, and how offensive in the Sight of God, and what Courfe is to be taken for delivering them from, or recovering any of them out of it. Nor indeed are all of them qualified to treat of fo nice and tender a Subject as this is, where without a folid Judgment and a great Meafure of Prudence, it can hardly be but a Man will fay either too much, or not enough.

2. In the fecond place, where thefe vocal Inftructions are wanting, it may be concluded that Recourfe fhould be had to Books ; but the Mifery is, that whofoever feeks for relief this way, will find himfelf deceiv'd for want of a fufficient Supply. There are very few Books adapted for People's Inftruction in this Cafe. And I muft confefs it is fomewhat ftrange, that this being one of the moft common Sins, there has yet been fo little publifh'd against it. I do not at all queftion but the Reafon why fo little Pains has been taken this way, whether in the Pulpit, or by private Inftruction, or by Writing, is becaufe of the fhameful Nature of the Sin. Yet it is not impoffible that People might without breach of Modefty have been better taught concerning it, than they generally have been. Some certain Rules for avoiding it might have been prefcrib'd the younger fort, whereby to beget in them a Nicenefs of Confcience in relation to it ; without defcending to fuch Particulars as it is not fit to mention to Perfons of their Age. And would but their Teachers apply themfelves ferioufly and diligently to this, they would not find their Endea-

yours unsuccessful. Though for want of such Application their People's Ignorance must inevitably be very great, and their Sin very common.

CHAP. II.

The Second Cause of Uncleanness, Bad Education.

A Second Cause of this Vice is a Want of good Education. Youth is a time in which Care should be taken to caution against all Sins, but in an especial manner against this. And so much the more are these Doctrines to be then inculcated, because Children in the earliest part of their Life are guided only by Sense ; and that Inclination to Corporal Pleasures, which is the great Temptation to this Vice, is then most prevalent in them.

Wherefore it is requisite they should be fortified against it by good Instruction in their tender Years, whereby to lay a Foundation for Religion and Virtue, and beget in them a mighty Veneration for Almighty God ; and after this by a Care to see them well brought up, in great Temperance, a Plainness of Apparel, an Unacquaintedness with bodily Pleasures, in Modesty, and an Abhorrence, not only of whatever is apparently destructive of Chastity, but whatever has the least Tendency towards Impurity. They should be taught a great Reservedness and Caution in their Discourse, and not be suffer'd to read obscene Books, or to talk wantonly, or any way that in the least offends against Modesty, and should never have anything of this nature said in their Hearing. For the bare Hearing and Repeating this sort of Language impairs

pairs their Modesty, and gradually wears it away, and this being once lost, they no longer have any Guard upon themselves.

Children and young People should likewise be put upon labour, and accustom'd to take pains to bear with Weariness and other Inconveniences, to abstain from Delights, and mortify themselves, and follow those Directions which Reason and Religion prescribe for the Government of their Passions. It is not to be thought what account these Means will turn to, what great Influence the Doctrines of the Gospel will have upon Children thus educated; and how much less susceptible they will be of any inordinate Passions; how they will find the Disposition of their Souls confirm'd and establish'd, so as to contribute very highly to the Happiness of their Life, and the Practice of Virtue.

But this is not now the Method of educating Children. It is seldom that Care is taken to instil the Principles of Religion into them, and in particular to train them up to Purity. Most Families are very regardless of their Children as to this part of their Duty, and more especially at those Years, when these Advertisements are most needful for them. No Instructions are then given them for guarding them against Uncleanness; little regard is then had to their Conduct, but they are commonly left wholly to themselves.

And yet what is much worse than this. They are wont to be bred in such a manner, as naturally inclines them to Sensuality and Lust; so negligent are most Parents of their Children's Education, and so little regard have they to see them accustom'd to the ways of Virtue. The Peasants, Artificers, Servants of both Sexes, and others of inferior Rank, have for the most part very weak and confus'd Apprehensions of Piety and Religion,

gion, having been carelefly brought up, with no Senfe of any thing but what concerns the Body. And thofe of better Condition are not much better taught ; fo that oftentimes their Eftates and Advantages as to this Life ferve only to make them the more vicious and fenfual. They are taught to live effeminately, and to mind only the things of this World. They are ruin'd while young by Luxury and Gluttony, by minding their Drefs too much, and feeding too high. And if any would be very obliging and kind to them, they have got an ill Cuftom of doing it, by prefenting them with fome fort of Ornaments, or by inviting them to eat fuch Meats as are not fit for them. By what they both hear and fee they are made to imagine that it is Defireable and Advantageous to wear fine Cloaths, and eat what is moft pleafing to their Taft. This is what they are very ready to harken to, and what they are eafily induced to comply with. And hence it unavoidably comes to pafs, that their Conftitution is depraved, and they foon become Lovers of Pleafures. It is infinitely dangerous therefore to encourage the Senfuality of young Perfons by ill Habits, of Delicacy, and Daintinefs in the Choice of Meats, or of Excefs in Eating ; this being the ready way to have them fwallow down a deadly Poyfon in their tender Years, and render them fenfual and intemperate all their Life after. But nothing is more pernicious than drinking Wine, which fome even of the Pagans have thought unfit for thofe who are under twenty Years of Age to drink. Yet now it is ufual in many Countries for Children and even for Girls to drink it unmixt. Thefe are vifible and neceffary Caufes of Impurity, and are therefore very unreafonable and improper. For young Perfons are fufficiently inclin'd to Pleafures by the Heat of their Youth, and the Plenty

and

and Briskness of their Spirits ; so that there is no need of cherishing and promoting such their Inclination, or of farther inflaming their Passions by a sensual Education.

Hereto may be added the Example which Children have set them, and the Discourse they hear in the Families whereof they are a Part, the Management of most Parents being a matter of great Lamentation. Great Care should be taken, and great Circumspection used, in what is said before Children ; because they are observant, and very apt to take notice, especially of what comes from their Fathers and their Mothers. Wherefore nothing should be said where they are by, that has the least Tincture of Impurity. And yet how many Fathers and Mothers have no regard to it ; though they thereby discover themselves very defective as to Chastity and Piety? They say any thing before their Children, tell immodest Stories, and use obscene and indecent Expressions, and possibly such as are remarkably so. Now such would do very well to consider whether any thing can more readily poison the Minds of Children than such Carriage. It was *Plato's* Saying, as is related by *Plutarch,* That Aged Persons should study above all things to shew their Modesty in the Presence of the Younger sort ; and that whenever they leave off to behave themselves accordingly, it is impossible to instill Shame and Reverence into their Children.

To conclude, There are two Faults to be observ'd, which are committed in the Education of Children, which tend very much to the Corruption of their Morals, and render them less pure and virtuous. The former of which is committed when they are Little, and the other when they are come to some Bigness. Whilst they are little, they have little Communication with Wisemen ;

and

and their Parents not willing to have the Patience to talk with them, nor to leave their Affairs or their Pleasures for them, put them into the hands of Maids or other Servants, from whom they can learn no Good, and by whom they are early corrupted, namely by Seeing and Hearing divers matters which are contrary to Virtue, and which teach them to know Vice, and to love it..

The other Fault I would mention is, That they are dismiss'd too young out of their Fathers House, and are left to their own Government, whilst they are not yet of Age to order themselves, but yet are susceptible of all sorts of ill Impressions. From Sixteen to Nineteen or Twenty, is the most dangerous part of all our whole Lives, that being the time when Youth enters into the World, and their Passions grow unruly, and there is a great deal of hazard in beginning to taft of Pleasures. By no means therefore should they be left to themselves at this Age; and if for Reasons taken from the manner of their Education they must be put out, all possible Care must be taken to commit them to the Inspection of Wisemen, who may watch narrowly over the Conduct of themselves, and not let them go out of their Houses, without having got them first well grounded in Religion. This is the great Duty of Fathers, and the greatest Good they can do to their Children. This is of a very different Consequence, from the other Cares that People are wont to take. And it is the most certain Method Parents can pitch upon, to promote their Children's Happiness in this World, and to save themselves a great deal of Expence, and a great deal of Uneasiness. The Neglect of which in Fathers, is the reason their Children thrive no better; but above all it is one of the Causes why they abandon themselves to Impurity.

CHAP.

CHAP. III.

The Third Cause of Uncleanness, The Way of Living.

A Third Cause of this Vice is a heedless inconsiderate manner of Life, which must be rectified in many Particulars, before People will be able to perform their Duty aright, in this as well as other respects.

I. And in the first place Devotion is absolutely necessary in order to a virtuous Conversation, and in an especial manner, in order to Chastity. Humble and fervent Prayer is the Method Almighty God himself has prescribed for obtaining Grace and the Holy Spirit of God. And those pure and solid Pleasures with which Devotion fills the Soul, are an admirable Defence against the most powerful Temptations of Voluptuousness. But then it is only a small part of Mankind that have attained to a true Sense of Devotion, that are both constant and hearty in their Addresses to God, and do not neglect these as well as Reading, Meditation, Religious Discourse, and other Instances of Piety; or that take any Delight in them. And what then can be expected, but that being no better guarded against the Temptations of the Flesh, they should be overpowered and captivated by them?

II. Idleness is a frequent Occasion of People's falling into this Sin of Uncleanness. Business chases away evil Thoughts, by employing the Mind to better purpose, and by mortifying the Body, and consequently the Passions. But whilst any lead a careless unactive Life, they are necessarily

sarily

ſarily expoſed to Luſt, unleſs their natural Temper and Conſtitution happily prevent it. And when the Lazy, and thoſe that live without any Employment meet with theſe Temptations, they readily yield to them, their Idleneſs having before weaken'd them, and render'd them unfit to encounter any Attempts that are made upon them. Having never been accuſtom'd to overcome their own Appetites, or to offer Violence to themſelves in whatever Caſe, the leaſt Oppoſition they meet with proves too hard for them. This therefore is one Cauſe why the younger ſort are ſo eaſily led aſide by their Paſſions; they are not enough engaged in Buſineſs. And for this Reaſon it is that in thoſe Places where Perſons are not intent upon any kind of Work, and have nothing to do for Part of the Year, the Crimes of Uncleanneſs reign much more than where the People are held to continual Labour.

III. Intemperance alſo leads to Uncleanneſs, theſe being two Vices that ordinarily go together, and promote each other; as the Holy Scriptures † Eph. 5. inform us. The Apoſtle St. *Paul* notes † *that Wine* 18. *leads to* * *Diſſoluteneſs and Exceſs.* And throughout Ἀσωτία. the New Teſtament Drunkenneſs and Gluttony are almoſt always joined with Impurity; as I have obſerved before. Intemperance naturally begets Laſciviouſneſs, in that on the one hand it depraves the Conſtitution, and enflames the Blood and Spirits, and on the other, it takes away the free Uſe of Reaſon, or at leaſt it leaves Perſons no longer upon their Guard, makes them leſs modeſt, and gives them a certain Freedom and Boldneſs in both their Speech and their Behaviour, whence they eaſily and in a very little time proceed to a farther Liberty. So that whereas in a Wiſeman, and much more in a Chriſtian, the Body ſhould be in ſubjection to the Spirit, and Reaſon ſupported

ported by Religion should govern and suppress the Motions of the Flesh; Intemperance subjects the Soul to the Body, and enfeebles Reason and Religion; and so subverts the natural Order of things, and plunges inevitably into Impurity. The Soul by this means becoming gross and sensual, is render'd unfit for Watching and Prayer, and tasting any other Pleasures, than those of the Body, whose Slave it is.

What I here speak of Intemperance concerns not those only who have arrived at the more scandalous and shameful Excesses of Debauchery, who eat immoderately, and drink till they have perfectly lost their Understanding; but those likewise who without exceeding in the Quantity of what they either eat or drink, seek after Delicacies, and the choicest and most dainty Food; and in general, all that are not sober and plain in their Diet, but set themselves to please their Appetite. There is no being chaste without living soberly, and accustoming ourselves to deny the Body its Demands, and especially as to Diet. When we have learn'd to govern ourselves in eating and drinking, we shall quickly become Masters of the Body and its Desires. And so we see the Gospel prescribes Sobriety and Fasting as one of the principal Means of subduing the Body, and taming the Passions. But when we neglect such Means we evidently run the hazard of sinking under the Temptations of Impurity; and this Danger is continual, in regard that Food is of inevitable Necessity for the Body, and what it every day calls for. When any therefore instead of practising Abstinence, study rather to satisfy their fleshly Appetite, their Soul then falls an easy Prey to Temptations.

IV. Too much Care of the Body, and the Love of Pleasures, is also another Step towards Lust.

One

One of the chief Doctrines of the Christian Religion is not to be too favourable to the Body. And it is very certain that a Love of Pleasures, is a Disposition diametrically opposite to the Spirit of the Gospel, which is a Spirit of Mortification, and Self-denial. *Make not Provision for the Flesh, to* † Rom. 13. *fulfil the Lusts thereof,* was St. *Paul's* Advice †. Our
14.
* St. Luke Blessed Saviour denounced * a dreadful Woe a-gainst them that live in Pleasures upon the Earth,
6. 24, 25. and think of nothing but Joy and Mirth. And his
‖ St. Ja. 5. Apostle St. *James* ‖ speaks to the same Purpose.
5. He that is enslaved to his Senses and Body, and whose Mind is set upon Pleasures, treads very slipperily. This Inclination grows every Day more violent accordingly as it is attended to, till at length the Man has so habituated himself to it that he knows not how to get rid of it.

Yet how dangerous soever this manner of Life be, it is nevertheless what too many love and are fond of ; who instead of mortifying their Bodies, by denying them what they call for, yield it almost readily, and make it their constant study, and the main Aim and Design of their Endeavours, to comply with and gratify their Desires. It is a Maxim own'd by many, not to cross themselves in any thing, but on the contrary to seek after all the Delights and Enjoyments of Life, in Eating, and Drinking, in Lodging, in Cloaths, and every thing else. There are abundance of People, especially amongst those whose Quality and Estates distinguish them from their Neighbours, and oftentimes also amongst those of inferior Rank, who never think of any greater Happiness than to waste their Time in doing nothing, to be merry, and continually in Company, or at Play, or some other Diversion. And in truth they know not how else to pass their Time. They divide it therefore betwixt their Sleep, their Dressing and

Adorning

Adorning themſelves, their Meals and other Entertainments, their Viſits, Amuſements and Pleaſures; ſome or all of which engroſs it wholly. And this effeminate ſort of Life, which daily obtains more and more, deſtroys Chaſtity, beſides a vaſt number of other Evils, which it is the Cauſe of. And if they that indulge themſelves in it do not fall into the Exceſſes of Uncleanneſs, it muſt be either becauſe they have no natural Inclination this way, or becauſe ſome worldly Conſiderations withold them from it, it being hardly poſſible that the Hearts of ſuch ſhould not be taken up with the inordinate Luſts of the Fleſh. Delights corrupt, enervate, and weaken the Soul, and render the Man tender, and unable to reſiſt the Allurements of Voluptuouſneſs. The ſame I ſay of Dancings, Balls, Vain Shews, and all that may be called the Pomp of the World.

Let us now imagine a Man, ſuch as we ſee abundance are, whoſe Temper diſpoſing him to Senſuality, ſtands in need to be corrected by Abſtinence and Mortification; let us imagine this Man, I ſay, to take all the ways he can to inflame and heighten his Luſt, that he feeds high, declines all Labour, and loves his Pleaſures, and is ſo far from ſhunning what gratifies the Senſes, that it is his buſineſs to find it out; and who inſtead of Abſtinence and Mortification is for Good Chear, inſtead of Work for Idleneſs, inſtead of Watching for Sleep and Reſt, inſtead of due Auſterities for Luxury, inſtead of a ſimple plain way of Living for Pride and Delicacies; now I ſay it is as impoſſible for this Man to be chaſt, as for a Fire not to kindle by blowing, and a conſtant Addition of Fuel, Wood, or whatſoever combuſtible matter. God muſt work Miracles, or rather muſt deſtroy the Nature of Man, if he will have ſuch an one, whilſt he remains in this Eſtate, not to be addicted

L   to

to Impurity. Sensuality and the Love of Pleasures have ever been the Ruine of Virtue, and particularly of Chastity. And it is always to be observed, that in those Places where such a soft, easy, and slothful Course of Life prevails, all both Men and Women lose the Sentiments that properly belong to their Sex. The Men become effeminate; and the Women by little and little part with their Modesty, and Bashfulness, till they grow shameless and venture upon the same Extravagances, and the same Debaucheries as the Men. And this makes way for such Enormities as I may not undertake to describe.

It has been observed in all Ages how dangerous the Love of Pleasures has proved, and it is at this time remarkable that where People live in Rioting, and Idleness, and Luxury, as is usual in the Courts of most Princes, and in those Countries where the Delights of Life abound, those that dwell in these Places are almost all vicious and ad-dicted to Luxury. † Gen. 13. The holy Scripture † propounds to us in this Case the Example of *Sodom.* The Country in which this City lay, was according to *Moses*'s Relation, and that of ‖ *Josephus*, one continual Garden, wherein grew great Plenty of Plants and the most delicious Fruits. The Advantages and Delicacies of this Country corrupted the Inhabitants; their Plenty produced amongst them Idleness and Wantonness; their Affluence of good things made them voluptuous and effeminate, and push'd them on to the most terrible Extravagances. *Ezek. 16. The Sin of Sodom,* says *Ezekiel* *, *was Pride, Fulness* 49. *of Bread, and abundance of Idleness.* And this Corruption grew at length to such a height, that God resolving not to bear any longer with this abominable People, executed upon them the dreadfullest

‖ *Of the War of the Jews,* l. 4. c. 27.

Ven-

Vengeance that has ever been heard of. A terrible Evidence to what intolerable Abominations a Man may become obnoxious, when a Love of Pleasures and Sensuality have got the Possession of him. These Passions are never to be satisfied, but grow more and more powerful by all the ways that are taken to please them, and never stop short of the last Excesses whensoever the Reins are let loose to them. They are as a Torrent swelling every Day higher and higher, till it carry all away with it. Thus the Heart grows soft and tender, Modesty and Chastity retire, and partly by Inclination, and partly out of Vanity and Point of Honour, People are drawn in to do as others do; and nothing less than some severe Calamity can stop the Course of these Impieties, and make Persons bethink themselves, and return to a better Mind.

V. Amongst other Causes of Impurity Excess in Apparel must by no means be omitted. This sort of Luxury is not only culpable as expresly forbidden in the Gospel, but upon several other Accounts which I may not insist upon here. Wherefore not to treat of it otherwise than as it relates to Impurity, I say Persons may offend in their Dress, either against Plainness, or against Modesty; and both the one and the other of these Offences leads to Impurity.

1. A Love of Finery and Gaiety is a frequent Companion of this shameful Passion. *Salomon* represents the whorish Woman, as one † that is adorn'd, deck'd, and perfum'd. Unchast Persons study to please; and those that employ their time in Dressing themselves to the best advantage, love to be looked upon when thus set forth; which may easily tend to beget impure Desires, whether in themselves, or those who behold them. Their Vanity this way makes them love to shew them-

† Prov. 7. 16, 17.

selves,

felves, and gives them free, open, and confident Airs, and thereby takes off from their Bafhfulnefs and Modefty, which naturally inclines to a more referved manner of Life, and a more prudent, ftay'd, and graver Deportment. The third Chapter of *Ifaiah* well deferves to be often read, as excellently fuiting with this Argument. The Prophet there paffes a long and fevere Cenfure upon the Luxury and Pride of the Daughters of *Jerufalem* ; but befides this he taxes them with want of Modefty and Shamefacednefs ; that they were *haughty, lifted up their Heads, and walked with ftretched-forth Necks,* fhewing apparent Tokens of their Immodefty by their Looks, their Gate, and their whole Carriage. Whence it is to be obferv'd, that as a Love of fine Cloaths and other Ornaments prevails very much amongft the Female Sex, fo is it apt to carry many of them very far ; and there are too many of them, who will not ftick wretchedly to expofe themfelves, even to the laft degree, for the fatisfying this Paffion.

2. But this Vanity becomes more culpable and more dangerous, when it prevails to the prejudice of Modefty. One of the firft Leffons we find in Scripture, was given in relation to Modefty and † Gen. 3. the Ufe of Apparel. *Mofes* † teaches that Garments were given to Man after his Fall for a Covering ; and accordingly Modefty and Decency require the Body to be cloathed. Which Rules are to be inviolably obferved amongft Chriftians, feeing we make Profeffion of fingular Purity ; though they chiefly relate to the Female Sex. The Apoftles moft exprefly admonifh Women of this * 1 Tim. Duty ; that * they *adorn themfelves in modeft Ap-* 2. 9. *parel, with Shamefacednefs and Sobriety.* St. *Peter* alfo fpeaks to the fame purpofe, 1 *Ep.* 3. 23. Of which latter place it is to be noted, that this Apoftle having recommended it to the Chriftian Wo men

men, to have their Converſation pure and chaſt, he immediately hereupon forbids Luxury, after this manner teſtifying plainly that this and vain Ornaments agree not with Chaſtity. *Let the Women, ſays he, be in ſubjection to their own Husbands ; that if any obey not the Word, they may without the Word be won by the Converſation of the Wives. While they behold your chaſt Converſation coupled with Fear. Whoſe Adorning let it not be the outward adorning, of plaiting the Hair, or of wearing Gold, or putting on of Apparel.* Wherefore there is no doubt to be made, but Modeſty ought to be moſt exactly preſerved in the manner of Cloathing ; and even to a Nicety. In other Caſes ſome Liberty is allow'd ; and a Chriſtian may follow the Mode where he lives, and accuſtom himſelf to the Faſhion and Uſage, in what concerns his Habit, ſo he does not fall into Exceſs, nor lay out upon it too much Pains, too much Time, or too much Charge ; and that he ſhuns Haughtineſs and Pride, and all Occaſion of Scandal. But with reſpect to Modeſty and Chaſtity, People ſhould be moſt nicely circumſpect, and never follow any Faſhion, or any way of Dreſſing, that is hurtful to Purity, in howſoever low a degree it be. This is an Article that requires great Exactneſs, eſpecially amongſt Women, whoſe Sex obliges them in a more particular manner to behave themſelves modeſtly.

Here then we may ſee a very ſenſible Proof, of the Remiſneſs of Chriſtians. In many places no regard is had to Decency in the manner of Cloathing, and Women are not dreſſed as Modeſty and Chaſtity demand ; they adorn themſelves after a free, indecent, and diſſolute manner, and appear publickly in a Dreſs favouring of Unchaſtity. Thus Modeſty is almoſt quite loſt, in this reſpect, and the Faſhion is become ſo cuſtomary, that People have no Scruple about it. This Immo-

I 3   deſty,

desty, these Nakednesses, and this want of Shame-facedness, were accounted very infamous amongst the Primitive Christians. *Tertullian* describing the barbarous and dissolute Manners of the Borderers upon the *Euxine* Sea, tells among other things, that the † *Women of these Countries had no regard to Modesty, and that they would appear with their Bosoms all uncovered.* Which this ancient Father noted as the Sign of an egregious Depravation; which yet is at this day too common amongst Christians. There is no need to prove that this want of Modesty in Apparel is a great Cause of Impurity, and the Source of numerous Temptations, and sinful Desires; that it will not fail to extinguish Bashfulness, and introduce Licentiousness and Lust, and I know not how many other dreadful Evils.

VI. Another Cause of this Vice is too frequent and too familiar Conversation of Persons of both Sexes, and especially whilst they are young. And not to mention here a frequency of Meetings with such as are known to be vicious and de-bauch'd; though it be certain the Company, the Discourse, and the Examples of such do very much corrupt Youth; not to mention this, I say that even too familiar a Conversation between Men and Women is the Cause and Occasion of many Transgressions; and that nothing more naturally tends to the Corruption of Youth. This breeds in their Hearts disorderly Passions and Desires, and so involves many in the Crime and the many Evils that follow upon it. Wisemen have always thought that young People, and chiefly Girls, should be brought up in private, and that it is dangerous and misbecoming to allow them too much Liberty. Amongst the *Jews,* their Girls

---

† Tert. adv. Marc. l. 1.

went

went little abroad, and when they did, went veiled as well as the Women. And we see the Apostle approved this Usage of theirs, in that he ordered the Women to appear veiled in the holy Assemblies, and with Tokens of Humility and Modesty; as was inviolably practiced in the Primitive Church. However these Injunctions are little observed in our Days, but rather the quite contrary; too much Liberty is given the younger sort, who are allowed to live freely, openly, and unreservedly. And so by degrees they lose their Modesty, Bashfulness, and Caution, their main Preservation against Impurity.

And here I cannot forbear touching upon one shameful and crying Enormity, very common in many Places; that is the promiscuous and scandalous accompanying of Boys and Girls together with each other, whereby they are seen, even in the Night, in a manner not only indecent, but very faulty. And which is very strange to think, this is done in the Sight and with the Knowledge of their Fathers and Mothers, who in their own Houses, and amongst their own Children suffer such infamous Familiarities, as ought by no means to be admitted of in any Nation professing Christianity. It is with great Reluctancy, that I commit these things to Writing, nor should I have done it but that the Disorders of this kind which reign in divers places compel me to it.

VII. It must be own'd likewise that War is to abundance of People a woeful School of Impurity. No doubt there are some that live chastly in this Employment, but for the Generality, every one knows that Souldiers give themselves a great Liberty in regard to Pollution, and that many of them are not ashamed to proclaim it. Nor ought this to surprize any who consider that Men of this Profession are ordinarily driven to it, either by

their

their Licentiousness, or a Prospect of Gain or Preferment, or through Misery and Poverty, out of which they are not willing to extricate themselves by honest Labour. Now this being the Case of most of the Souldiery, that they have wanted the Happiness of a good Education and Instruction, and have ventured upon a Course of Life, where they meet with continual and very strong Temptations, particularly Idleness and bad Examples, and where the Helps to Piety are very rare, and they think they have a Dispensation to live as they please; Can it possibly be expected that in these unhappy Circumstances their Manners should not be very corrupt, and especially as to Incontinence? And which is worse yet, being thus corrupted abroad, at their return home, they bring their Vices back with them, and so both abandon themselves, and invite others to all sort of Licentiousness.

VIII. Almighty God has appointed Means, and especially Marriage, for preserving from the Defilement of Impurity. But many refuse to enter upon this State, or at least neither enter upon it, nor live in it as they ought. The Injunction of Celibacy has done abundance of Mischief, and has introduced infinite Crimes and Abominations into the World and the Church. But many besides, no way concern'd in this, forbear Marriage; some through Libertinism, and to be less confined in their Passions, or to avoid some Inconveniences they apprehend to accompany the Married Life; and others, because they cannot meet with a Fortune to their mind, or helpful Relations, or other Advantages they aim at. And in the mean time not being chast, they hereby expose themselves to continual Temptations, and cannot avoid being ever and anon overcome by them. They that are married likewise oftentimes bring

bring themselves into the same Difficulties, either, by not living in that Purity wherein they ought to live, or because they married only out of Interest, or Ambition, and not by Inclination and mutual Affection. Now such Marriages cannot be expected to prove happy ;-and in truth the Effects of them are often very dreadful. Want of Kindness and Esteem is sometimes the Cause of breaking out into Adultery, as well as an unagreeable Temper, and a Failure in point of Easiness and Compliance in the Married Persons.

CHAP. IV.

The Fourth Cause of Uncleanness, Ill Books.

THE Fourth Cause of Impurity I shall instance in, is unchast Books. I have formerly shewn in † my Treatise *Of the Causes of Corruption*, how many sorts of Books tend to corrupt the Readers Manners ; but this must not totally prevent my touching upon the same Head in this place ;. the Mischief that is done by this means among Christians being greater than can be sufficiently lamented.

It has been long complained of that young Men who have learned the Tongues, have been corrupted by reading and interpreting the Poets and other Heathen Authors, where they have met with divers foul and immodest Expressions, fitted to excite their Curiosity and their Passions. And yet were there no Books of this nature except in the learned Languages, and which therefore are

---

† *Part* II. *Cause* VII.

not generally underftood, the Cafe were not near
fo bad. But alas! how many are there to be feen
in the modern Languages, that are of no lefs pernicious Confequence? It is oftentimes not fo
very eafy to put even Books of Religion into the
Hands of Children, where we can be fure they
fhall meet with nothing that may any way do
them hurt. Such extravagant Liberty is allowed
in fome places, that Authors make no difficulty
of publifhing whatever they pleafe againft Religion and good Manners. Neither do the Spiritual
Governors, though perhaps ftrict enough in Matters of far lefs Importance, nor the Civil Magi-
ftrate, fet themfelves with any concern to fupprefs thefe dangerous Writings; but they have
free Permiffion, are bought and fold publickly,
and poffibly *With Licence.*

There have been from time to time, and are
now in our own Days, certain mifchievous Books,
full of Libertinifm, Obfcenity, Naftinefs, fhameful and fcandalous Stories, againft the very Principles of Religion; which betray fuch a Stock of
Licentioufnefs and Impiety as is not eafily to be
conceived. But what is more furprizing and more
fcandalous is, that thefe Works find Patrons not
only amongft profefs'd Libertins, but even amongft
thofe whofe proper Bufinefs fhould be to undertake the Defence of Religion againft thefe and all
its Adverfaries. Thefe Books have done infinite
Mifchief; have made a great number of Libertines and Atheifts, and taught People in general,
and even fuch as had never ftudied their Religion,
to difpute againft it, to call it all into Queftion,
and fophiftically to cavil at it, not excepting the
Fundamental Articles of our Faith, and the Hiftories of the holy Scripture. But it is impoffible
to tell what Mifchief they have done, and do every day in refpect to Impurity. Here therefore is
one

one confiderable Caufe of this Vice; which is alfo
at the fame time a fenfible Proof of the exceffive Licentioufnefs that reigns amongft Chriftians. We
havealready taken notice that it is more offenfive to
fpeak unchaftly, than only to think fo; but yet it
is much worfe to write than to fpeak in this manner. And the Reafon is plain; in that what is
faid hurts only the Hearers, and is prefently over,
but what is committed to writing is more lafting,
and is difperfed all abroad. This is expofed to the
view of all, and fo unchaft Books become for a
long time together, and to Multitudes of Perfons,
a Caufe of publick Impurity.

As Books of this Character are not fit to be read
by any, fo thofe who have any Senfe of Religion
will not know how to allow themfelves to read
them. I know fome will plead, that a Man
fhould read all forts of Books, that he may improve his Underftanding by the Diverfity of Subjects that will occur in them. But there are other
Books befides thofe which are inftructive; and it
is much better not to know feveral things which
fome Authors have laboured to amafs together,
which yet ferve little to any other purpofe than to
endanger and pollute the Heart. And moreover
befides this Danger of being defiled and corrupted,
there is another Reafon for not reading thefe
Books, namely, left they fhould leave fuch Impreffions on the Mind, and fuch Ideas in the Memory, as will not readily be banifhed thence, and
yet which, if they do not feduce the Heart, caufe
a great deal of Uneafinefs and Trouble to the Soul.
It is no ftrange thing to hear People bewail the
Misfortune they had in converfing with improper
Authors in their Youth, and getting Love-Poems
by heart, which long after recur to their Thoughts,
and many times very unfeafonably, and upon the
moft ferious Occafions. Some have found no
fmall

fmall Trouble and Difquiet from them when lying upon their Death-beds. So that there is abundant Reafon to abftain from Books of this nature, which may prove very hurtful, but can do no good.

But above all it is a matter of the higheft Confequence to prevent young Perfons employing themfelves in this manner, and take from them not only all impure and unchaft Books, but all wherein is any thing that tends to Impurity, all Books of Love and Gallantry, which moft certainly ferve to no other Ufe than to feduce the Mind and Heart. I might have added other Reflections upon this Subject; but I am not willing to repeat what I have already faid in a former Difcourfe *.

CHAP. V.

The Fifth Caufe. Impunity, *and Want of good Government.*

THE Laft Caufe of this Vice is Impunity, and Want of a due Execution of Government both Civil and Ecclefiaftical.

I. In the Civil Society, Princes, Magiftrates, and Judges fhould confider that this Sin is, as I have proved, contrary to the Publick Welfare, and fhould therefore make it their ftudy, to put a ftop to fo great a Nuifance. But where is this Care taken? Where doth the Government inflict any Punifhments upon the Impure? Or if any be inflicted, are they not fo light, as that few are afraid of expofing themfelves to them for the Sa-

* *Treatife of the Caufes of Corruption. Part II. Caufe VII.*

tisfaction

tisfaction of their Passions ? There are in *Chri-stendom* two grievous Faults, with relation to the Society, as well as to the Laws of the Gospel ; the One in respect to Adultery, the Other to Divorces.

1. In respect to Adultery, it must be acknowledged to the Shame of almost all Christian Princes and Magistrates, that this Crime is not punish'd as it ought to be ; either sufficient Provision is not made against it by good and wholsome Laws ; or else those Laws are not duly put in execution. Even the Pagans surpassed us Christians herein ; for they put Adulterers to death, as I have shewn ; whereas in most Christian States they are very gently prosecuted. I will not enter in this place upon that Question, which some make, whether Death ought to be the Punishment of Adultery ; but shall only propose another Question ; which is, Whence it comes to pass that Christian Rulers have taken upon them to enhance the Punishment of Thieves, and at the same time to lessen that of Adulterers ? † God's Law adjudged Adulterers to Death, no less than Murderers, but did not pass so severe a Sentence upon Robbers. And yet Offenders in this kind lose their Life for it ; many times stealing what is of no great Importance is attended with Death ; now some make a great question whether this be just ; whether capital Punishments for Theft be warrantable, and if this

---

† *Our Author's Argumentation in this place being founded upon a political Law of the* Jews, *seems to favour the Doctrine of* Carolostadius *and* Castellio, *who asserted the Validity of the Judicial Laws of that People,* (Wilhel. Zepper. l. 1. c. 2.) *Whereas it is to be consider'd, that as we are not now under the Theocracy as the* Jews *were, so we cannot be obliged by their topical Laws, but all Governors are at liberty to make, and their Subjects to obey such other Constitutions as seem most to conduce to the Good of the People where they are established.*

Crime

Crime were not better proceeded againſt in another manner, more conformable to the Divine Law, and the Spirit of the Goſpel, and more conducing to the Publick Welfare. But without taking upon me to decide this Queſtion, I only ask by what Right the Proceedings againſt Robbers are ſo rigorous, whilſt Adulterers are ſuffered to live, though guilty of a much greater Injury, and which by the Law of God was to be puniſhed with Death? However if Magiſtrates think they have good Reaſon not to proceed to capital Puniſhment of Adulterers, they ought certainly to uſe all the Severity towards them that is conſiſtent with the Preſervation of their Lives. Which would be a ready way to prevent the commoneſs of this Crime. But on the contrary they are wont to be uſed with very great Indulgence, and ſuch Remiſneſs as conſiderably leſſens the Horror that every one ought to have of ſo flagitious a Crime as this is.

2. The other Fault reſpects Divorces. In relation to which the Law of our Bleſſed Saviour † is ſo expreſs, as might well caution all Judges never to grant Divorces, but in conformity to its Direction. Yet in many Countries they admit of them upon very ſlight grounds; ſeparating Huſbands and Wives upon other accounts beſides the Crime of Adultery. And what is yet a greater Abuſe, they have upon too eaſy Terms granted to the Perſons thus parted a Liberty of remarrying. It is obvious to obſerve the terrible Effects of theſe pernicious Cuſtoms. The Hope of finding a way to get rid of a Companion not beloved, or of marrying another, may tempt, and actually does tempt many Perſons to the Sins of Uncleanneſs, and ſometimes to other grievous Crimes.

It needs not be added in this place, that this Law touching Divorce, is very difficult to be obſerv'd.

† St. Mat.
5 & 19.

serv'd. *Tertullian* relates * that six hundred Years * Apolog.
had passed without the knowledge of any one Divorce in the Families of the antient *Romans*, and
that they came not into common Use, till their
Manners began to be very corrupt. If the Heathens had this regard for Marriage, how can
Christians, who have abundantly greater Light
vouchsafed them, think the Law of Christ too
hard, and too burdensom?

I shall mention one thing more in this place,
which is the Occasion of manifold Miscarriages,
and that is the Convenience young People find in
many places of being privately married, and in
strange Churches, without the Knowledge of their
Relations. This Abuse ought to be reformed, and
no Marriage should be celebrated except publickly,
according to the Order and Rites established, and
in the Churches to which they belong. I must say
farther before I leave this Article of Marriage, that
to oblige People to reverence it and live chastly,
the Ecclesiastical Discipline ought to be exercised
upon such who marry only the better to conceal
their Lewdness, and that when their vicious manner of Conversation comes to be discovered, they
should not escape the Church's Censures, as they
too often do in many Places.

II. In the Church the Neglect of Discipline,
which is one of the grand Causes of Corruption,
is more particularly one of the principal Sources
of Impurity. The Apostles who have appointed
and so earnestly recommended the Exercise of
Discipline, have more especially appointed it for
the Impure; as is declared 1 *Cor.* v; where this
Matter is particularly treated of. There St. *Paul*
delivers it as an inviolable Law, that those who
indulge themselves in this Sin are not to be suffer'd
in the Church, but to be cut off, and not to be
looked upon as Christians, till they shall have given
ven

ven good evidence of their Repentance. And
feeing there was amongft the *Corinthians* a Man
guilty of horrible Impurity, he complains that
fuch a Crime had been committed amongft them,
but he complains more of the Church than of the
Criminal; he cenfures the *Corinthians*; he acquaints them how dangerous it was to permit fuch
vile Trangreffors amongft them; and tells them
the Fault of this Man hereby became the Fault of
the whole Church; he does what the Church had
negle&ed to do, makes ufe of the Power he had
as an Apoftle of delivering egregious Sinners over
to Satan; and then again he repeats the Order he
had given the *Corinthians*, not to look upon the
Unclean as their Brethren, but to caft them out
from among them. I have otherwhere recited
the exprefs Words of St. *Paul*, and have fhewn how
in the Primitive Church Difcipline was ftri&ly
exercifed upon Adulterers. It would be requifite
alfo to put in pra&ice what the Apoftles fo often
enjoined, namely to avoid Familiar Converfation
with fuch who gave occafion of Scandal by their
impure Lives. By which means many might be
reftrain'd; and befides if any had offended the
Church by their Extravagances, their Fault could
not then be imputed to the whole Church, nor
would the Religion of our Bleffed Saviour be
difhonour'd by it.

But the Apoftolick Difcipline is fo far from being duly obferv'd, that in divers Churches it is totally laid afide. Inftead of proceeding againft the
Impure in excommunicating them for a time, the
Minifters of the Church are compelled to admit
to the Communion thofe who are chargeable with
infamous Sins, and to give holy things to Dogs
and Swine. Heretofore a Bifhop or Prieft that
had receiv'd to the Communion known Adulterers
and Fornicators, before they had given publick

Proofs

Proofs of their Repentance, would have been de=
pofed, and the whole Church would have reckon=
ed fuch an Action as a horrible and unheard of
Sacrilege. But now there are Places where he
that fhould deny the Communion to thefe Men,
would be depofed for denying it.

If in fome places where there are Laws in being,
and Punifhments determined for the Unclean, either thefe Laws impofe only civil and corporal Cor-
rections, or elfe they are fome other way defective,
or are but badly put in execution: The Crime is
often tolerated, and goes without any Punifhment
at all; and the Actors of it know how to find out
Methods of fheltering themfelves. And where
there is any fhew of Difcipline it is unduly admi-
niftred, either by admitting Sinners to the Peace
of the Church without having given good Teftimony of the Sincerity of their Repentance; or by
not making a juft difference between their Offences, in that oftentimes the Proceedings againft A-
dultery are no more fevere than thofe againft Fornication; or againft thofe that relapfe into their
Sin, than if they had only once fallen into it. Befides, in thofe places where this Difcipline is in
fome fort fettled, it has not the force that were to
be defired, not only upon account of the Defects
already mentioned, but likewife becaufe not being
exercifed every where, Sinners being excluded
from Communion in their own Churches, need
only go to fome other Church to be admitted to
the Lord's Table; which is a woful Irregularity,
and the ready way to introduce a Contempt of that
facred Ordinance, and of the Cenfures of the
Church, and confequently great Impiety. In the
midft of this general Remifnefs of Difcipline, it
ought not to be thought ftrange if People give
themfelves up to the Sins of the Flefh; fince there
is nothing encourages Wickednefs like Impunity.

K   Thefe

Thefe are the Caufes of Impurity which I thought my felf chiefly concerned to take notice of ; and by what has been faid concerning them, it is obvious to infer what are the proper Remedies for the Suppreffion of this Vice. But thefe I fhall have occafion to fpeak to in the following part of this Difcourfe.

SECTION

SECTION IV.

An Answer to the Excuses that are made for Uncleanness.

AFter what has been said of Uncleanness and the mischievous Effects of it, it is just matter of Astonishment that it should be so common. And it must be either because these forementioned Considerations are not attended to, or because People deceive and flatter themselves with a Persuasion that Uncleanness is no such great Offence, and that they may safely indulge themselves in it. Both of which is too true. The Ignorance and the Negligence of Mankind is very great in this Case; so that either they do not understand their Duty, or do not mind it. But it is certain too that there are false Reasons and insufficient Excuses whereby they make a shift to impose upon themselves. It is ordinary with Sinners to flatter themselves, and try to excuse their Miscarriages, and even to justify them. And as in other cases they do this, so no less in relation to Impurity. For which cause the Apostle St. _Paul_ expresly requires that no one deceive himself in this respect, nor suffer himself to be deluded by any vain Appearances of Reason. † _Be not deceived_, says the Apostle; and again * _Let no Man deceive you with vain Words._ I come therefore now to enquire into and answer the principal Excuses whereby Men pretend to palliate this Sin.

† 1 Cor. 6. 10.
* Eph. 5. 6.

K 2 I. Some

I. Some may appeal to the Propensity of Nature, and plead that God Almighty would never have given this to Mankind if they were not allowed to comply with it. But this by no means proves the lawfulness of Incontinence. For it is very certain God has given to Men a natural Inclination to those things which are for the Preservation of Life, and the Propagation of Mankind; and it is a signal Instance of his Wisdom that he has done it. It was requisite likewise that this Inclination should be strong towards those things, without which Mankind could not continue in Being. This is well worth our serious Consideration, but it is what I must content my self to have but just touched upon. But the Inclination which thus appears in Men, does in no wise authorize the Excesses into which they may fall, and unless we would set Mankind upon the same level with the Beasts, it must be acknowledged that this Inclination is to be kept under Rule and Government. Men have an Inclination to eat and drink; but can any be so senseless as to infer from hence that they are to observe no Rule or Measure in either of these? And would this natural Inclination be allowed as a good Excuse for Drunkenness, or Gluttony, or the other Excesses of Intemperance? All that can reasonably be urged against this is, that this Inclination proves that something is permitted to Men. But I hope it does not prove that every thing is lawful for them; and that they are not oblig'd to a moderate use of whatever God has given them for their Nourishment. And just so it is in the Case before us.

In short, It does not follow that because Mankind are liable to certain Inclinations of their own, therefore these Inclinations can carry them away by an inevitable Force and Fatality, so as that they will be no longer able to resist them. St. *Chry-sostom*

ſoſtom very effectually † confutes this Imagination, as extravagant and wicked, in a Diſcourſe againſt the *Manichees*, who charged the Work of God with being evil, and the Nature of Man with carrying him on inevitably to what is evil. He tells them it is Mens Will, not their Nature or their Body, which cauſes the Exceſſes into which they fall, and that the Inclination God has planted in them, was not given them to be abuſed to Wantonneſs and Luſt.

Our own Nature proves this. For if God has endued us with Deſires and Senſations which may tempt to divers Extravagances, he has alſo afforded us Means and Power to reſiſt their Motions. God has beſtowed two Bleſſings upon Mankind, which ſhould be ſure to keep them within their Bounds. The former is Reaſon and Modeſty. The carnal Appetite is brutiſh and blind, and is to be found in the Beaſts alſo ; but Reaſon was given Man to ſubdue this Appetite, and he has it in his choice either to follow this or not, and can judge what he ought to do, and what to refrain from. And accordingly his Reaſon is to direct him as to the Paſſion now under conſideration, as well as in relation to what he eats and drinks. But in regard that Reaſon alone is not of force enough to reſtrain theſe Paſſions, I ſay farther, that God has vouchſafed Man a Supernatural Principle, namely Religion and Faith, which by the Light it gives us, the Motives it lays before us, the Hope of Eternal Happineſs, and the Fear of Hell-Torments, together with the Grace of the Holy Spirit which is hereby communicated to us, enables us effectually to reſiſt our Paſſions. Theſe Power-

---

† Ad Galat. Ἡ ἐπιθυμία εἰς παιδοποιίαν, κỳ βίυ σύστασιν, ἐ πρὸς μοιχείαν, κỳ πορνείαν, κỳ ἀσέλγειαν, &c. Τὸ γὸ μοιχᾶ̓ ἐτ ἐ τ ̔ ἐπιθυμίας ἐτι τ̓ φυσικῆς, ἀλλὰ τ̓ ὕβρεως τ̓ ωρα φύσιν.

ful

ful Confiderations fhould raife us above a fhameful and brutifh Inclination; and with thefe Affiftances we may overcome ourfelves, and fet ourfelves free from the Bondage of our Lufts. If thefe things were weighed as they ought to be, and all the ufe that might be were made of thefe Advantages, an Inclination to Impurity would not be able to govern Men as now it does.

II. And by this time we may fee what Anfwer to return to a fecond Excufe, taken from the Difficulty of refifting this Paffion. I readily agree there are fome Pains required for taming the Paffions; the Gofpel fuppofes it when it exhorts to deny ourfelves, to watch, and fight, and mortify our Defires. But this is no more than is required in the other Parts of our Duty. There is without doubt fome trouble in curbing a Fit of Anger, or withftanding the Temptations of Avarice, Pride, and Intemperance. But this is no reafon why we fhould not be oblig'd to conquer thefe Paffions, nor any Proof that we cannot do it. Nor ought any more ftrefs to be laid upon the Difficulty of refifting Impurity

1. Becaufe this Difficulty is not univerfal, is not to be found in all Perfons. Divers overcome their Paffions eafily and with no great trouble; this being the happy Condition of fuch who have been blefs'd with a pious Education, and whofe Youth has been pure. And again, as to thofe who may have been hurried on with a great deal of force by a vicious Inclination, I have two things to offer. The one, that they are in this Condition is their own Fault; and had they been forewarned againft their flefhly Lufts in their younger Years, they wou'd not have been in fubjection to them as now they are. The other, It is not yet wholly out of their power to get rid of them. God has furnifhed them with Remedies againft Incontinence, and

Means

Means of avoiding it. So that it is not yet too late to retrieve themfelves out of the State they are in, if they will be but at the Pains of heartily endeavouring it. As I fhall fhew when I come to treat of thofe who are guilty of this Sin, and the Means of obtaining Chaftity.

2. It is really not impoffible to live in Purity, and avoid the Exceffes of the Flefh ; there being no ground to conclude that this Duty is out of Man's Power. Which if it were, we may affure ourfelves Almighty God would not exprefly require it of us, and under pain of Damnation. When the Pagans commended Chaftity and Continence, they believed it might be preferved ; and can Chriftians to whom God has granted fo many Graces, pretend the Practice of it to be impoffible. The Laws of Chaftity might indeed have been thought too fevere, and not without an appearance of Reafon, if we had been left wholly to ourfelves and had been made only for this World. But we are Chriftians, to whom God has granted a new Birth, and whom he invites to a Supernatural State of Happinefs. And what can be too hard for the Grace and divine Power of the Gofpel, the Example of Jefus Chrift, and the Expectation of a Life to come ? Ought not all thefe Bleffings to make us fpiritually minded, to infpire us with fublime and noble Thoughts, and to difengage us from the Allurements of our grofs and brutifh Paffions ? God who calls us to Chaftity, lets us know on the other hand what is incumbent upon each one of us in order to it ; he prefcribes us Means that will confiderably facilitate the Practice of this Duty. As will be fhewn more particularly hereafter.

3. But I fay farther, Wifemen do not fuffer themfelves to be affrighted with Difficulties , but keep their Thoughts fixed upon the Confequence of their Endeavours, the Benefit or Difadvantage

K 4 *that*

that may be expected to enfue upon them. And this Confideration fhould put thofe who meet with Difficulties in the Duty here treated of, upon encountring it with Courage and Refolution, tho' it had been much greater than it is. On the one fide, by doing this they procure to themfelves an infinite Happinefs, and advance themfelves to the moft bleffed and moft glorious State that can be imagined. Befides the Felicity whereof they fhall be poffeffed in Heaven, who had taken care to keep their Bodies undefiled, they take the fureft courfe to be truly happy in this prefent Life. They may find fome trouble in refifting Temptations, but when they have got the Victory, they will never repent of having denied themfelves the gratifying of their Senfes; and the more Difficulty they have met with in this fpiritual Conflict, the greater Comfort and Satisfaction will they enjoy when they are got well through it. Wherefore the Pleafure that arifes from having fhook off the Yoke of thefe inordinate Paffions of the Flefh, fhould engage us all to mortify ourfelves, and earneftly to ftrive after this happy State. On the other fide, the Mifchiefs and Punifhments of Impurity call for our Attention, and make it neceffary for us to compare Pains with Pains, and Difficulty with Difficulty, the Pains of overcoming our own Defires, and fhunning the Gratifications of Senfe, with the dreadful Confequents of this Sin, the Wounds it gives the Soul, and the Remorfe whereto it fubjects it. We fhould confider the feveral Misfortunes with which this Vice is attended here in this Life, and which make the guilty Perfon pay dear for infamous and tranfient Pleafures. But above all we muft bethink ourfelves, that if there be trouble in preferving Chaftity, and † S, Mar. if for this end it were neceffary to pull out our Eyes, 9. 43. 47. and cut off our Hands, as our Saviour fpeaks †, it
will

will be an incomparably greater trouble to be cast into Hell-Fire, there to undergo the Tortures which Almighty God has prepared for the Unclean. These fleshly Pleasures are but little, and are over in a Moment, but the Pains of the Life to come are terrible, and yet will never have an end.

III. It may be farther urged That every one has not the Gift of Continence, for so some wrest that of St. *Paul,* 1 Cor. 7. 9. But the Apostle answers this in the very same place, declaring that for those who cannot live single, Marriage is ordained as a holy and honourable State, provided they live chastly in it. Again, if this Argument were good, there is no Sin that might not be excused. All Virtues are the Gift of God as well as Continence; his Grace being alike necessary in order to the Government of Mens Anger, and for rendring them sober, Affable, or Charitable, as it is for resisting Uncleanness. And one that allows himself in Transports of Anger, or lives in Drunkenness and Debauchery, and will neither forgive an Injury or Affront, nor relieve a poor Neighbour, may as well say for himself, that he has not the Gift of Meekness, of Patience, of Sobriety, or of Charity. The Case thus stated, who sees not that this is a vain and frivolous Excuse, and indeed a wicked and impious one? For to say Uncleanness is no way to be avoided, because God has not bestowed the Gift of avoiding it, is to accuse God himself, and impute to his divine Majesty all the Excesses whereinto any are hurried by this infamous Passion.

Grace is certainly necessary for us, and it is a Gift of God without which we can do no good thing. But then it is as certain that God is ready to vouchsafe us this Gift, on condition we will do our part for obtaining it. And this is to be done † St. Lu. by Prayer, God having engaged † *to give his Holy* ii. 13. *Spirit*

Spirit to them that ask him, and by Fasting, Working, and other Methods which I shall touch upon in their proper place ; which Means when made use of as they ought to be, are not so difficult as is ordinarily apprehended. And God does yet more than this ; he freely bestows his Grace, and prevents us by his Spirit, and so puts it into our Power to be Masters of this Gift of Chastity, if it be not through our own Fault. Who are they then that complain for want of this Gift ? Are they not such who will not have it, such who neglect Prayer and all other Means, and will not hearken to all the good Motions which the Holy Spirit excites in them, and the other Advantages that are vouchsafed them ; but rather on the contrary do all they can to deprive themselves of this Gift if they had it, loving Temptations, and wilfully putting themselves in the way of them ? No better can be expected of such, than that they should want this Gift of Chastity. And it is highly unreasonable therefore to insist upon so frivolous an Excuse. If People will not perform their own Duty, yet at least they should not dare to charge God as the Author of all the Wickedness they commit.

IV. I astly, Those who are guilty of this Vice may seek to shelter themselves under the Examples they find in Scripture of several that have fallen into the Sins of Uncleanness. Which Excuse I have formerly considered * in another Work ; and so it will suffice at present only to alledge, that

1. No Examples can justify the Violation of the Divine Laws, and that the Sins of which we have any Relation in the sacred Volumes, serve only for Admonitions that we be constantly upon our Guard. We must not judge of what is allowed or forbidden by Examples, but by the Law of God,

---

* *Causes of Corruption, Part I. Cause IV.*

which

which is the Rule whereby he will judge us at the Last-Day.

2. We have admirable Patterns of Chastity proposed to us in Scripture, that we may be invited to the imitation of them, as that of *Joseph*, of *Job*, and other holy Men who have been eminent for this Virtue.

3. It is to be considered that these Sins with which some of the Faithful recorded in the Old Testament were overtaken, were grievous Sins, and wherein they must have inevitably perished, if they had not recovered out of them by a sincere Repentance. And if it should be objected as the Consequence of this Assertion, that Sinners may recover of themselves and obtain the Pardon of their Sins, and so the Danger of falling into them is not so great; I answer that God is ready to shew Favour to the Penitent; but that it is the utmost height of Folly, and extremely dangerous to live in Sin upon this Consideration; and it shews an exceedingly depraved Mind to offend and provoke God, only because he is so very good. And he that does so imposes miserably upon himself, in promising himself that he shall be sure to repent; this being what he can have no certainty of. And if any find themselves disposed to take encouragement from the Example of those who have risen again after terrible Falls, let such know they have much more reason to tremble at the Remembrance of others who have fallen in like manner, and have been utterly undone by it.

4. Once more, The Difference that is betwixt the Times of the Gospel and those that were before, may justly silence all these vain Excuses. What our Saviour *Jesus Christ* says St. *Matt.* Ch. V. and XIX. concerning Divorce and Adultery, shews clearly that the Duties of Chastity under the Old Law were very different from what is now required

red of us, and that God, out of regard to the
Estate of the *Jews*, and the carnal Temper of their
Mind, passed by many Defects by reason of which
Christians will be excluded the Kingdom of Heaven. And no one that well understands to what
a Degree of Holiness we are called by the Gospel,
will ever dare to alledge the Falls of those who lived before Christ, in Excuse of their Impurity.

SECTION

SECTION V.

The Duties of Offenders in this kind.

AFTER having treated thus largely of Uncleanneſs, before I leave this Subject, it will be requiſite to enquire what is incumbent upon ſuch as are chargeable with this Sin, in order to the Pardon of it. This is a moſt important Article, and concerning which all have great need to be well inſtructed. And the rather becauſe theſe Duties are little underſtood, the greateſt part of thoſe who are moſt concerned in them not knowing what they are to do that they may recover themſelves from their Fall. Some will pretend to expiate this Sin by I know not what defective and inſincere Repentance, and by this means lead many into Perdition. And hence my Deſign in this Section is to give ſome account of what all that are guilty of this Sin are obliged to. And it is what thoſe who have fallen into the Crime are in a peculiar manner concerned to read with great Attention. And thoſe who have not proceeded to the Crime, but are chargeable however with other leſſer Species of Impurity, will find ſeveral Particulars in what I am about to ſay, that will relate to themſelves. Nor is there any Perſon whatſoever that may not make ſome good uſe of it. The Conſideration of what an Unclean Perſon is to do for obtaining the Pardon of his Offence, is a powerful Motive for perſuading to refrain from this Sin. And were every one throughly inſtructed in this Point, People would be far more fearful
ful

ful of yielding to the finful Lufts of the Flefh, than they ufually are.

In general, Every one is convinced that there is no obtaining the Pardon of this Sin, any more than of others, without Repentance. But People are apt to deceive themfelves concerning the Nature of Repentance, as not well knowing in what it confifts. That I may therefore explain this with fome exactnefs, I fay that to repent favingly of this Sin, it is neceffary firft to be Sorry for it ; fecondly to Confefs it ; thirdly to endeavour a Reparation of it ; and laftly, to renounce and forfake it.

CHAP. I.

The firft Duty of Offenders in this kind, Sorrow for their Sin.

THE Firft Branch of Repentance, and the Firft Duty of the Impure is a Sorrow for what they have done. But now that they may not deceive themfelves, they ought to be made fenfible what is to be the ground of this Sorrow, and what the Degree and Meafure of it.

I. It is abfolutely neceffary to enquire into the Principle whence the Sorrow they feel in themfelves proceeds ; inafmuch as this Sorrow is not always faving, nor ought it to be believed that all who are afflicted and mourn for the Irregularites of their Lives, are to be accounted true Penitents. The Grief which many feel in themfelves, or at leaft pretend to, is for the moft part no better than a worldly Grief. That which fticks fo clofe upon them is very often only a Fretting and Vexation, Shame and Difpleafure to find themfelves in Difgrace;

grace, or expofed to other Temporal Misfortunes, which their Incontinence has brought upon them. One Proof of this is, that the greater part give no Token of their being inwardly afflicted till their Crime comes to be difcover'd, and fo they come experimentally to find in what Evils they have involved themfelves by their ill Conduct. Whilft they can fin fecretly, and without fear of Difcovery, they continue in their Licentioufnefs, and take Delight in it. Such a Sorrow is not faving, unlefs the Sinner make a farther Progrefs, and improve the Almighty's Chaftifements to the begetting in him an unfeigned Abhorrence of his paft Tranfgreffions. Wherefore the Principle and Caufe of his Grief muft be the Greatnefs of the Sin it felf, and the woful Eftate whereinto it brings Men in relation to God and their own Salvation. Without repeating here all the Confiderations which may juftly raife in us an Abhorrence of Impurity, I fhall content my felf to note, that no Repentance is acceptable in the Sight of God, that does not arife from fuch Meditations as thefe. For which reafon thofe who know themfelves guilty, fhould weigh them well with themfelves, and have them always prefent to their Mind. And forafmuch as fome are more guilty than others, every one fhould confider the Nature and Circumftances of the Sins which he has committed, that fo his Senfe of them and Repentance for them may bear a proportion to the Heinoufnefs of them.

II. As to the Degree and Meafure of this Sorrow, two Qualifications are to be attended to, that is, the Greatnefs of it, and its Duration.

1. It is not enough to be fomewhat grieved, and afhamed, but this Grief muft be affecting, fuch as enters deep and pierces the very Heart, filling it with Sadnefs and Remorfe, Deteftation and Fear; or if it be not fuch at the beginning, it muft be

fuch

such at length. This is above all others the one infallible Mark of a hearty Sorrow and sincere Repentance; that the Sinner finds no longer any Pleasure or Satisfaction in the things he had formerly delighted in, but seeks to withdraw and get out of the way of them, and finds more Comfort in his Sadness and Tears for them. Sometimes those that have renounced their Uncleanness, have turned aside another way, and betaken themselves to Pleasures of another nature. But so long as they retain an Affection for worldly Pleasures and Joys of whatsoever kind, this is a certain Sign of their not being touched with a true Repentance.

2. But above all Care must be taken that this Grief be lasting. And this Observation serves not only for the Instruction of the Guilty, but is useful also for the Encouragement of such who do not at the first feel themselves so throughly grieved as they ought to be. For Mens Sorrow is oftentimes but light at the beginning of their Conversion; as will easily be apprehended if we but call to mind that there are two sorts of Sins. Some there are for which a Man is apt to have an extreme Concern as soon as ever he has committed them; and they are such as he is not betraied into by his own Inclinations, nor can take Delight in: Thus when one has committed a Murder, or spoken Blasphemy, he will perhaps be immediately struck with the Horror of his Crime, and a stinging Remorse by reason of it. But it is quite otherwise with those Sins into which Men are drawn by Pleasure, and which gratify their Inclinations, and especially when they are become Habitual. Tho' they take up a Resolution of quitting these, they do not at first look upon them with the Aversion due to them, they could yet please themselves with them, and it is not without doing Violence

to

to themſelves, and reſiſting their own Inclinations, that they get rid of them.   So that their Diſlike of theſe ſort of Sins is but ſmall at the firſt, the Fire of Luſt not being yet wholly extinct.   But the chief Commendation of it is, that it is Laſting, and encreaſes continually.   And this is what they ought to have an eſpecial Regard to, the Cauſe of moſt Mens Failings in theſe Attempts being, that in time the Senſe of their Crime abates, and at laſt wears quite away.

The Repentance of thoſe who are polluted by Uncleanneſs, ſhould remain with them to their Lives End.   Theſe are not Sins which a Man can forget; and the Memory of them ought to be always freſh, that the Penitent may truly ſay with *David*, † *My Sin is ever before me.*   Not only the †Pſ. 51.3. Time that has paſt ſince the Commiſſion of it, but even an Amendment of Life does not take away the Senſe of ſo great a Fault; but on the contrary he becomes more and more ſenſible of it. Even this Thought, that the Sinner has had the Happineſs to obtain the Pardon of his Guilt, will render the Remembrance of it the more bitter. And the greater Progreſs he makes in Holineſs, the more abominable will his Wickedneſs appear; the greater Experience he has had of God's Mercy, the more will he accuſe and loath himſelf; and the more Hope he has of Salvation through God's Goodneſs, the more will he be affected with the Danger of being excluded from it, to which he had expoſed himſelf.   In a word, The greater Mercy God has ſhewn in Pardoning, the more reaſon has the pardoned Sinner to love God; And the more any one loves God, the more nearly will he be touched with the Thought of having offended Him.

This is the Firſt Duty of ſuch as are chargeable with Impurity, to have a lively, a hearty and piercing

L   cing

cing Sorrow for it. And if thofe who find not in themfelves fuch a Sorrow as I have been defcribing, are not in a State of Salvation, what can we think of thofe who have no fenfe at all of their Sin, but inftead of condemning, feek to excufe themfelves, and are fo far from having a pungent Regret, and being in Confufion by reafon of their Sin, that they take delight in thinking and fpeaking of it, and even boaft of and glory in it.

CHAP. II.

The Second Duty, Confeffion.

THE Second Duty incumbent upon fuch as are guilty of this Sin, is Confeffion. I need not fay that there is no repenting fincerely of our Sins without confeffing them, this is fo evident of itfelf. But then feeing there are two forts of Confeffion, the one made to God alone, and the other made to Men, it will be requifite to enquire, What is the Duty of thofe who are guilty of Impurity, with refpect to each of thefe?

I. Now forafmuch as none doubts of the Neceffity of Confeffing his Sins to God, I fhall not enlarge upon this Article, but fhall content myfelf to mention only thefe two Obfervations concerning it. Firft that this Confeffion is to be made with an unfeigned Sorrow of Heart, and not with the Mouth only. For confidering to whom it is made, that it is to Almighty God, who is the Searcher of Hearts, and throughly knows whatfoever paffes there, it highly concerns every one to beware of pretending to own his Sins before Him, and to beg his Pardon for them, if the Cafe be not fo, and he is not truly touched with a Senfe of them.

them. Secondly, that this Confeſſion is a moſt effectual Means of raiſing more and more in us a hearty Compunction, and utter Abhorrence of our Sin ; it being impoſſible for a Sinner who conſiders himſelf as in the Preſence of God, and calls to his Remembrance the heinous Immoralities he has lived in, and makes a particular Confeſſion of them, who acknowledges in the Preſence of the Moſt Holy God his ſinful Actions, together with thoſe impure Thoughts and Motions to which he has ſuffer'd himſelf to hearken ; it being impoſſible, I ſay, for ſuch a Sinner, at ſuch a time, not to conceive an Abhorrence of his Impieties, and that a Confeſſion ſo made, ſuch a black Catalogue expoſed to the Eyes of the Almighty, ſhou'd not fill his guilty Soul with Shame, and Confuſion, and Indignation againſt himſelf.

II. Confeſſion made to Man is either publick or private.

1. Publick Confeſſion is ſuch as is made either before the Church in general, or before thoſe who repreſent it, according to the different Cuſtoms of Places. Now ſuch who have fallen into the Sin of Uncleanneſs, muſt Confeſs their Fault publickly, when it is come to the knowledge of the Church, and they are called upon to tell the Truth. In this Caſe it ought to be believed, that God having permitted the Fault to be publickly known, it is his Will to have Confeſſion made of it. And accordingly the Offender is to own it ingeniouſly, and diſcharge his Conſcience of it, whenever he is ſummoned to do it, by thoſe to whom God has committed the Government of his Church with a Power of Excluding notorious Tranſgreſſors. Nor will any one ſtick at ſuch an Acknowledgment, who is touched with a ſincere Repentance ; but whoſoever refuſes in theſe Circumſtances to confeſs his Sins, thereby gives certain Evidence of his Impe-

nitence, and so can hope for no forgiveness. Besides there is an Obligation to confess the truth in order to the removal of that Scandal these sort of Vices give in the Church, for the Comfort and Edification of good People, who cannot but be afflicted by reason of these Vices, and to set an Example to others, this Confession being a most likely means of restraining those who find themselves inclined to Wickedness. So that a Man cannot refuse this Duty without aggravating the Sin he has committed. Besides that in denying what he is justly charged with, he thereby charges his Accuser with having published an Untruth, and made a false Declaration; which is equally inconsistent with Piety, Justice, and Charity. Not to add that Persons by denying their Guilt in this case of Uncleanness, oftentimes engage themselves in another horrible Crime, of refusing to own such Children as they are under an undoubted Obligation to take care of.

Yet how great soever their Crime be, who refuse to confess their Sin, nothing is more common with the Impure, and especially the Men, than to deny the Truth. They betake themselves to Lying and sly Pretences, seeking to defend themselves by all the Tricks they are able to invent. Nor are there wanting some, who though bound by the most tremendous Oath to confess their Fault, deny it upon Oath, and labour to conceal their Wickedness by Perjury, and the most solemn Protestations accompanied with Imprecations against themselves. Which is doubtless one of the most heinous Wickednesses a Man can be guilty of, one of the most dismal Estates a Man can cast himself into. Besides the flagitiousness of the Crime, the Effects of it are terrible; and what is yet more formidable is, that hereby a Door is shut against Repentance. It cannot be denied but a Man

may

may recover himſelf by confeſſing what he had denied, but it is what is hardly ever reſolved upon. And the longer the time paſſes on, the greater Impreſſion thoſe falſe Reaſons which are offered to conceal his Fault, will make. A ſolemn Declaration alſo being once made, he holds himſelf engaged in Honour to ſtand to it, and to do this puts himſelf upon a neceſſity of perſiſting in his Impenitence. Or perhaps he enters upon Marriage, or has a Family of his own, or is in ſome Employment, or finds himſelf in other Circumſtances, which withold him from owning afterwards, what he had once endeavoured to conceal.

The Caſe of ſuch is exceeding dreadful, and all their religious Performances no better than ſo many Acts of Sacrilege. How can they pray to God, or offer themſelves to the holy Communion? And what Uneaſineſs then, what Frights muſt they be in, having ſuch a Load upon their Conſcience, and eſpecially when they are about to leave this World? Then will theſe miſerable Wretches who have covered their Sin by Lying, Perjury, and other Crimes, and have perſevered in ſo doing to the laſt, be racked with horrible Remorſe. They will then begin to open their Eyes, and to judge of things after another manner than they had done formerly, and will abominate their own blind Madneſs, and won'd give all the World, were it at their diſpoſal, that they had made a ſincere Acknowledgment of their Sin. It is undoubtedly an exceſſive degree of Folly and Madneſs, to chooſe rather to throw oneſelf into ſo frightful a State, and ſo to be brought within the Bonds and Snares of the Devil, than by a free and impartial Confeſſion to ſet the Conſcience at eaſe, and enjoy the Happineſs and Satisfaction that would follow hereupon. And all therefore who are concerned in what I am ſaying, ſhould be ſure to conſider it

well

well in time, and fhould take care to Confefs their Sin whilft they may ; left hereafter they be far lefs willing to do it.

The chief Obftacle to People's Confeffion of their Faults of this kind, is Shame and the Fear of being Difgraced. But this is a wicked Shame, and a Procedure every way unreafonable. For firft they are grofsly deceiv'd in thinking that by a Denial of the Truth they fhall efcape the Shame they are fo afraid of. For for the moft part it is obfervable that they are not the lefs expofed, though they do deny their Guilt, after it has taken Air, and they are required to make a publick Confeffion of it. They are not thought the lefs faulty in this cafe, but on the other hand are had in greater Contempt. But farther it is a Miftake to think Confeffion of Sin to be juft matter of Shame. If the Cafe were rightly ftated, it is rather honourable than fhameful to acknowledge the Evil we have done. The Shame is only in doing wickedly; but it is a laudable Action to Confefs the Wickednefs we have done, fuch an Acknowledgment being fome fort of Reparation for it. Hereby the Sinner wafhes off the Stain which Sin has caufed in the Soul ; hereby he is reftored to Peace with God, he rejoices both the Angels in Heaven and the Church on Earth, and all Wifemen look upon him with an Eye of Love and Compaffion.

But fuppofing a Man were hereby expofed to Shame in this World, and that Men would be fure to pafs their Cenfures upon him, he ought not to be deterred by this. The Fear of another fort of Shame, and another greater Punifhment fhould fet him above the Dread of Men. And yet after all, Are the Confequences of a fincere Acknowledgment to be feared even in this World? Though a Man expofe himfelf to the Contempt of Men, and to be reproached and reviled by them, what

signifignifies this Contempt? The Judgment Men make of us, whether in our Favour or to our Dif-advantage, is of very little confideration. Their Approbation or Diflike of us determines nothing, and is quickly forgotten; but the Effects of a Lye perfifted in are very dreadful. The Shame which one may fuffer in this World is prefently over, it vanifhes away, and the Men themfelves dy; but the Mifchiefs whereto Obftinacy in Wickednefs renders Sinners obnoxous will never have an End; but they muft be expofed in the Sight of God him-felf, of his Holy Angels, and of Men, to an Ig-nominy infinitely more formidable than all that is moft fhameful and moft painful here below.

Shame will never prevail over that Man who is heartily grieved for the Sins he has committed, A true Penitent accounts of the Shame as a fmall matter; and he no longer ftands in awe of Men's Judgment, when once he is heartily affected with the Terrour of God's Judgments. *David* finned; but he was not afhamed, though a King, to own his Crime, not only before the Prophet *Nathan,* but in a far more publick Manner, by compofing the Fifty-firft Pfalm upon this Subject, to be to the End of the World a lafting Teftimony of his Repentance. A Sinner who is really fenfible of his Fault, ftands not to hefitate with himfelf, as to his Behaviour when called to Confefs; nor does Shame any way withold him from it. Being over-whelmed with a much greater Shame, for having defiled himfelf, offended God, and fcandalized the Church; he does not fo much attend to his own prefent Intereft, or any worldly Confiderations, but that he efteems it his Honour to wafh off his Defilement by fuch an Acknowledgment as may make fome Amends for it. And how fenfible fo-ever he be of the Shame that follows upon fuch an Acknowledgment, he willingly fubmits to it, as a

good

good degree of Mortification. He looks upon it as one fort of Punishment, and an Occasion of humbling himself, and subduing his vicious Inclinations, and is very glad of an Opportunity of giving such evidence of his Sincerity and Repentance. A true Repentance fills the Sinner with Indignation, and a Desire of taking all possible Revenge upon himself, and being convinced that he has deserved yet more Shame than he has met with, he readily submits himself to whatsoever is most mortifying to him, and most useful for taming his Flesh and its Passions.

I have treated somewhat largely of this Article, because of the Necessity there is of pressing it, and because it is ordinarily by reason of an unaccountable Shame that the Impure suffer themselves to perish.

And yet it is not to be thought that all who acknowledge their Sin make a saving Confession. Many confess their Fault, but not except in case of Extremity, and when they can deny it no longer. And this Confession they make with so little of Frankness, and such Reserves and Shifts, that it is easily seen it is all forced, and drawn from them by pure Necessity. An evident Token of an Evil, a Wicked and Hard Heart! Every one sees also that they live afterwards in such a manner, as shews no true Amendment. Yet it is only a sincere and ingenuous Confession of Sin that will be available in order to Forgiveness.

2. I have hitherto discoursed of such whose Guilt is known. But it may farther be enquired, Whether those whose Fault is still concealed are obliged to Confess it; and how they are in this case to behave themselves? Which is a weighty Question, and concerns a great part of Mankind, only that it is as nice as weighty.

I say therefore in the first place, that Whilst a Fault is not come abroad, the Offender is not only not obliged to confess it publickly, but that he ought not to confess it in this manner, that he scandalize not the Church, by bringing to its Knowledge a Sin it had otherwise heard nothing of. But then I say this purely upon supposition that this Sin has been kept secret, and he has never been required, nor enter'd into any Obligation to own it in Publick. It is not to be imagined that it was ever allowed to use any unlawful courses for preventing these Faults being made known, such as Lying, false Declarations, the Exposing or Abandoning Children, or those other sinful Means Unclean Persons are wont to make use of for preserving their Faults from a publick Discovery. It were much better that a Fault should become publick, than to conceal it after this manner, this being a means of aggravating it, of putting the Sinner out of a Capacity of Amendment, and of engaging themselves in a Necessity of remaining all his Life in a state of Impenitence, which it is impossible to get out of whilst he makes it his Business to conceal one Wickedness by the help of another.

Well, but suppose the Sin not to be known, what is to be done in this Case? I answer in general, the guilty Person is to endeavour to ease himself of it by a true Repentance. He must omit nothing that is necessary to this purpose; must privately humble himself before God, must amend his Fault, and use all means possible for disburdening his Conscience, must deny himself for some time the participation of the holy Communion, and observe those Duties incumbent upon Offenders, which I am about to mention. But still it may be questioned Whether these Persons are to confess their Sin in Private.

I say

I say a Private Confession may be of very great Advantage, and that upon some Occasions it must be made use of ; it may happen that a Man may be indispensably obliged to it, if the Sinner is perplexed with Scruples, or cannot well enform himself what course he must take to rise again after his Fall, or is in doubt concerning the truth and reality of his Repentance ; it is certain that being in these Circumstances, and so having need of Assistance and Advice, he cannot do better than to apply himself to some Person of known Understanding and Probity. Generally those who are guilty of great Sins, will not know what to do without some help. And it is certain that Multitudes perish for want of Courage to lay themselves open to their Spiritual Physician. Unless the Sinner throughly understand his own Case, and his Conscience be tender enough to direct him, a Happiness rarely to be met with amongst the Impure, it is of necessity that he consult some other Person. He may address himself to whomsoever he shall think fit upon such an Occasion, and freely open his Mind to him. But the Ministers of the Gospel being ordained to watch over Men's Souls, and Almighty God having authorized them to pronounce Pardon upon the Terms of the Gospel ; and since it is besides to be presumed that they are better skilled in matters of Religion than their Neighbours, the best course the guilty Sinner can take will be to address himself to his own Spiritual Guide. This was the Practice of the Primitive Church. Publick Penances were appointed amongst the Ancient Christians for publick Sins. But when any had committed a Sin in private, which had it been known, would have required a publick Confession, he then betook himself to the Ministers of the Church, to receive by their means such Advice, Exhortation, and Comfort as his Condition called for.   But

But now in order to the putting this in practice, a Man ſhould be fully aſſured of the Ability, and eſpecially the Probity of theſe Miniſters, ſo as to have an entire Confidence in them ; and they on the other hand ſtand engaged to keep what is Confeſſed as an inviolable Secret. Whence by the way it may be obſerved, of what mighty importance it is that none but wiſe, prudent, and diſcreet, underſtanding, and truly religious Perſons be ever admitted to this ſacred Function.

When Sinners thus addreſs themſelves to their Spiritual Guides, it is Their Part to give them all neceſſary Advice, to repreſent to them the Heinouſneſs of their Sin, to ſee what Tokens and Aſſurances they can give of the Sincerity of their Repentance, and to acquaint them what they are to do by way of Reparation for their Sin, or in order to their own Recovery out of it. They ſhould alſo examine whether their People be fit to receive the holy Sacrament, and to deny them it for ſome time, till they diſcover in them the Signs of a real Reformation, and pronounce the Pardon of their Sins.

I ſpeak not here of the private Admonitions they ſhould give to ſuch as live looſly, as they have opportunity, and though never conſulted by them, becauſe this is not the proper place for it.

It is not only before † the Prieſts that People ſhould acknowledge their Faults, but there are ſome Caſes wherein it ſhould be done before others. Thus they ought to own them in the preſence of ſuch as are to take cognizance of them in order to their Edification. It is certain they

---

† *Here I render* les Paſteurs, *the Prieſts, becauſe it is to the Prieſts only that our Lord has committed a Power of abſolving Penitents.*

are to confess them in secret, when there is no
other way to prevent the great Mischief that might
ensue from a more publick Confession of them.
It is a ruled Case, that rather than permit an Ince-
stuous Marriage between two Persons, who neither know nor suspect themselves to be Brother
and Sister, but yet are so, one of them being of
an impure Birth, the guilty Father or Mother, if
no other Method can be contrived for hindring
such a Marriage, ought to declare his, or her,
Crime, yet with all the Secrecy that may be. But
out of this Case of absolute necessity, these kind
of Sins are not to be discovered, for fear of the
Consequences such a Discovery might have, the
Breaches in, and Dishonour of Families, and many other Mischiefs it might produce. A Man
should rather seek the Reparation of his Offence
by secret Means; only he must be sure to do it
with great Sincerity and Honesty, and so as that
Conscience be no way entangled by it.

C H A P. III.

The Third Duty of the Unclean, A Reparation of the Evil they have done.

THE Third Duty whereto the Impure stand
obliged is to make Reparation for their Sin.
It is an uncontroverted Principle of Religion, as
well as of natural Justice, that every one must
make Satisfaction to the utmost of his Power, for
all the Evil he has done; it being evident that
without this there is no Repentance, and by consequence no Pardon. He that labours not with all
his might to repair a Fault he has committed, or
an Injury he has done to another, hereby testifies
that

that he does not unfeignedly repent of it, and that he has no true Sense of either Justice, Charity, or Piety. Which Remark I make for the Information of such who conceit that their Sins may be forgiven them, though they do not make Reparation for the Mischief done by them, only upon condition that they repent and fly to the Mercy of God. This is utterly impossible. For Repentance and Recourse to the Divine Mercy are never sincere, till the Sinner uses his hearty endeavour to Repair the Evil he has done.

Now the Reparation Persons are bound to for the Sin of Impurity, respects our Neighbours Interest either Temporal or Eternal.

I. In respect to Temporal Interest a Man may prejudice his Neighbour in his Honour and Reputation, in his Goods, or upon other accounts; and he should therefore make it his Business in each of these Instances, to Repair the Evil he has done. We see in the Law, that God who had ordered Thieves * to make a full Restitution, has ordered the same likewise for the Sins of Impurity, † He that had abused a Virgin was to *take her for his Wife;* and moreover the Law imports that whosoever had espoused a Woman after this manner was *never after to put her away.* Whereby it appears ♪ that one Method of making Amends for this Sin is by marrying the Person who has been seduced. And this is especially to be done when any Promises have been made to each other; supposing withal that they are both free, and in a Capacity of Contracting. If this cannot be, as in many Cases it plainly cannot, and there is no Repairing these Sins by Marriage, some other course must be taken for making Reparation of the Damage done to the

* **Exod.** 22. 3.
Numb. 5.
† Deut. 22. 29.

♪ Grot. de Jure belli ac pacis. l. 2. cap. 17. 15.

Person

Perſon enticed. The Law of God points out this Duty, ‖ enjoining that *if the Father of the Damſel* refuſed to give her in Marriage to him who had ſeduced her, the Perſon ſeducing ſhould pay a Summ of Money. Whence it follows that one of the ways of Repairing this Crime, when it cannot be done by Marriage, is by giving a Portion, or a Summ proportionable to the Condition of the Perſon, other Circumſtances alſo conſidered.

‖ Exod. 22. 17.

Another Duty, and indeed the moſt indiſpenſable of all with reſpect to this World, is to procure that no harm be done to the Children born of theſe unlawful Mixtures, but moſt diligently to provide for their Support and Education. I have already † treated of this Duty, and have proved that it would be a horrible Crime to caſt them off. And not only ſo, but Proviſion muſt be made for their Education and for their Maintenance with ſo much the more care, becauſe the Condition of theſe Children is ordinarily very uncomfortable, and they are born into the World in a ſtate of Shame and Miſery.

† Sect. 1. Ch. 1.

Laſtly, There is no manner of doubt but in the Crime of Adultery, Reſtitution is to be made to thoſe who ſuffer by it ; as when a Father is put to the charge of maintaining a Child that is none of his own, and when a Child that is come into a Family by Adultery, partakes, with the lawful Children and Heirs, of an Eſtate that does not at all belong to him. In either of theſe Caſes, the guilty Perſons are indiſpenſably obliged to Reſtitution to the Father or the Children. Only this muſt be ſure to be done privately, ſo long as the Crime is not known ; though if it were known, then the Reſtitution ſhould be publick: Nothing can excuſe from this Duty ; without which it is impoſſible the Offenders ſhould have

their

their Crime pardoned, save only when they have it by no means in their Power to make such Restitution. And yet even in this Case, they must be sincerely and constantly resolved, to make it as soon as ever they shall be able, and must endeavour it heartily, and to the utmost of their Ability. Nor are they Divines only and Moralists, who prescribe this Duty as indispensable; * the Lawyers also declare the Justice and Necessity of it.

This Article should beget a great Abhorrence of Sensuality, and make People tremble at the thoughts of giving themselves up to it. And would they seriously consider it, certainly they could never suffer themselves to be enticed to the filthy Lusts of the Flesh, nor would those who are guilty of it be near so easy as they are for the most part. They would quickly see that by committing this Sin, they plunge themselves into abundance of Misfortunes, they entangle themselves in strange Difficulties, and prepare for themselves terrible Remorse, and cruel Uneasiness. This Reflection Mr. *Placette* most judiciously makes in his *Treatise of Restitution*, at the End of the XIIIth Chapter. Having discoursed of the Restitution whereto Persons are obliged in case of Adultery, he concludes thus, *What I have said shews into what Snares, and Troubles, they that commit this great Sin, cast themselves. Which if People would at all mind, perhaps they would shun them more carefully than they do. But they either do not know them, or are not willing to consider them. In a word, Mankind lead their Lives, as if the Violaters of this*

---

* Grot. de Jur. b. ac p. l. 2. c. 17. 15. *Adulter & Adultera tenentur non tantum, indemnem præstare maritum ab alendâ prole, sed & legitimis hæredibus rependere, si quod damnum patiuntur, ex concursu ita suscepta prolis ad hæreditatem,*

Law

Law had neither Justice to overawe them, nor Punish-
ment to stand in fear of. I beseech all whom this
concerns to reflect upon it in time ; and that they
will give themselves the trouble of reading the
XIth, XIIth, and XIIIth Chapters of that same
Treatise, where this Matter is handled at large.

II. I added that Reparation is to be made for
the Damage any one has done his Neighbour as
to his Spiritual Interest. And this requires two
Duties, the one general, and the other particular.

1. The general Duty is to make amends for
the Scandal which has been given, either to some
who have come to the knowledge of the Crime,
or to the whole Church. In the former Case a
Man should omit nothing that is necessary for
the Edification of those he has scandalized, for
comforting such good Christians as are greatly
afflicted at these sort of Sins, and above all for
hindring those whom he has set so bad a Pattern
from sinning after his Example, and for retrie-
ving them from their Sin, if through his fault
they have been already drawn into it. In the
other Case, He is to make amends for the Scandal
he has given the Church, which can be done only
by shewing publickly that he is sincerely and
humbly Penitent. This was the Practice of the First
Christians, and it was exactly conformable to the
Spirit of the Gospel. It is clear that scandalous Sinners, and amongst others the Unclean, testifying by
their Conversation that they are no true Christians,
and separating themselves from the Communion
of *Jesus Christ,* as S. *Paul* speaks, 1 *Cor.* 6. are not
therefore to be looked upon as true Members of
the Church, till they change their course of Life,
and beg to be restored to the Communion from
which they have departed. Thus by the bye it
appears, what Notions we should have of Publick
Penance. Divers account of it as a Punishment
and

and Correction executed upon Sinners, which it
is not: It is on the contrary a Favour that is
granted them And hence it was that in the Primitive Church, the Penitents entreated this Favour with Tears, and a great deal of Earnestness.
But this holy Practice is now abolished in many
Places; and it is very rarely that either Excommunication or Penance is made use of in relation to the Impure.

Which obliges me to add one Consideration more,
with respect to those who commit this Sin in places where Ecclesiastical Discipline is grown into
disuse; and that is, that they must not be careless and secure upon Pretence that they are not
liable to the Laws and Duties of Penance; nor
suffer themselves to be prevailed upon by the Liberty that is allowed them of coming to the Holy Mysteries, and enjoying all the Privileges of
the External Members of the Church. They
should bethink themselves, that neither the Bad-
ness of the Times, nor the Opposition of Men,
nor the Customs and Laws established by those
in Authority, can alter the Laws of Christ. Excommunication is not the less of Divine Right,
for being grown out of use. If egregious Sinners
are not excommunicated by Men, they are however in the sight of God; they have cut themselves off from Jesus Christ by their disorderly
Life; they have broken the Communion they
had with the Saints by scandalizing them. So that
whatsoever Judgment Men make of them, they
ought to judge and condemn themselves, and
look upon themselves as separated from their Saviour. Let them therefore be very wary how
they approach his Table after the commission of
this Sin, but let them abstain for a time, and let
them groan by themselves in private; and if
their Fault be known, let them give publick Signs

of

of a profound Humiliation and Repentance. These are the Advices proper to be given to the Guilty, and which they ought to follow as they would secure their own Salvation. This is what might be said upon this Subject in the mean time, till it shall please God in his good Providence to re-settle Discipline in the Church, and Princes, Magistrates, and People, shall all submit to the Laws of Christ.

2. Besides this general Duty, there is another more particular, and that is to Repair the Injury which has been done to, and provide for the Salvation of, the Person with whom this Wickedness has been committed. For this Sin, putting two Persons at the same time into a State of Damnation, it is evident, that whether one has been solicited, or has solicited, the other, he is obliged to procure by all ways possible, the Conversion of that other with whom he has been engaged in this Crime. This is an important Article, but which is very little thought of. Far from this, the Impure oftentimes put the greatest Impediments in the way of their Accomplices Repentance, and employ all their Art to immerse them deeper in their Guilt. As all those do who tempt them to conceal their Fault by Lying, and making false Declarations, and entice them to use other unlawful means to prevent the Truths being brought to Light.

CHAP.

C H A P. IV.

The Fourth Duty of the Unclean, Conversion.

THE Fourth Duty of such who are chargeable with this Sin is Conversion and Amendment; which is to be wrought by these Four
Steps.

I. First to forsake their Sin, and continue no
longer in it. When our blessed Saviour pardoned
the Woman taken in Adultery, he said to her,
* *Go and sin no more.* The Crime must therefore *S. Jo.
be totally Renounced; and they which do not 8. 11.
this, but relapse into it, have not Repented of it.
Every Act, and every Repetition of their Sin, is
an Aggravation of both their Guilt and Punishment: This is so easily comprehended, that there
will be no occasion to shew it more at large.

II. But this is but the Beginning of Conversion; and this first Step will be to no purpose if
the Offenders stop here. It is not enough to renounce their Crime, without renouncing likewise
all the Approaches to it, all the several Species
of Impurity, and all the Defilements of either
Body or Mind; all lewd Actions, wanton Glances,
impure Thoughts and Desires, together with such
Familiarities as expose to Temptation, all obscene
Discourse or Expressions; and which are contrary to Chastity. It is true this Renunciation may
appear Difficult at first, and will occasion no
small Trouble, to those that have contracted a
vicious Habit of giving themselves up to all sorts
of Passions. But People must couragiously resolve to overcome themselves, it being far better
to deny themselves in some things, and to cross

their own Inclinations than to perish eternally. †*It is profitable for them that one of their Members should perish; and not that their whole Body should be cast into Hell-fire.* Moreover, the Difficulty that is herein is of no long Continuance; and I shall shew that it is not too great to be overcome.

†S. Mat. 5. 29.

There are two Reasons, why it is necessary to renounce all these Species of Impurity. First because they will be apt to make Men fall again into the Crime. And then because a true Repentance is inconsistent with Defilement. The Soul is not changed, whilst it is not pure, but preserves a Kindness for these filthy and shameful Passions. The Soul and the Body are polluted by unchast Desires and Actions. In a word, wheresoever there is any love of Sin, there is no true Reformation.

By this Rule any one may know that there are many false and hypocritical Conversions. Many abstain from the Crime and renounce it, who in the mean time are neither chast in Body, nor in Heart. Their Soul is always full of lascivious Desires and Imaginations; they are dissolute in their Actions and in their Speech; they give themselves a full Liberty, and satisfy themselves in every thing but only the very Crime. This is an evident Mark of Corruption, and Impenitence; and they may assure themselves that it is only upon worldly Considerations, they do not deliver themselves up to the utmost Excesses.

III. It suffices not barely to fly Impurity, but in the Third Place, they must shew forth their Repentance by a Life of Mortification, partly for the satisfaction of those who have been scandalized at them, and partly for defending themselves against Temptations and Relapses. It being the Flesh that has put them upon sinning, it is but reasonable that this be tamed by Severity and

and Fafting. The carnal Appetite, and love of
Pleafures and worldly Joy, muft be brought into
fubjection. A Man muft in token of his Humiliation, and by way of Prevention for the future,
mortify himfelf in all things, and efpecially in
thofe he has moft kindnefs for, and where they
are not expreſly forbidden him. If it be a general Doctrine among Chriftians, * *not to take*   * Rom.
care of the Flefh, † to mortify the Body, or *to keep*   13. 14.
it under and bring it into fubjection, none has more   † 1 Cor.
reafon for the Obfervance of thefe Injunctions,   9. 27.
than thofe whom the Paffions of the Flefh have
drawn into Sin. A Love of Pleafures, and Compliance with the Flefh are no where more highly blameable, than in fuch as are guilty of Impurity. And it muft alfo be granted that when
any one is touched with a lively Senfe of this
Crime, he goes no longer in queft of thefe vain
Delights, he is not then in a Condition to rejoyce
and pleafe himfelf, but places his Confolation
rather in the Exercifes of Repentance. Diverfi-
ons and frivolous Entertainments, reading vain
Authors, Dreffing, and the care of the Body,
all thefe make but faint Impreffions on him. And
no lefs on the contrary, when thofe that have
been Impure, and Diffolute, and who have left
off to fin as they have grown into Years, do not
mortifie themfelves, when they love their Eafe,
and make it their ftudy to obtain the Pleafures
and Advantages of Life, paffing their Time in
Idlenefs, or at Play, and fetting their Minds upon
Dainties and fumptuous Entertainments, moft certainly thefe are yet in a ftate of Impenitence,
and have never been truly fenfible of their Fault,
nor duly fet themfelves to make amends for it.

IV. In the laft place, The fincerity of a Sinner's
Converfion muft appear not only in the things
which

wh'ch have relation to Impurity, but in the whole course of his Conversation. So great a Fall should render a Man wise, pious, circumspect, in all things.   All that is in him is to become new. He should take occasion from every thing to shew his Repentance, to discharge his Duty towards God, to edify his Neighbour, and to purify himself more and more.   He ought with great exactness and sincerity to practise the Duties of Religion, to give himself to Meditation, and Prayer, and to be constant in holy Exercises. He ought to do all the good Works he shall be able, and especially to employ his Goods to the Uses of Piety and Charity, following the Counsel of the Prophet *Daniel,* † *Redeeming their Sins by Alms, and their Iniquities by shewing Mercy to the Poor.* In one word, He should be sure to neglect nothing of all that may evidence a sincere Conversion.

† Dan. 4. 27.

See here one way whereby to distinguish betwixt a true and a false Repentance ; and how a great part of the World deceive themselves. The Guilty of Lasciviousness think it enough to leave that Sin ; yet they stick not at others, and their Conversation is very disorderly upon many accounts.   Now to what purpose is it to lay aside one Sin, and take up others in its room? This alone is an abundant proof that such have never truly Repented ; What they call a Reformation being only an Exchange of one Passion for another.   He that lived in Sensuality has left off his wonted Extravagances, because Age has cooled his Passion, or else he is Married and has a Family to provide for, or is in an eminent Post, or such other Circumstances as require him to live regularly, and suffer him not to follow his own Inclinations.   But he is not at all the better Man for this ; but is still Covetous, or Ambitious, or a Swearer,

Swearer, or an Incendiary, or an † Uſurer, or a
Drunkard: It is very uſual after People have ſpent
their Youth in Pleaſures, to devote the remainder
of their Life to Ambition and Covetouſneſs. Yet
all the while they impoſe upon themſelves, and will
by all means believe that they are well amended,
becauſe they do not go on in the ſame Sins they had
practiſed formerly. They do not now commit the
ſame Sins they did in their younger Years, but yet
they commit others inſtead of them that they were
not then acquainted with. Wherein there is ſo
little Amendment that it is rather an Enhancement
of their Condemnation, as being an addition of
Sin to Sin. And yet after this Manner do a great
number of Perſons become ſucceſſively Slaves to
theſe three Paſſions, Pleaſure, Pride, and Avarice.
Beſides abundance of others in whom none of theſe
Paſſions is extinct, but they reign all at once, and
though grown into Years they are nevertheleſs impure, ambitious, and miſerably addicted to their
Intereſt. I conclude therefore that there muſt be
a general Reformation. If a Man be a real Penitent, he will ſhew this in his whole Converſation,
in his outward Deportment, in his Diſcourſe, in
his Employment, in his Family, if he has one,
and in all his Affairs ; throughout the whole his
Management will be according to the Rules of the
exacteſt Juſtice, and the Dictates of a tender Conſcience. This is the Character of a true Penitent.

† This I take to intend one that is very griping and unreaſonable in his Demands; ſince if all it means were only one
that takes a moderate Intereſt for Money, ſuch a Practice
though forbidden amongſt the *Jews* to thoſe of their own
Nation, will however be very hardly proved unlawful
amongſt Chriſtians, our Bleſſed Saviour having nowhere
condemned it in his Goſpel. As has been fully proved not
only by *Salmaſius* and Others formerly, but by a learned Wri-
ter to whom our Author himſelf appeals upon another Occaſion.
Mr. La Placette, Second Traité ſur des Matieres de Conſcience

And

And thus I have shewn what are the Duties of those who have fallen into the Sins of Impurity. But as I have said, they are not so appropriated to the guilty of the Crime, but that all others who, though free from the Crime, are not yet every way pure and chaft, may and ought to apply them to themselves.

Happy are the Guilty that discharge these Duties aright, who with the sinful Woman in St. *Luke's* Gospel, weep bitterly for their Faults, who have confessed them, and made Reparation for them, and have renounced and forsaken them !   * *Their Sins, though great, shall be forgiven them.* These are by no means to be despised. For there is a great deal of Love and Tenderness due to all Sinners, but more especially to such as forsake their wicked ways, and cause *Joy in Heaven* by their Return. And it would be a great Sin to reject those whom God has taken into his Favour.

  But what shall we say of Sinners that neglect these Duties, and continue in their Pollution and their Crime ? How sad a state must that Man be in, who not only feels his Conscience accufing him of this Sin, but who besides has taken no care to make amends for it, and who, miserable Wretch as he is, heaps Sin upon Sin, and Crime upon Crime ? But above all, what can be thought of those who, laden with their Sins, live however in Security ? How is it they are so blind as not to see into what a deplorable Condition they have brought themselves ? Or whence is it they are so easy under these Circumstances ? How and in what manner do they hope to end their Lives ? Can they promise themselves to obtain the Pardon of their Sins, before they leave this World ? I entreat, I beseech, I conjure them to enquire what Ground they have to flatter themselves with any such Hope. I beg of them to reflect upon
what

* St. Lu. 7. 47.

what they have read, but withal to do it very ſeriouſly, for after all it is what deſerves to be well
conſidered. It is not their Buſineſs to drive theſe
Thoughts from their Mind, and live like Beaſts,
letting looſe the Reins to their Senſuality, and har-
dening themſelves in their Guilt, and ſo to go
down unconcernedly to the Grave. This is the
utmoſt height of Blindneſs and Brutality; in as
much as Death is every day drawing nearer, after
which every one muſt enter upon an Eſtate from
whence there is no Returning.

If to obtain the Pardon of this Sin, the Duties I
have mentioned are neceſſarily to be performed, it
ſeems to me plainly to follow, their Hope is every
way groundleſs and deceitful, who put off their
Converſion, and yet promiſe themſelves to find
Favour with God at the end of their Life. For
Death may ſnatch away the Sinner without allow-
ing him time to bewail his Sin. But admitting his
Circumſtances to be ſuch as will allow him time for
Reflection; what ſort of Reflections will he make,
when his Conſcience ſhall ſet before him the Miſcarriages of his Life, and ſhall eſpecially reproach
him for thoſe Sins which draw others after them,
and for which he ought to have made Reparation.
Oh the miſerable ſtate, will he ſay to himſelf,
whereto I find myſelf reduced! Oh that whilſt I
was in Health, and had Time allowed me, I had
taken care to clear my Conſcience! But I have
perſevered in my Sins, I have added one Provocation to another, I have put Obſtructions in the
way to my Repentance; and have brought myſelf to that paſs, that I know neither how to confeſs, nor how to make amends for them. And
now at length I am come to my laſt Day, I am
laid upon that Bed from whence I ſhall riſe no
more, but muſt go to appear before my God, and
thither ſhall I carry into his Preſence a guilty Con-
                                                    ſcience,

fcience, a Body and a Soul polluted and laden with Filth. Now things appear with much another Countenance than they had formerly. Now Terrors and Remorfe begin to fhew themfelves, and the Sinner is feized with horrible Anguifh. Now he would make Reftitution. Now he condemns himfelf for having deceived a Parent, and done Injury to the Children. Now he would crave the Prieft's Advice, and would fain learn how to fet his Confcience at eafe. But it is now too late, he has no more time left, he is dying, and has already loft his Strength and Underftanding.

I am well aware that Man muft not pretend to fet bounds to Divine Mercy ; nor exclude a Sinner from Pardon upon condition he be touched with a lively and unfeigned Repentance, and which proceeds not meerly from a fear of Death; fuppofing alfo that he in good truth does all he is able to confefs and make amends for his Sin, and gives all the Tokens poffible of a fincere Repentance, not being withheld from it by Shame, or any worldly Confideration whatfoever. But befides that this is a very uncomfortable manner of a Chriftians ending his Life, and he will meet with a great deal of diffatisfaction in it ; it is farther to be remembred that there are very few, that after a Life of Senfuality, end their days with a faving Repentance, efpecially amongft thofe who have committed fuch Faults as have need of Confeffion and Reparation, and have endeavoured by one Sin to conceal another. Some have been racked and tortured upon their Death-bed with thefe dire Reflections : And fome being called upon and exhorted to confefs and make amends for their Sins, whereof they have been publickly accufed, and of which they were certainly guilty, but yet had folemnly protefted themfelves innocent, have died without ever being brought to own the
Truth.

Truth. When Men have made theſe advances to-wards the concealing their Wickedneſs, it is very rarely that they will recede from them ; but they will chooſe rather to damn themſelves through a falſe Shame and point of Honour.

Whence it appears that all who abandon them-ſelves to the Crime, caſt themſelves into an Abyſs of Miſeries. A dreadful State indeed ! No wiſe Man ſure would ever knowingly bring himſelf into ſuch cruel Perplexities; it is ſo eaſy, and ſo reaſonable to prevent it by diſcharging his Con-ſcience, and doing as he ought. How then ought ye to enter upon theſe Reflections, all you that have contracted a Habit of Licentiouſneſs. You are called to do it now ; and if ye do it not, you will one day bewail and deteſt your own bru-tiſh Security. No doubt you perſuade yourſelves that you ſhall never be ſo unhappy, and that you ſhall have better Sentiments hereafter ; but the longer you ſhall expect, the worſe you will find it with you ; the longer you ſhall live, the more un-willing you will be to take up a Reſolution that you will not be invited to at preſent. Your Re-turn to God is not the work of a Moment ; but there is need of Time to free yourſelves from the Bonds and Snares whereinto Men are brought by Incontinence, to make amends for your Sin ; to root out evil Habits, and to purify the Heart. To be informed of all which Truths, and not to make a good uſe of them, is but to run upon Deſtructi-on, and prepare for yourſelves an extremely doleful End.

These Conſiderations are alſo offered you, who are yet in the Age of Youth. Be affected with them, and hearken rather to the Voice of God and the Counſels of Wiſdom than to your own Paſſions. You are young, you are in Health, you put from you the thoughts of a Reformation, but

you

you are haſtening continually towards Death, and may be ſurprized by it much ſooner than you imagine. Wherefore reckon not upon the time to come; nor flatter yourſelves that you ſhall be converted when Age ſhall have worn off your impure Paſſions. The Flames of Impurity burn even in thoſe of elder Years; and if they dye away in ſome, thoſe of other Paſſions are kindled in them. There is too much Danger in ſuffering ourſelves to be ſurprized by the Temptations of Voluptuouſneſs; but much more in wilfully delivering ourſelves up to them, in deſpite of all the Admonitions we meet with to the contrary. From one Sin People paſs on to another, and ſo their Habits come to be confirmed; they ſin, and think of nothing but hiding their Sin whatſoever it coſt them, till at length they find themſelves in an Eſtate out of which there is no Recovery; becauſe they can no more reſolve to do what is neceſſary for the diſcharge of their Conſcience. Bleſſed therefore is he that waits not till Death to amend his Faults! But much more bleſſed he, whoſe Youth is chaſt, and always kept within Bounds! His Life cannot fail of being Pure, or his Death of being Happy.

Here I conclude the former part of this Work, in which I have propounded to treat of Uncleanneſs. I ſhall now proceed to the other, wherein I am to diſcourſe of Chaſtity.

The End of the Former Part.

PART II.

OF

CHASTITY.

VICE and Virtue being two Oppofites, in keeping at a diftance from the One, we by this means approach the Other. And fo Chaftity being the oppofite Virtue to Uncleannefs, what has been hitherto difcourfed of that Vice, has a natural tendency to render Perfons Chaft. Yet not fo fully but that it will be requifite to treat alfo of Chaftity in particular. And the rather becaufe this Virtue is not throughly underftood; a great part of Mankind not knowing the Nature and Duties of it; few apprehending what is to be done in order to it; and fewer yet being willing to be at the Pains of acquiring it. My Defign therefore in the Second Part of this Work is to fpeak of Chaftity, and to fhew thefe three things. Firft, what Chaftity is; Secondly, what are the Motives to it; and thirdly, what Means are to be made ufe of in order to our being Chaft. The firft of which Articles will explain the Nature of this Duty; the next will invite to practife it; and the laft will render the Practice of it eafy.

SECTION

SECTION I.

CHAP. I.

Of Chaſtity in General.

CHaſtity is a preſervation of ourſelves both Souls and Bodies pure and exempt from the Pollution of Uncleanneſs. St. *Paul* deſcribes it in theſe terms, 1 *Theſ.* IV. 3, 4. *This is the Will of God, that ye ſhould abſtain from Fornication ; that every one of you ſhould know how to poſſeſs his Veſſel in Sanctiſication and Honour.* Whereby he firſt ſhews that Chaſtity conſiſts in abſtaining from Uncleanneſs, and preſerving the Body pure. For this term of *Veſſel,* or * Inſtrument, ſignifies the Body, which is as a Veſſel wherein the Soul dwells, or as an Inſtrument by the help of which it executes its Deſigns. St. *Paul* ſpeaks of the Body, becauſe Uncleanneſs is properly a Sin of the Body and Fleſh, as is ſaid 1 *Cor.* 6. 18. and *Rom.* 1. 24. But though the Apoſtle ſpeaks of the Body, Chaſtity concerns the Mind alſo. The truth is, the Apoſtle would have us poſſeſs our Bodies in Purity ; but we cannot keep our Bodies pure without the help of the Mind. It is the Soul's Buſineſs to guard the Body, to govern it, and keep it in ſubjection ; and it belongs not to the Body to have dominion over the Soul. When a Man follows the Motions of the Body, then the Body guides the Soul and drags it along ; it is the Fleſh that rules, and the Soul is become its Slave. But when † *through the Spirit we mortify the*

Deeds

So the Word ſeems to be uſed Act. 9. 15.

† *Rom. 8. 14.*

Deeds and Paſſions *of the Body,* as St. *Paul* ſpeaks, then the Body is brought into ſubjection, and the Soul preſerves its Authority over it, as in reaſon it ought.   It is plain therefore that Chaſtity reſpects both Body and Mind, and that it conſiſts in the Purity of both the One and the Other of theſe Parts of ourſelves. As is implied in theſe Words of St. *Paul,* wherein he gives a Deſcription of one who lives in entire Chaſtity. ||*The unmarried Woman careth for the things of the Lord, that ſhe may be holy both in Body and in Spirit.* || 1 Cor. 7. 34.

But the Apoſtle teaches that to keep our Bodies pure, it is not enough to refrain from all unlawful and immodeſt Behaviour, and abſtain from Impurity ; but there is ſomething more than this required, and theſe Words *to keep the Body in* Holineſs, or *Sanctification, and Honour,* import that we are to uſe them purely, and to employ them to holy Purpoſes, worthy of that Chriſtianity we make Profeſſion of, and acceptable in the ſight of God. This is the general Notion a Man ſhould form to himſelf of Chaſtity.

CHAP. II.

Of the First Branch of Chaſtity, with reſpect to what is forbidden.

BUT to give a more diſtinct Character of Chaſtity, it contains two general Duties. The former of which reſpects the Government of our Lives as to things forbidden, the other as to things allowed us.

To begin with the former of theſe Duties, we muſt obſerve there are four Degrees of Chaſtity. The Firſt is an Abſtinence from the Crime ; the
Se-

Second is a Refraining from other Impure Actions; the Third is a Resistance of evil Desires; and the Fourth is an Exemption from, or Mastery over them.

I. The First Duty of Chastity is to renounce the Crimes of Uncleanness, such as Adultery and Fornication; as is plain from the Words of St. *Paul* I *Thess.* IV. 3, 4. recited in the foregoing Chapter. Every one easily perceives that this is the first degree of Chastity; this is so manifest, it needs only to be hinted. But however there are two Inferences proper to be mentioned in this place. First, if to abstain from the Crime be the first Degree of Chastity, then is it the lowest Step or Degree of it; and this alone that a Man is not plunged into the Crime, is neither the Effect of true Virtue, nor the Subject of any great Praise. Secondly, We must beware of accounting all those chast who are free from the Crimes of Uncleanness. It must be enquired upon what grounds they refrain from them; because if it be only for want of Ability, or because they dare not gratify their brutish Passion for fear of exposing themselves to some worldly Disadvantage, there is no Chastity in this, nor will they be reputed innocent before God. Those only are chast, who have abstained from the Crime out of a Principle of Virtue and Piety. And accordingly as this Principle is more or less powerful, so is Chastity more or less advanced.

They who shun the Crime out of an unfeigned Fear of displeasing God, but yet with Difficulty and Conflicts, have together with their vicious Inclinations some measure of Chastity; but those have carried their Virtue to a great height, who have such an Abhorrence of the Crime, as to find themselves under no Temptation to the commission of it. It was by this that *Joseph* deserved the Praise of a consummate Chastity, when being solicited

licited to the Crime, exposed to a most infinuating Temptation, and this in an Age, and in other Circumstances the most capable that might be of enticing one not firmly addicted to Virtue, he resisted this Temptation, he resisted it divers times, and at last rejected it with Detestation and Horror; saying, * *How can I do this great Wickedness, and sin against God?* * Gen. This Victory obtained over the Temptation presents 39. 9. us with an Instance of an accomplished Chastity, and which includes in it the other Degrees of this Virtue. But all that abstain from the Crime are not arrived at this measure of Purity; they do not all reject the Temptation with this firm, ready, and generous Resolution, which not only causes a Man to hesitate, but shews him to be smitten with Horror at the first appearance of the Crime. However they do refrain; and do it because witheld by a Principle of Religion and Conscience. This is the first Degree of Chastity.

II. But to proceed. This Duty of Chastity implies in it an Abstinence from all impure Actions, whether unchast in themselves, or only conducing to what may defile. I have noted in the former part of this Treatise some Actions that are prejudicial to Chastity, and have laid down some Rules whereby they may be distinguished. And it shall therefore suffice in this place only to observe, that it is the part of Chastity neither to do nor say any thing that is immodest, but to be very pure and very circumspect in both Actions and Words, that nothing that is dissolute or too wanton may escape us. Chastity governs the Hands and the whole Body, that none touch themselves, or others, or suffer themselves to be touched in too free and indecent a manner. Chastity governs the Eyes, and causes to withdraw them from such Obejcts or Writings as might seduce the Heart, that we never read nor look at what may tend to excite impure

N   Thoughts.

Thoughts. This Virtue is alſo a profeſt Enemy to Luxury and Immodeſty in Cloathing, and teaches a grave and inoffenſive Carriage, and baniſhes vain Diſcourſe, fooliſh Mirth, and exceſſive and ſcandalous Diverſions. Laſtly, this Virtue when once well ſettled in the Heart, makes a Man exact and cautious in all theſe Particulars, and to keep his Body and his Senſes under great Reſtraint.

III. The Third Degree of Chaſtity is a Reſiſtance of thoſe Thoughts and Motions of the Soul which tend to Impurity. Theſe kind of Thoughts ſeduce Perſons, when they raiſe ſuch Luſts in them as obtain their Deſire, and the full Conſent of their Will, or when they barely entertain them in their Minds, but ſo as to take pleaſure in them. Both which are contrary to Chaſtity. And the chaſt Man therefore is one who not only allows not himſelf to be tranſported by irregular Motions, nor only juſt forbears the Deſire of the Crime, but who does not pollute himſelf with the ſimple Thoughts of the Pleaſure, and with fooliſh and impure Imaginations, but rejects and repels theſe Thoughts. Then a Man has attained to this Virtue, when he has learned to be Maſter of his own Heart, and to keep his Thoughts and Deſires in ſubjection. When the Objects that preſent themſelves, or the Diſcourſe we hear, or the Imagination or Memory raiſe up ſenſual Thoughts or Ideas, a chaſt Perſon will not allow them to enter the Heart, or ſo much as to come near it. This is one of the great and principal Duties of Chaſtity, to reſiſt thoſe Motions of the Soul which tend to Luſt, ſo as that if a Man unhappily feel ſuch Motions in himſelf, he ſtudies to repreſs them, and at leaſt to prevent their becoming Voluntary.

IV. Laſtly, There is a Fourth Degree of Chaſtity, which is the higheſt of all, and that is to be

entirely,

entirely; or at least very near exempt from these
Thoughts and Desires I have been speaking of. It
has been observed upon this Occasion, that there
is a difference between Continence and Chastity. The former of these Vertues is said to consist in containing ourselves, and refraining when
we find ourselves solicited to Evil; that it is a
Resisting the sensual Motions that arise in the
Soul, and keeping the Passions in order, which
supposes a Person to be tempted, and that he is not
chast without some struggle and conflict. But as
to the other it is said that a Man has attained to
true Chastity, when he is free from evil Desires,
and the Rebellion of his Passions, without being
exposed to any conflict with them. It was S. *Je-*
rom's Saying, * that *He who is Continent is in the way*
of Vertue, but is not yet arrived at the top of it, in as
much as the Desires of the Flesh spring up in the Soul
of him that contains himself, and pollute his Soul,
though they do not prevail over, and draw him into the
Crime. But this Article has need of some farther
Illustration.

For it is questioned whether there is a possibility of being exempt from impure Thoughts and
Desires, and whether any have attained to that
pass as to take no Pleasure in Thoughts that tend
to Impurity, so as to have no Sense of any vicious Motion in their Soul with respect to this Sin.
For my own part I doubt not but this State may
be attained to, and that there are Persons to whom
Almighty God has vouchsafed this Favour; and
especially amongst those who from their Youth,

---

* *Hierm.* in *Gal.* cap. V, Continentia in viâ quidem virtutis est,
sed nec dum pervenit ad calcem; quia cupiditates adhuc in
ejus qui se continet cogitatione nascuntur, & mentis polluunt
principale, licet non superent, nec ad opus pertrahant cogi-
tationem.

toge-

together with a happy Constitution, and good Education, have had a solid Piety and a large share of Modesty and abhorrence of this Vice, and have always kept themselves at a distance from it. The greater Progress any one makes in Chastity, and the more rarely wanton Thoughts disturb him, the more they lose of their force; and there is no reason why it may not be believed that there are some who have them not; and that what is a Temptation to others, is to these no more than as a Spark that lights in the Water, or an Arrow shot against a Rock.

I will add something here concerning Sleep. A chast Person is so when he is asleep. Men are ordinarily such in the Night, and in their Dreams, as they are in the Day-time. I speak not of what is involuntary and purely natural. The Constitution of the Body, and the Imagination may produce unusual and strange Effects in Sleep and Dreams; but Chastity is not impaired by this, provided there be nothing of the Will in it, and that a Person do not give occasion for it, but all the time he is awake endeavours a great Purity. Moreover impure Dreams and Fancies, and disorderly Motions, are a sign that the Flesh is not yet brought into subjection. These are the Fruits either of a vicious Inclination to Sensuality, or of Intemperance in Eating or Drinking, or of a Memory and Imagination filled with sensual Ideas, and impure Objects. I have touched this Point concerning Sleep in very few Words; but there is a great deal included in them, that deserves larger and serious Reflexions.

CHAP.

CHAP. III.

Of the Second Branch of Chastity, with re-
spect to what is Lawful.

TEmperance prescribes Rules not only with
respect to things forbidden and sinful, but
likewise to things allowed and lawful; and if we
are obliged wholly to abstain from the one, so
are we not always to make use of the other. This
latter Duty is of very great Importance, and calls
for our particular Consideration.

For Men are more easily drawn to sin in things
allowed, than in those forbidden. In regard to
these latter, the knowledge of their being forbidden keeps many in awe; but in things allowed
the most part observe no Rule, but think themselves free to use their utmost Liberty; and so
destroy Vertue and Piety; it being impossible
in this Case not to pass from what is permitted to
what is forbidden. A thing may be allowed to a
certain degree, and in some Circumstances only;
but how few contain themselves within these
Bounds, and do not proceed farther than they
ought? It is slippery treading here, and there is
infinite Danger in being willing always to have
our fill of things allowed. By satisfying our Desires in these things the Passions get such Dominion over us, that we shall not be able to refuse
them any thing; and so by pleasing ourselves with
what is allowed, shall be carried on to what is
not. Besides Persons should stint themselves in
things allowed, lest by being wont constantly to
please themselves, they come to be enslaved to
their Passions. It is essential to Piety and Vertue

N 3

to

to mortify the Will and bring it into subjection.
But especially Care should be taken and great
Circumspection used in those things which are
pleasant and delightful, and so become strong
Temptations. Though a Man should never venture upon what is unlawful, too great an Affection for sensible things, and too ready a Compliance with the bent of our own Will, will not easily consist with true Piety; it will make the
Heart too fond of the World and its Enjoyments,
and will necessarily abate its Love of God, and
its Diligence in seeking after the heavenly Trea-
sures, and that submission, which all are to pay
to the Divine Will. Which shews it to be a Maxim in the Christian Ethicks, that things Lawful
are not to be abused. *All things are lawful for
me, but all things are not expedient,* 1 Cor. 10. 23.

To apply this to our present Subject, it is observable that Temperance lays down two Rules
in respect to lawful things; never to use them but
with Moderation; and sometimes wholly to refrain from them. When we speak of Chastity
there is but one thing permitted, and that is Marriage; and we must therefore take notice of two
Degrees of Chastity in this respect; 1st, A Care
not to abuse this State; 2dly, An entire Renunciation of it.

I. In the first place we must be sure not to abuse
it. Marriage is common to all the People in the
World; but it will by no means become Christians, who know it is a holy State instituted by God,
to enter into, and live in it after a sensual manner,
as the Pagans do, and those Nations who have never been blessed with the Light of the Gospel.
Here therefore are two Duties to be attended to,
to enter upon it purely, and to live purely in
it.

1. Mar-

1. Marriage being a holy Society, Christians are to enter into it holily and with Reverence, and to order their Conversation in it, not according to the Directions of the Flesh and Senses, but according to those of Reason and Religion. That general Rule of the Apostle, who orders † *all things* † Coloss. *to be done in the Name of the Lord Jesus,* is more espe- 3. 17. cially to be put in practice upon this occasion, as being one of the most important affairs of our whole Life. And it is not therefore without great reason that the usage of beginning Marriage with Acts of Religion has been established in the Church. As indeed it had also been among the Heathens. Christians should always perform this Office so as that they may be able to assure themselves our Lord Christ is present with them, and sanctifies them by his Blessing. But Piety has commonly little to do in Marriages; and though the Church's Blessing, and Prayer are used at them, these solemn Devotions are not attended to, nor looked upon otherwise than as a Formality. Marriage is often no better than the effect of sensuality; This Estate so holy in it self is with many people only as a Cover for their Shame. They marry to avoid Disgrace, and upon force, because of the ill consequents of their impure manner of Life. Such Marriages are rather a continued Impurity veiled under a creditable Name, than a chast and Christian Ordinance. Not to say any thing here of the strange Licentiousness and Dissoluteness that accompanies these Weddings, and the foolish, immodest, and scandalous Merriment which is usual upon these Occasions. Which things considered it is not to be wondered, that so many Matches succeed no better; that such as marry not out of a wise and reasonable Affection, or an Esteem founded upon Vertue, but upon some sudden Passion, or Necessity, or to save their Honour,

N 4

nour, do in a little time diſlike one another; that they agree very ill, that their Children are badly educated, and that they fall ſometimes into great Crimes.

2. The other Duty of Married Perſons is to live purely and free from Senſuality. The remains of Natural Light in the Heathens taught them that Marriage was to be chaſt and modeſt, and that every thing was not allowable in it. St. *Paul* ſhews what Notion we ſhould have of it, when he tells us ſuch as are coupled together by this ſacred Bond ſhou'd ſeparate themſelves ſometimes to betake themſelves to Faſting and Prayer. Theſe Rules which the Scripture lays down in regard to whatſoever concerns the Body, the World, and the Things of this Life, that † *all that is lawful may not be done at all times*, that * *Proviſion muſt not be made for the Fleſh to fulfil the Luſts thereof*, and that ‖ *they that uſe this World are not to abuſe it*; theſe Rules, I ſay, reſpect Marriage likewiſe, and make it very clear that Perſons ought to live chaſtly in it. We may ſin, and that very grievouſly too, againſt Purity, in that Eſtate though lawful. Our Religion requires us to mortify our Paſſions, and above all our ſenſual Deſires. And therefore we muſt manage ourſelves ſo as may correct our Senſuality, but may by no means promote it. We muſt labour to become ſpiritual, not voluptuous and animal. In every Eſtate we muſt try to obtain ſuch a diſpoſition of Mind, as that we may apply ourſelves to what is well pleaſing to Almighty God, and may make us everlaſtingly happy. And if Marriage has been ordain'd as a Remedy againſt Uncleanneſs, we muſt not turn our Remedy into Poiſon. Thoſe that do ſo are highly culpable, and have enſnared themſelves by marrying. This Article is of ſingular importance, and affords matter for many Reflections, but it is one of thoſe that I am conſtrained to ſhorten.

II. The

† 1 Cor.
6. 12.
* Rom.
13. 14.
‖ 1. Cor.
7. 31.

II. The second degree of Chastity with respect to what is lawful, is to renounce Marriage, and live in Celibacy.   St. *Paul* comparing the State of the Married with that of the Unmarried, gives the Preference to the latter, as to a sort of Life, which frees a Man from many Inconveniences, Distractions, and Troubles, which attend Marriage, especially in times of Persecution. He says, * that *that this Estate gives more Liberty for the Service of God ;* that ‖ *the unmarried Woman careth for the things of the Lord, that she may be holy both in Body and Spirit ;* that ‡ *it was good for the unmarried to abide even as himself ;* and that * *he who gives not his Virgin in Marriage does better than he who gives her.* But then he speaks this only upon supposition of living chastly in Celibacy, and being inviolably continent ; inasmuch where this is wanting, he declares ∴ *it is better to marry than to burn.*

† 1 Cor. 7. 33.
‖ v. 34.
‡ v. 8.
* v. 38.
∴ v. 9.

The Primitive Christians were likewise of the same Persuasion. They condemned not Marriage, no not in either Bishops or Presbyters ; but yet they commended a single Life, and many amongst them of both Sexes chose to continue in it ; though without ever obliging themselves by an irrevocable Vow to remain so all their Days. A forced Celibacy is a most dangerous State, and inevitably entangles Persons in a thousand Temptations, and terrible Miscarriages. I have already observed that the Law of Celibacy has been the Cause of infinite Irregularities ; and that abundance of People live in Uncleanness, because they will not enter into a married State. Not but that Celibacy is assuredly a very happy State, where Continence is carefully preserved.

Here those who are not married ought to learn their Duty ; nor can they be too studious of Purity. This is what the Younger Sort should above all things apply themselves to ; their great Duty,

the

the Mark they should always have their Eye upon, being to preserve Chastity. To this purpose they are to be vigilant and scrupulous as to whatever wounds this Virtue, and not to give themselves any Liberty in this respect, considering the great Hazard there is in offering Violence to Chastity, and that the Breaches made here are rarely to be cured. He that is not chast in his younger Years, is sure to feel either sooner or later dreadful Consequences of his Folly. There will continue sad Remainders of it, its Ideas will return, the Fire will kindle again in his full Age, perhaps when he is grown old ; and if he do not repent he is irrecoverably ruined ; if he does repent, how is he forced to condemn and reproach himself ? But on the other hand, Oh the Happiness of such an one who has kept himself pure from his Youth, and has never been acquainted with these corrupt Passions ! How many other Delights does he meet with, besides those of sensual Pleasure ! Virtue is always lovely wheresoever it appears ; but more especially in young Persons, it being highly commendable to follow its Precepts, in an Age wherein the heat of the Passions may be so easily blown up, and such a Beginning promising moreover happy Fruits to follow through the several Stages of their Life. But of all the Virtues none shines in young Persons more gloriously than Chastity and Continence. Nothing is more beautiful, nothing more worthy of Esteem, or more acceptable in the sight of God, than to be pure in Youth.

What I have said to those in Celibacy calls upon me to give some Direction to those in Widowhood. For the same Duties are incumbent upon them, and they ought to be so much the more careful to preserve themselves chast, because of their being more exposed to Temptations, and

in

in more Danger of sinking under them; because Purity is a harder Task to those that have been married, than if they had always continued single. This chiefly concerns Widows, who are not to abuse the Liberty which their Estate gives them, and the easiness of satisfying their Passions, which they had not whilst they were under the power of a Husband. No, their principal Care should be to live in great Purity, and more than usual Reservedness, they must not content themselves to abstain from the Crime, and whatsoever is impure or unchast, but they must live prudently, modestly, and retiredly, and not seek after vain Ornaments, Pleasures, Feasts, and the Company and Conversation of those of the other Sex. They must apply themselves to the Education of their Children, if they have any, and to do good Works. These are the Duties the holy Scripture enjoyns Christian Widows; as may be seen in the Character given of them by St. *Paul*, 1 Tim. v. 5, 10. *She that is a Widow indeed trusteth in God, and continueth in Supplications and Prayers night and day; she is well reported of for good Works, for having brought up Children, having lodged Strangers, having washed the Saints Feet, having relieved the Afflicted, and diligently followed every good Work.* See also what a Description he gives of Widows that have abused their Estate by living in Pleasure, *v. 13. They are idle, wandring about from House to House; they are Tatlers also and Busy-bodies, speaking things which they ought not.* He professes likewise *v. 6.* that *Widows who live in Pleasure, are dead while they live.* Than which nothing can be said more expresly to shew that Widows ought to live in Modesty, Circumspection, and great Purity.

SECTION

SECTION II.

Of the Motives to Chastity.

HAVING shewn the Nature of this Virtue of Chastity, I proceed now to the Motives which oblige us all to be chast. And the truth is, very powerful ones may be inferred from what has been hitherto discoursed. If we attend to what has been said of Uncleanness, and all the Reasons alledged for proving the Turpitude of this Vice; or to the Consequences of it, and the Condition to which People are brought by it; the other Sins into which it draws them, and the Misfortunes to which it exposes them; or to what is necessary in order to a Recovery out of it, and for making Amends for it, where it has been committed; or lastly to what has been said of Chastity, these are all so many powerful and pressing Motives to this Virtue. But it is not my Design to go over these Considerations again, but only to present the Reader with the chief Motives we have to Chastity.

C H A P.

CHAP. I.

The First Motive, The Nature of the Virtue.

I Take my first Argument for Chastity from the Nature of the Virtue it self ; wherein I find three things that ought strongly to incite to the Practice of it, the Necessity, the Beauty, and the Easiness of it.

I. Chastity is a Virtue absolutely necessary. I do not stand to prove here that it is a Duty which Almighty God has most expresly required ; because if we insist only upon the Nature of the Virtue itself, it must be owned to be of indispensable Necessity.

1. It is utterly impossible to practise the Christian Virtues without mortifying the Senses and the Inclinations of the Flesh ; a fondness for the Passions and Pleasures of Sense being inconsistent with Virtue. This is so undoubted a Truth, that there is no need to have recourse to the Testimony of the Gospel for the proof of it. The Light of Nature teaches it ; and each one's own Experience will convince him, that the progress any makes in the Practice of Virtue, bears a proportion to the Care he has taken to moderate his Passions. But this is also very evidently asserted in the Gospel. St. *Peter* admonishes, us that it † *is dangerous to follow the Lusts of the Flesh, and that they war against the Soul.* † 1 S. Pet. The holy Scripture represents the Flesh as the 2. 11. Cause of Sin, and the Spirit as the Principle of all Virtues. St. *Paul* declares these two to be plainly irreconcileable to each other ; that the Inclinations of the Flesh are opposite to those of the Spirit, and

that

that the motions of the Spirit are no less contrary to those of the Flesh. *The Flesh,* says the Apostle, *lusteth against the Spirit, and the Spirit against the Flesh, and these are contrary one to the other,* Gal. 5. 17. Which being the true state of the Case, one of them must necessarily yield to the other. Where the Flesh prevails those Christian Virtues which are the Fruits of the Spirit, such as *Love, Joy, Peace, Long-suffering, Gentleness, Goodness, Faith, Meekness, Temperance,* v. 22, 23. are made to give way. And where the Spirit governs those Sins which are the fruits of the Flesh such as *Adultery, Fornication, Uncleanness, Lasciviousness, Idolatry, Strifes,* and the rest of the Sins the Apostle reckons up, *v.* 19, 20, 21. can no longer domineer. Whence we see the great and principal Advice Religion gives us is to resist the Flesh and its Desires, to crucify it, and to bring the Body into subjection ; in a Word, to live after the Spirit, and not after the Flesh. And forasmuch as amongst all our fleshly Passions, there is none more violent than that which tempts to Impurity, nor that is attended with more dreadful Consequents, when it has got the mastery over the Heart, it follows from hence that this Passion is a grand Obstruction to Virtue, and by consequence, that one of our chief Duties is to keep it under. So that unless People can persuade themselves there is no necessity of being virtuous, or observing the Precepts of Religion, it must be granted that Chastity is absolutely necessary.

2. I add, this Virtue is so necessary; that there is no knowing how to love God, or to serve him without it. We are all bound to serve God, to pray to him, to give him Thanks, these being Duties all that have not renounc'd Religion readily agree to be of absolute Necessity. But bodily Pleasures are a Hindrance to the Performance of them ; they extinguish Devotion, the Love of God,

God, and the Fervor of Prayer. To serve God and pray to him as we ought, we must be sure to do it with Sincerity, Love, and Delight. But it is impossible to take delight in the spiritual Exercises of Devotion, whilst a Man is possessed with a Love of carnal Pleasures. The more devout any one is, the more nearly he is touched with the Love of God, and the more he has tasted of spiritual Pleasures, those ravishing Delights which are to be found in Communion with God, the more is he affected with a hope of the Heavenly Glory; and the more indifferent he is towards sensual Pleasures, the greater disgust he has of them. On the contrary, the more addicted one is to the Pleasures of Sense, the more does he seek after them; and the less relish he has for spiritual Pleasures, the less disposed he is for the Exercises of Devotion. For this I refer my self to my Readers own Consciences, and what they feel in themselves, whether Whenever they begin to love the World passionately and immoderately, the Love of God doth not thenceforward decline in them? And yet what an unpardonable Affront is it to the holy and glorious God, the God who would make us happy, and give himself to us, to prefer vain, brutish, and transient Pleasures before him?

3. It appears likewise that Chastity is of absolute Necessity, that we may attain to that Salvation and Happiness which Religion aims at. Such is the nature of the Heavenly Felicity, that without being chast, there is no possibility of seeking after it, relishing it, or possessing it. But I forbear to insist upon this at present, designing it for the Subject of one of the following Chapters.

I presume I have said enough to shew that the Nature of Chastity itself, and the Relation it has to our other Duties, call loudly upon us to cultivate this Virtue, as we esteem it necessary to be

Reli-

Religious, and to use our Endeavours for obtaining another sort of Happiness than what our carnal Passions can furnish us with, during the short Stage of this Life.

II. What I next take notice of in this Virtue is its Beauty. St. *Paul* teaches this when he says, that *by this we keep our Vessel in Sanctification and Honour,* 1. Thes. iv. 4. By which Words he represents Chastity as fair, honourable, comely, and which makes an essential part of the Holiness to which we are called; whilst Impurity is in the mean time infamous and the Turpitude of it apparent by the very Light of Reason. But Chastity is most worthy of a Man, and does honour to. and perfects his Nature, and disengages him from the Slavery of the Body and of Sense. A fondness for Pleasures is unbecoming one who has a spiritual and immortal Soul. Sensuality is a dull Passion, and debases the Soul, stupifies and renders it a Slave to the Body, and the more a Man is given to this Passion, the nearer he approaches to a Beast ; as on the other hand, the greater Stranger he is to it, the more does he advance his Nature, and the more Care he takes of his Soul. But now if Chastity be worthy of a Man, much more lovely and more honourable is it in a Christian, who is devoted to God, and called to Holiness and Glory, and whose principal Character should be to have spiritual Inclinations, † *to seek the things that are above, and not those which are upon the Earth,* and in short, to be a ‖ spiritual and not a carnal Man. Upon this account it is that Chastity has been called an Angelick Virtue, because by it we resemble the Angels, and the state to which the blessed shall be advanced in the World to come ; when, as our Saviour Christ says, * they shall be like those pure and glorious Spirits the Inhabitants of Heaven.

† Col. 3. 1, 2.
‖ Rom. 8. 6.
* St. Lu. 20. 35, 36.

III. In

III. In the laſt place I mentioned the Eaſi-
neſs that is to be met with in the Practice of
Chaſtity. Virtue always brings its own Reward
with it, by reaſon of the Compoſure of Mind
and the Peace of Conſcience with which it is accompanied. This is the certain Effect of it, that
by purifying the Soul it renders it alſo quiet and
eaſy. St. *Peter* has declared of *fleſhly Luſts* that they
* *war againſt the Soul.* And it is obvious to obſerve   * St. Pet.
that Impurity raiſes in it Fear, Trouble, and Re-   2. 11.
morſe ; but Chaſtity fills it with a ſettled Tranquillity and Peace. By denying himſelf the Entertainments which the Fleſh is wont to promiſe, a Man
procures to himſelf infinite Joys ; and by how
much the ſtronger the Aſſaults of his Paſſion are,
ſo much the more Pleaſure does he find in Reſiſting them. An inward Satisfaction follows cloſe
upon a Victory over Temptations, a Man being
always well pleaſed to come off Conqueror ; but
it muſt be confeſſed that he taſts moſt of this Peace
and Satisfaction in reſiſting thoſe Temptations
which invite by Pleaſure. The more the Sacrifice coſts, the more acceptable it is concluded to
be with God. If herein a Man offer Violence to
himſelf, he finds himſelf abundantly recompenced,
and enjoys a Satisfaction which infinitely ſurpaſſes
whatever could be had in following a ſhameful Inclination. And here again I refer my ſelf to the
Experience every one may have had, and I beg
of thoſe who ſhall read this to declare, whether
when they have got the Maſtery over a Temptation, have turned away their Eyes from an alluring
Object, and refuſed in any reſpect to gratify their
Senſes, they have not preſently perceived an inward Peace and ſecret Satisfaction filling them
with Conſolation and Joy. With what ſort of
Comfort is the Soul then filled when it has reduced the Body to that condition, that its Tempta-

O   tions

tions have loft their force, and there is no more fear of the Revolt of Senfe, and the Affaults of this dangerous Paffion ! Then it enjoys a moft delightful Calm, is delivered from a thoufand Dangers, and freely performs the Functions of the fpiritual Life.   And moreover in this ftate of Peace and Purity, the God of Purity and of Peace communicates himfelf, in a moft intimate and moft comfortable manner.

C H A P. II.

The Second Motive, The Divine Will.

THE Second Motive to this Virtue is the Will and Command of Almighty God. There is no room for doubting whether God would have all be chaft. We have already feen that he has declared his Mind moft fully in his holy Word, and that there is no particular Sin oftener forbidden in the New Teftament than Uncleanneſs. I fhall mention in this place only thoſe Words of St. *Paul,* 1 Theſ. iv. 3, 4. *This is the Will of God, even your Sanctification, that ye ſhould obſtain from Fornication, that every one of you ſhould know how to poſſeſs his Veſſel in Sanctification and Honour.* As he had alfo ſaid before, *v.* 2. *Ye know what Commandments we gave you by the Lord Jeſus.* Which Words taken together intimate Chaftity to be one of the principal Commands of the Gofpel, and an indifpenfable Duty which God requires to be obferved by all. Whereto may be added alfo the Promiſes made to thoſe who are chaft, the Punifhments denounced againft the Impure, and the feveral Judgments which have been executed upon them

from

from time to time.   A fufficient Proof of its
being the Will of God that we live in Chaftity.

And of what force ought this fingle Motive to
be, That it is the Will of God ? We are undoubtedly all nearly concerned to fubmit to whatfoever
he enjoins.   He has a fovereign Authority over us,
and we cannot without great Offence and Injuftice refufe to obey him.   How prevalent foever
our own Inclination be towards any thing, whenever it appears that God has forbidden it, a Fear
of difpleafing him muft over-rule all other Confiderations ; and we muft be fure to obey him even
in the moft difficult cafes ; it being unqueftionable
that he has a Right to demand of us the Sacrifice
of whatfoever we love beft, and even of our own
Lives.   How much more fhould we offer up to
the Refpect and Love due to Him, thofe fhameful Paffions which are not only difpleafing to his
Divine Majefty, but do ourfelves an infinite Mifchief.

· That we may the better apprehend how powerful an Argument this is, let it be confidered, that
it is not only out of Duty and Reverence to Almighty God ; we ftand obliged to pay an entire Submiffion to his moft holy Will, but it is
what our own Intereft alfo claims of us.   This Will
of God is *Good*, † as St. *Paul* fpeaks, it is for our
Profit and Advantage, and enjoyns us nothing
but what is for our own Benefit.   Can any one
imagine that God would command fuch things as
feem grievous to us, that he would forbid what
we are apt to take delight in, and would impofe
fuch Duties as offer Violence to the Flefh, without juft reafon for it, and meerly that he may
fhew his Authority in tormenting us ? This would
be an abominable Mifreprefentation of a God
who is all Love and Goodnefs.   And in truth he
does it only becaufe our Welfare requires that we

† Rom. 12. 2.

O 2   be

be uſed in this manner. He acts only as a tender and wiſe Father, who witholds from his Children ſuch things as would be hurtful to them, and who never croſſes them, but when it may conduce to make them wiſe and virtuous. We cannot ſatisfy our Paſſions, and take up with Creature-Enjoyments, without great Wrong and Ruine to ourſelves. This were the way to involve ourſelves in manifold Evils here in this Life, to ſet Almighty God at enmity with us, to leave us no hope of any greater Happineſs than what the things of this World afford, and ſo wholly to ſenſualize our Souls as to put them out of a capacity of ſeeking after the everlaſting Treaſures of the other Life. And we have therefore abundant cauſe to adore the infinite goodneſs of our gracious God, who has condeſcended to direct us how we may effectually prevent our own Deſtruction. Wherefore we ſhould readily and chearfully ſubmit ourſelves to this Will of our Lord, ſo juſt in itſelf, and ſo highly for our Advantage, ſhould ſilence all the Murmurings of the Fleſh, and take delight in fulfilling thoſe holy Laws whoſe great deſign is to conduct us to God, to imprint his Image upon us, and render us like him, and to prepare us by this means for the Enjoyment of the moſt conſummate Felicity.

C H A P. III.

The Third Motive, The Preſence of God.

THe Preſence of God is likewiſe a great Motive to Chaſtity; which as it is of ſingular efficacy for withdrawing from all ſort of Wickedneſs, ſo has it a particular Influence whereby to render us pure. And it is certain People would not give
them-

themselves, as they do, to Sensuality, if they would seriously remind themselves, that they are continually in the sight of the Most High.

This is a Sin of which Mankind are usually ashamed, and this Shame has such Power with them, that there are few who can bring themselves to such a degree of Brutishness, as to conquer it, and lay it wholly aside. The Unclean study to hide themselves from the Presence of Men. And even the Suspicion or Fear of being seen will put a stop to their Intrigues, and cool their hottest Passion. There are many in the World who if they were convinced that all the Wickedness their impure Passions had put them upon were known, and that the shameful Excesses of their Thoughts and Desires were any way discovered, would wish to buy it off, if it were possible, with all they are worth; nor would they know how to live in Society, nor would have the Confidence to appear abroad, but would be covered with Confusion, and would choose rather to betake themselves to some foreign Country, where their Extravagances were never heard of. How then does it come to pass that the Fear of God does not deter Men from this Sin? How dare they commit it in the sight of a most holy and most just God, who † *is not far from every one of us,* but beholds every thing we do, or think, and to whom Uncleanness is infinitely more odious than it is to Men? Or how can they be easy when they are conscious to themselves of having abandoned themselves to infamous Actions or Desires? Must not every one acknowledge it a most outrageous Provocation of Almighty God, to have less regard for his Divine Presence, than for that of a Man, or even of a Child? They are ashamed and reserved before Men; and is it not intolerable that when Men are not in the way, and they are

† Act. 17. 27.

O 3   only

only in the Presence of the Almighty, this Shame should immediately vanish? To this purpose speaks the Son of *Syrach,* Ecclus. xxiii. 18, 19. *A Man that breaketh Wedlock,* the Lustful and Adulterer, *saith thus in his heart, Who seeth me? I am compassed about with Darkness, the Walls cover me, and Nobody seeth me; what need I to fear? Such an one only feareth the Eyes of Men, and knoweth not that the Eyes of the Lord are ten thousand times brighter than the Sun, beholding all the ways of Men, and considering the most secret parts.*

It is of mighty use therefore to get this Thought well impressed upon our Minds, That God is everywhere, and takes notice of whatever we do. And Oh that we would often revolve it in our Minds, and would endeavour that it may in some sort be always present with us! Let us remember we are continually in the Presence of God, and moreover that it is a most Holy and most Just God in whose Presence we are; that being Holiness itself, he can bear no Impurity, and being perfectly Just and the Judge of the World, we have all the reason that can be to be afraid, whensoever we offend his pure and holy Eyes by any Pollution. It was his own express Command to the *Jews,* Deut. xxiii. 14. *The Lord thy God walketh in the midst of thy Camp; therefore shall thy Camp be holy, that he see no unclean thing in thee, and turn away from thee.* And if God exacted even an outward Purity in the *Israelites* Camp, upon this Consideration, That he *was in the midst of them;* can it be conceived that he will suffer the Filth of Vice in Christians, in the midst of whom he dwells in a more particular manner, than ever he did among the *Jews?* We should be sure therefore to render this Meditation familiar to us; and especially when we are attacked by a Temptation, should recollect that God's Eye is upon us; that he is near us, and observes and sees

what

what we are doing at this very inftant, and whether we have the Courage to refift the attraction
of a brutifh Luft for his fake; or whether we prefer
an infamous Paffion before the Reverence we owe
to Him.   This Reflexion well attended to would
conftrain us to cry out with *Jofeph, How can I do
this great Wickednefs, and fin againft God?*

This Motive will not only be of ufe for withdrawing from the Crime, but will oblige us to
keep our Defires and the Motions of our Heart
in good order.   For if God be prefent to our
Thoughts, if he be within us, and fearches and
examines us, and * *all things are naked and open to his* * Heb. 4.
Eyes; it neceffarily follows that whenever we give 13.
up our Hearts to Senfuality, God is witnefs of all
the Vanity, Lafcivioufnefs, and Immodefty that
is in our Thoughts and Imagination.   And how
unagreeable an Object to the Eyes of God muft
a Heart be, where Luft reigns, and the Flames of
a thoufand corrupt Defires are perpetually blowing
up? Did the impure Perfon weigh well with himfelf, that from the time this abominable Paffion
began firft to take poffeffion of him, God has be-
held all that he has done or thought, and that he
ftill is, and always will be with him, he would
find it a very difficult matter not to be affrighted,
And if Perfons would often make thefe Reflexions,
they would affuredly become much purer and
chafter than they are.

Q 4   CHAP.

CHAP. IV.

The Fourth Motive, The Life and Sufferings of our Blessed Saviour.

IT has been hitherto made sufficiently apparent that the Doctrine of our Lord *Christ Jesus* calls for Chastity, and that the Consideration hereof is a very powerful Engagement to apply ourselves to this Virtue. But it is not by his Doctrine alone that the Son of God was willing to dispose us to Chastity, but farther also by his Life and by his Sufferings. He came into the World to raise Mankind to a supernatural State of Happiness, and to wean them from the Earth. To this end he lived here below in an entire Freedom from the things of the World; and this was one reason of his Sufferings and his profound Humiliation.

I. To begin with our Saviour's Life, I need not say that it was completely pure, and that none could discover any the least or lightest Defilement in it. He ate, he drank, he was subject to our innocent Infirmities, he made use of indifferent things, but yet he lived in a total unacquaintedness with carnal Pleasures; hereby teaching plainly that all who profess themselves his Disciples and Followers are to be extremely moderate in this respect. We must propose our Lord to ourselves as a Pattern for our Imitation, to tread in his Steps being the great Duty of a Christian; and must endeavour to resemble him as far as possibly we can, in all his Virtues, and more particularly in his Purity and Temperance, no less than in his Charity and his Zeal. † *He that saith he abideth in him, ought himself also so to walk even as he walked.* And

† St. Jo. 2. 6.

can

can it be thought after this, that Chriftians are at liberty to lead a life wholly Carnal and Senfual? Or if they do, what manner of agreement is there betwixt them and their Head?

I am very fenfible that in the Condition wherein we are in this World, we can never hope to be as pure as our Lord and Saviour was. Nor does he require it of us. Only he would have us imitate him as far as we are capable, and to this end to abftain from whatfoever he has forbidden us. Moreover I muft note here, that the Difference which is betwixt our Lord Chrift and us, is fo far from Authorizing any to let loofe the Reins to their Paffions, that on the contrary it is even this Difference that obliges us all to be upon our guard. Our Lord being exempt from all Corruption had no need of being forewarned to arm himfelf againft Temptations, whereas we are in great danger of fuffering ourfelves to be led afide by them, and by confequence this fame Thought that we are liable to the Paffions of the Flefh, fhould in a peculiar manner make us the more vigilant and circumfpect, and fhould wean us the more effectually from all Senfuality.

II. The Sufferings of our Saviour teach us the fame Leffon. The Crofs of our Lord which makes up all the knowledg of a Chriftian, and ought to be the continual Object of our Meditation, is a moft powerful Motive to Chaftity. This Crofs was the loweft degree of our Saviours Humiliation, and that which compleated his renunciation of the World. He not only tafted no carnal Pleafure, but he came to fuffer whatever is moft dolorous; and for this caufe he ended his Life upon the Crofs. And why wou'd he do this, if not in the firft place to make Expiation for the Sins of Mankind, and next to teach them by his own Example, what he had before delivered and enjoined

as

St. Mat. 16. 24. as the Sum of his Doctrine; that * *they muft deny themfelves and take up their Crofs?* This is the weighty Doctrine which Chrift crucified prefles upon all that profefs to believe in him. The Crofs of our Redeemer *crucifies the Flefh, mortifies the Lufts, and caufes the Chriftian to be crucified and dead to the World;* as St. *Paul* teaches in his Epiftle to the *Galatians.* And after this will it become us to fearch after the Pleafures and Delights of the World? Whofoever well underftands the great Myftery of the Crofs of Chrift, cannot but know that he ought to bear his own, and to lead a mortified Life, and that without this he can never attain to eternal Glory. Our Lord *Jefus* went thither by the way of Sufferings; and let not us think to accompany him there by that of Delights. A Man cannot have the heart to give himfelf up to Pleafures, when he reprefents to himfelf Chrift in the midft of his Sufferings.

† *Rom. 6. 4, 6.* A Chriftian † *that has been crucified and buried with Jefus Chrift in his Death by Baptifm, walketh* thenceforward *in newnefs of Life,* he *knows that the old man is crucified with him, that the Body of Sin might be deftroyed, that henceforth we fhould not ferve Sin.* He is very far from plunging himfelf in grofs and fenfual Pleafures, and giving up his Soul to the foolifh and corrupt Delights of the Flefhly-minded. His Body is brought into Subjection, his Soul is united to his Saviour,

‖ *Gal. 2. 20.* and he can fay with St. *Paul,* ‖ *I am crucified with Chrift, neverthelefs I live; yet not I, but Chrift liveth in me: and the Life which I now live in the Flefh, I live by the Faith of the Son of God, who loved me, and gave himfelf for me.* And thus it appears how the Life and Sufferings of our Lord *Jefus Chrift* are a Motive to Chaftity.

CHAP.

CHAP. V,

The Fifth Motive, The Glorious State we are in.

CHRISTIANS have another Motive to Chastity, arising from the Glory of their own Condition, and the happy State to which God has advanced them.   They are Men formed after the Image of God, and resemble him in the excellency of their Nature, and the Difference that is between them and Beasts.   So that their own Qualifications as Men engage them to govern themselves by the Principles of Reason and Virtue. But the Character of Christians may well put them upon labouring to bear this Image in a perfecter manner.   They are called † to be *holy as God is holy*, and * *pure as He is pure*, and by consequence to abstain from all Pollution.   St. *Paul* teaches this most manifestly, *Ephef.* iv. 20, &c. He makes the Image of God to consist chiefly in being free from Impurity.   For having given an account of the Abominations of the Pagans, see how he applyes himself to his Christian Readers. *Ye have not so learned Christ ; If so be that ye have heard him, and have been taught by him, as the truth is in Jesus : That ye put off concerning the former conversation the Old-man, which is corrupt according to the deceitful lusts ; and that ye put on the New-man.*   And again he delivers almost the very same Doctrine, *Col.* iii. 9, 10.   In both which places the Apostle opposes the Image of God to the Impurities of the Heathens, evidently supposing that this Image is defaced in a Christian who is not pure.

† 1 S. Pet.
I. 16.
* 1 S. Jo.
3. 3.

Thus

Thus it appears that the Character we bear as Christians in a particular manner obliges us to live in Chastity ; this being the great Motive the Apostles insisted upon for banishing all the Pollutions of the Flesh from amongst the Disciples of our Lord ; || that *they should not walk as other Gentiles* ‖ Eph. 4. 17, 18, 19. *did, who having the Understanding darkened, had given themselves over to Lasciviousness, to work all Uncleanness ;* * *should not live in the Lust of Concupiscence, as the Gentiles which know not God ;* but † *the time past of their Life should suffice to have wrought the Will of the Gentiles, when they walked in Lasciviousness, and all sorts of Lusts, Debauchery, and Excess.* Whence we see that as Impurity was next to Idolatry, the most prevailing and most abominable Sin of the Heathens, so on the other hand Chastity is one of the chief and principal Virtues of a Christian.

* 1 Thess.
4. 5.
† St. Pet.
4. 3.

And it will highly become us therefore to be seriously and frequently reflecting upon it. God has granted us to be born in his Church, he has honoured us with a holy Calling, such as aims at preserving us from the Defilements of the World. ‡ *Our Bodies and our Souls are his,* says St. *Paul* expresly, to dissuade from Impurity, and to instruct us that it would be a horrible Prophanation and Sacrilege to abandon ourselves to our shameful Passions of the Flesh. We are invited by our Religion to ∴ *present our Bodies and Spirits a living Sacrifice to God, and glorify him with both these parts of us.* But to offer to God a Body and Soul polluted and infected, would be to tender him an Abomination, much as if the *Jews* should have taken upon them to sacrifice a Dog or a Swine. The Scripture compares such as are enslaved to their carnal Lusts, to the nastiest and filthiest of Beasts. *For if after they have escaped the Pollutions of the World,* says St. *Peter,* 2 Ep. ii. 20, 21, 22. *through the Knowledge of our*

‡ 1 Cor.
6. 20.

∴ Rom
12, 1. &
1 Cor. 6.
20.

Lord

*Lord and Saviour Jesus Christ, they are again entangled
and overcome, the latter end is worse with them then the
beginning.* *For it had been better for them never to
have known the way of Righteousness, then after they
have known it, to turn from the holy Commandment delivered to them.* *But it is happened to them according
to the true Proverb, The Dog is turned to his own vomit
again ; and the Sow that was washed to her wallowing
in the Mire.* Which Comparison lets us see that
the Sensualists dishonour their Christianity, and
cast themselves down from the most glorious Condition Mankind is capable of attaining to, into a
most contemptible State.

Many other excellent Observations might be
made from the several Methods the Sacred Writers
take for describing the glorious State of Christians.
For instance we are told, that ||*they have Commu-* || 1 St. Jo.
nion with God and with his Son Jesus Christ, and 1, & 2.
that they are in Jesus Christ, and Jesus Christ is in them.
Can a stricter or more honourable Union be imagined, than this ? Or can any thing be conceived
that requires greater Purity ? So says St. *John* † *If* † *ibid.*
*we walk in the Light we have Fellowship with God,
and with his Son Jesus Christ, but he who walks in
Darkness lyes if he says that he is within this Communion.* But now who walks more in Darkness than
the Impure, who indulge themselves in those very
Sins, which the Scripture calls * *the Works of Dark-* * Rom.
ness ? St. *Paul* tells us likewise that Christians have 13. 12.
the Honour and Glory of being Members of *Je-
sus Christ,* and the Temples of the *Holy Ghost ;*
which we have already seen are infinitely glorious
Names, as importing a most intimate Communion
with our Lord ; but that without Chastity these
Relations cannot be preserv'd ; but Impurity will
break the Links whereby we are fastened to our
Saviour ; it defiles and dishonours our Body ; is
drives

drives away the Spirit of God ; and by this Sin we lose all the Privileges of our Christianity.

Those August Titles, and so many others which the Scriptures ascribe to us, as of Saints, the Elect, the Children of God, the Redeemed of the Lord, New Men, &c. will by no means allow us to wallow in beastly Pleasures, and bring ourselves into bondage to infamous Passions ; but should on the contrary inspire us with Desires and Aims, worthy of the Grace which God has bestowed upon us, and the Glory whereof he would have us Partakers. This St. *Paul* affirms in the sixth and seventh Chapters of his second Epistle to the *Corinthians.* He speaks there of the glorious State whereto we are called, and the Advantages of the divine Covenant. He says *we are the Temple of the living God, that God dwells in the midst of us, that he will be our God and our Father, and will own us for his People and Children ;* and then concludes, that *we ought to separate ourselves from among the Wicked, and not to touch any unclean thing, but to cleanse ourselves from all Pollution both of Body and Spirit.* These are without doubt very charming and powerful Engagements to Chastity, and to look well to ourselves, and reverence the Characters of our divine Vocation, which are imprinted upon our Bodies, and upon our Souls.

These are not only Motives in point of Decency, but of Justice, and which lay upon us an indispensable Obligation to live chastly. Because God in raising us to so honourable a Condition, furnishes us with most effectual Means of guarding ourselves against impure Passions. He makes use of his Gospel ; he sets before our Eyes the strongest Arguments ; he fortifies us by his Spirit ; he † *gives us according to his Divine Power, all things that pertain to the Life of the Soul, and to Godliness.* And let it be particularly remembred that the Use of

† 2 S. Pet. 1. 3.

the

the Sacraments tends to keep us off from Impurity, and that a Man cannot reflect upon thefe Sacred Ordinances, which it has pleafed our Lord to eftablifh in his Church, but he will immediately perceive what an Obligation they lay upon us to be pure. The Ufe of them fhould fanctify our Bodies, inafmuch as thefe fame Bodies, our Hands our Mouths are the Veffels which receive thefe holy Signs ; and who will fay thefe Veffels ought not to be kept pure ? The Sacraments are of the number of holy things, which are not at all for Dogs and Swine. By Baptifm we have been confecrated to our Lord, God has fet his Seal upon us, and we have made a folemn Vow before him, to renounce the World, and the Flefh with its Defires. And in Communicating in the holy Eucharift, we repeat this Vow, and engage ourfelves anew to refrain from Sin. So that Chriftians who live not chaftly, defpife the Glory of their own Eftate, tread under foot their fingular Advantages, violate their Engagements, and leave themfelves entirely inexcufable.

I fhall beg leave farther to add one Reflection upon the difference of the Times we live in from thofe of former Ages. Men have been known to be chaft when they had not fuch Advantages for it as we enjoy. St. *Chryfoftom* * preffes this Confideration ; when fpeaking of the Chaftity of *Jofeph*, and that of *Job*, he proclaims it admirable, confidering the Time in which they lived. He remarks that they lived before our Saviour's Incarnation, and had never heard the Voice of St. *Paul* faying, *Know ye not that your Bodies are the Members of Jefus Chrift ?* neverthelefs they believed that fuch as make a Profeffion of ferving God ought to have the Command over their own Defires, and to pre-

* Serm. de Contin.

serve

serve themfelves in Continence. He profeffes it a wonderful thing, to have feen fuch Examples of Chaftity, at a time when they had not fuch ftrong Motives to this Virtue. And upon the whole, he concludes, That Chriftians are under a much greater Obligation to live in the Fear of God, and in Chaftity, whereby to render themfelves worthy of the Honour they have of being Members of *Jefus Chrift :* And that it is not to be expreffed, what an Indignity and Affront it is to the Mercy of God, to abandon themfelves to Senfuality, after fo fignal an Honour done them. Laftly, This pious Father adds, That whenfoever Evil Defires arife in the Mind, our Courfe muft be to recall thefe Reflections, as being the proper Means of delivering from impure Temptations.

C H A P. VI.

The Sixth Motive, Death.

IF we find great Invitation to Chaftity, from the State wherein we are in this World ; our Future State prefents us with other not lefs cogent Arguments. And upon this Account it is that I now defign to touch upon the Eftates through which we are to pafs after this Life.

And the Firft thing that here prefents itfelf to our Thoughts, is Death.

It has been a long time faid, That the Meditation of Death, is moft ufeful for repreffing our Paffions. But it has a particular Efficacy, in relation to the Duty I am treating of. Death being a Deftruction of the Body, the Confideration of our Mortality fhould over-rule us in our Searches

after

after Bodily Pleasures, and should breed in us a disgust of them. If Persons were to live in this World for many Ages, they would seem more excusable in a passionate pursuit after the Pleasures of Sense, because so they might flatter themselves with the hopes of enjoying them for a long time; and yet the thought, that they must one day lose them, would be ready to trouble them in the height of all their Mirth. But when we call to mind, that we are to make but a short Stay in this World; that our Life is passing on, and whatsoever is the Object of our Passions passes together with it; that this Body of which we are so over-fond, will speedily be laid in the Grave, and will become an Object of Horrour, and a heap of Stench and Putrifaction; these mortifying Thoughts must doubtless tend to allay the Heat of our Lusts. And accordingly St. *Peter* tells us, * *our being in quality of Strangers and Pilgrims, obliges us to abstain from fleshly Lusts.* Whosoever then has these Thoughts duly imprinted upon his Mind, that weighs with himself how soon it may fall out that he shall be no longer in this World, and, for ought he knows to the contrary, Death may seize him in the midst of his Pleasures, will find it necessary to abate of his Earnestness in seeking them, and will be far less influenced by their Allurements.

* 1 S. Pet. 2. 11.

But withal, it is farther to be remembred, That the Death of a Sensualist must needs be very miserable; and the Separation whereby he is snatched from his Pleasures, cannot but be exceeding sad. For the more any one has lov'd his Pleasures, the greater Grief will it be to him to part with them; and the more he has sought after the Delights and Diversions of this Life, the more bitter will Death be to him. None is ever more afraid of Dying, or betrays more

P
of

of Cowardise and Pusillanimity at the approach of his Latter End, than the Effeminate and Voluptuous. And the Condition of one who is in fear of Death, and dreads the thoughts of being taken hence, is so disconsolate, that no wise Man would venture to end his Days in this manner. Especially seeing, on the other hand, it is such a Happiness, to be able to leave the World without Regret, and to look Death undauntedly in the face, that one would think every one should earnestly labour after so desirable an End; to which yet nothing conduces more, than to accustom one's self, in time, to refrain from what he desires, and to fortifie his Soul and his Spirit, by a contempt of Sensual Pleasures.

To improve this Argument a little farther, it will be requisite briefly to consider the State whereto Men are reduced by Death, whether in relation to the Body, or to the Soul. The Body is laid in the Earth, a lifeless, senseless Carcass, incapable of any sort of Pleasure, and never to taste of it more. The Soul, indeed, does not perish with the Body, but subsists after Death, lives, and retains its power of Thought and Reflection. Thus much the Heathens confess'd, and every one may easily perceive, that will but attend to it; but Revelation puts it beyond all doubt. Now, in what Condition must a Soul be, which knows no other Pleasures but those of Sense, and which, during its continuance in the Body, was become wholly Sensual: In what Condition must such a Soul be, when it finds itself transported into a New World, where it can discover nothing of what it is so much in love with?

It is no sooner parted from the Body, but it immediately begins to bewail its own unhappiness, that it is lost, and undone, and is for ever separated from God, and its soveraign Good.
What

What is paft, ferves only to raife in it an afflicting
Regret and Remorfe ; and Futurity gives it no
Expectation of any thing but what is highly Tormenting. It has no hope now of any manner of
Comfort ; can no longer enjoy any of thofe Pleafures it had formerly been acquainted with, and is
fadly unqualify'd to tafte of thofe which alone
could render it happy in the State whereinto it is
now tranflated. Thus wretched and miferable is
the poor Soul, deprived of all Comfort, and over-
whelmed with Sorrow, upon a melancholick
Profpect of its approaching Judgment. This is
the woful Condition of the Sinner. But, oh, the
unfpeakable Happinefs of a pure Soul ! What
Confolation does it enjoy in the other Life ! How
does it rejoyce, to think that it had taken care, in
time, to difengage it felf of all fenfual Pleafures,
and accuftomed itfelf to feek after that Felicity
which is only to be found in God ! Such a Soul
can readily leave its Body, whenever it is called
for, and will be fure to find itfelf much nearer to
its God than ever it had been before, and will be
all filled with Joy, and a fweet and delightful Expectation of a Refurrection, and Eternal Glory.

C H A P. VII.

The Seventh Motive, The Refurrection.

WE have now feen, that a Confideration of
Death, and the Deftruction of the Body,
pleads hard with us to keep our felves pure. But
it is a much more powerful Confideration, to
think that this Body muft be at length reftored by
a Refurrection. Our Bodies do not wholly

perish, and for ever ; but God will reanimate and enliven them. *Jesus-Christ* will come to rescue these Parts of us, for which he has shed his own Blood, from the Power of the Grave ; and to raise up these Temples, which he had consecrated to himself, but which had been destroyed by Death. But then it is to be noted, that if our Bodies must rise, it will not be that they may serve to the same Uses they had formerly, but to very different Purposes. * *They shall be raised, not to be then sensual, or natural Bodies, but to be spiritual Bodies ;* † *made like to our Blessed Saviour's Glorious Body ;* and they shall inhabit the other World, where will be nothing carnal, sensual or earthly.

This is a very glorious Hope, but which at the same time tends naturally to our Sanctification. This Glory whereto our Bodies are appointed, gives us to understand, that they were not made only for this short, transitory Life, but that our Gracious God has design'd them for a more Perfect and Eternal State. Wherefore we must by no means perswade ourselves, that they are to serve only for Pleasures, and that the Gratification of our sensual Desires is the End they were made for. There is a far more noble and more excellent Use to be made of them ; in order whereto, we must look upon ourselves as concerned to have such a Regard for them, that we may, as much as in us lies, even before Death seizes us, approach to that blessed State whereat we hope one day to arrive. Our Regeneration should beget in us a Change like that which our Resurrection will effect, that is to say, it should render us Spiritual Men, should take away, as much as may be, what is dull, earthy, and imperfect in us, and set us free from the Slavery of Lusts. Our Bodies are at present Members of the *Lord Jesus Christ,* and the Temples of the *Holy Ghost* ; and this obliges us to treat them

*Cor. 15. 44.

† Phil. 3. 21.

them with Respect, and to preserve them in Purity.   Which we shall find ourselves the more strongly obliged to do, if we consider that these Bodies are to be the Members and Temples of our Lord, in a far more perfect and glorious manner, at the Day of the Resurrection.   How unspotted then ought the Purity of that Body to be, which is ordained to Immortality and Glory, above in Heaven?

It is upon this Consideration, that St. *Paul* dissuades Christians from Impurity, 1 *Cor.* vi, 13, 14. *The Body* (says the Apostle) *is not for Fornication, but for the Lord ; and as God has raised up Jesus Christ, he will also raise us up by his own Power.*   In the 3d Chapter of his Epistle to the *Philippians,* ver. 20, 21. he declares, That *the true Christians, who expect the Lord Jesus Christ from Heaven, to come and change their vile Body, that it may be fashioned like his glorious Body, demean themselves as Citizens of Heaven, and have quite different thoughts from those of carnal Men, who have their Belly for their God, and who mind earthly things.* He again urges the same Consideration, *Rom.* viii. 5, &c. assuring us, That *if we live the Life of Christ, and take care to mortifie our Lusts, our Bodies, which are subject to Death because of Sin, shall be raised by the power of the same Spirit of Christ, by which we had overcome our fleshy Desires in this World ; and that they who shall have thus mortified the Works of the Body, and their Passions, shall live thenceforward a glorious and immortal Life : but they that had lived after the Flesh, shall have Misery and Eternal Death for their portion.*   Whence the Apostle draws this Consequence ; That *we are under an indispensable Obligation not to live after the Flesh, and not to employ the Members of our Body to Uncleanness and to Sin, but to consecrate them to Holiness and Righteousness.*

How

How dreadful then will be the Refurrection of thofe, who inftead of ordering their Converfation aright, according to the Laws and the Spirit of Chrift, fhall have chofen to plunge themfelves in Uncleannefs? They fhall indeed arife, but, as the Prophet *Daniel* fpeaks, *Dan.* xii. 2. *to Shame and everlafting Contempt.* This Shame will be the Inheritance of thofe who fhall have made their Bodies Veffels to Difhonour, Inftruments of a brutifh Senfuality, and Receptacles of Filth and Impurity. The Voluptuous are Slaves to their Bodies, and do all for their fakes, and think to procure them the greateft Good, and moft delightful Satisfaction. But in reality, they difhonour and deftroy them, they expofe them to Eternal Mifery and Reproach, and, in fhort, prepare them for Hell, And fo they become Murderers of their Bodies, afwell as their Souls. Whereas thofe who, in obedience to the Precepts of our Lord *Jefus Chrift,* keep the Body pure, treating it with fome rigour, and bringing its Appetites into fubjection; thefe are the true Lovers of their Bodies; thefe promote their real Welfare, and do them all the Honour that is in their power: This being the only way of attaining to the Refurrection of the Juft, and fecuring an Intereft in thofe Joys and Pleafures, which fhall be referved in the Life to come, for fuch as fhall not have fuffered themfelves to be enflayed by the Lufts and Vanities of This.

C H A P.

CHAP. VIII.

The Eighth Motive, The Laft Judgment.

AFter the Refurrection, all Mankind fhall appear before the Tribunal of God to be judged for what they had done in the Body, to give an account of their paft Converfation, and to receive according to the tenor of it, whether well or ill. At whichtime the Impure fhall meet with a moft fevere Judgment.

There is no queftion to be made, but all Men whatfoever, the very Heathens not excepted, muft be judged. St. *Paul* fays of thefe, *Rom.* ii. 12, 13, 14. that they fhall be judged by the Law of Nature. The fame Apoftle likewife teaches us † that Impurity is one of thofe Sins they will be to account for. St. *Peter* declares alfo, 1 St. *Pet.* iii. 3, 4, 5. that *the Gentiles who walked in Lafcivioufnefs, and all excefs of Riot, fhall give an account to him who will come to judge the Quick and the Dead.* And if the Heathens who had not any other than the dim Light of Nature to guide them fhall be thus judged, what a heavy Doom muft thofe Chriftians expect, who fhall have violated both the Laws of Nature, and thofe of the Gofpel too, fhall have defpifed fo much Light, fo many Arguments, fuch peculiar Affiftances, as fhall have been vouchfafed them in order to Purity, and fhall have abandoned themfelves to luftful and diforderly Paffions? Thefe, we know, are in a particular manner threatned with the Judgment of God. So fays the Apoftle to the *Hebrews*, ch. xiii. 4. *Whoremongers and Adulterers God will judge.* Nothing can be more exprefs than this. At another time St. *Paul* affirms, that *We fhall all appear before*

† *Rom.* 1. 24, &c.

the

the Judgment-seat of Christ, that every one may receive in the Body according to what he had done, whether good or bad, 2 Cor. v. 10. In which Words there is something that deserves to be more especially attended to by the Impure, namely that mention is there made of the Body. For whether these Words signify that Men shall be punished or rewarded in their own Body; or as some understand them, that God will render to Men according as they shall have done *in the Body,* that is to say, whilst they dwelt in the Body, during this Life, every one must needs see that one way or other the Body will contribute very much to our Happiness or Misery; and that therefore the use we shall have made of the Body will then prove of vast Importance. Whereby we may see what such are to expect, as shall have committed that Sin which is in a peculiar Sense stiled the Sin of the Body, and who shall at the Last Day appear before God with Bodies and Souls that had been polluted by Incontinence.

But what we read in the second Epistle of St. *Peter,* ch. ii 4, &c. ought above all to be considered with great attention. This Apostle denounces the Judgment of God to those false Teachers whose chief Character was Licentiousness and Impurity; and proves the certainty of this Judgment by the Punishment of the wicked Angels, by that of the Inhabitants of the old World, and by the Destruction of those abominable Cities of *Sodom* and *Gomorrah;* and concludes from all these Examples, that Sinners, and most certainly the Impure, shall be punished at the last Day. *If God spared not the Angels which had sinned, if he spared not the old World, but brought a Flood upon the World of the Ungodly, if he condemned Sodom and Gomorrah, with an Overthrow, reducing them to Ashes, and making them an Example to those that should after live ungodly, and delivered just Lot vexed*

vexed with the filthy Converſation of the Wicked; the Lord knoweth how to reſerve the Unjuſt unto the Day of Judgment to be puniſhed; but chiefly them that walk after the Fleſh in the Luſt of Uncleanneſs. Theſe Words are directly levelled againſt Impurity. Theſe Threatnings, though relating to all the Workers of Iniquity, have yet a particular reſpect to the Unclean, and ſuch as follow the Luſts of the Fleſh; and are ſupported by terrible Inſtances of the Wrath of Heaven upon ſuch as give themſelves over to the filthy Luſts of the Fleſh. For we have ſhewn that it was chiefly this Sin which gave occaſion for theſe dreadful Judgments of God; as is more ſenſibly evident in the Deſtruction of *Sodom* and *Gomorrah.* St. *Jude* alledges the ſame Example, and to the ſame purpoſe with St. *Peter. Sodom and Gomorrah and the Cities about them giving themſelves over to Fornication, and going after ſtrange Fleſh, are ſet forth for an Example, ſuffering the Vengeance of eternal Fire,* Ep. St. *Jude* 7. And this he ſays to prove that *the Lord will not ſuffer thoſe to go unpuniſhed, who defile the Fleſh, and turn the Grace of God into Laſciviouſneſs.* Theſe Conſiderations are of ſingular force; theſe Examples, and particularly that of *Sodom,* ſhould make the Impure to tremble, and ſtrike them with a Dread of their approaching Judgment.

There is one thing more to be obſerved in relation to this Sin, which is that it is very often committed in ſecret; but yet if God be obliged as Judge of the World to puniſh other Sins, he is more eſpecially engaged to puniſh hidden Sins. The Crimes of Uncleanneſs are, as St. *Paul* ſpeaks, † *Works of Darkneſs,* and *things committed in ſecret,* † Epheſ. 5. but they ſhall however be brought to light, at that 11, 13. Great Day which will make all manifeſt. Theſe ſecret Sins and unknown to Men, will be the more certainly and more ſeverely puniſhed, becauſe thoſe

who

who commit them, though in truth highly culpable, yet pass for innocent, and are not put to disgrace by them ; whilst others who have not had Cunning enough to conceal their Crimes, or did not think fit to do it, but chose rather penitently to confess them, have suffered Reproach and Punishments in this Life. But it is more especially to be observed of Impurity, that many of those who conceal their Guilt, die without Repentance, and for this reason, because they have betaken themselves to Lying, and other wicked Courses, as I have shewn, whereby they lay themselves under a sort of Necessity of persevering in their Sin, and dying without either Confession or Reparation. Whence it comes to pass, that generally speaking, such as have sinned in secret, are in a far more dangerous State, than those whose Faults are most taken notice of, because these are in a better disposition to discharge their Conscience, and rise again after their Fall. They that judge themselves in this World shall not be judged in the other.

From what has been said it follows that the Unclean shall not escape the Judgment of God ; and therefore the Prospect and Apprehension of this Judgment should make us all chast. Oh how dreadful must the Approaching and the awful Appearance of the Great Day, which shall determine the eternal Fate of all Mankind, be to those who shall have lived in a State of Pollution ! It is easy to guess what Distress and Anguish will then seize them, with what Confusion they will be covered; and what on the contrary will be the Confidence and Joy of all that *shall have lived in this present World in Chastity and Temperance ; waiting for the blessed Hope, and the glorious Appearance of our Lord and Saviour Jesus Christ.*

CHAP.

CHAP. IX.

The Ninth Motive, Hell-Torments.

FROM the Confideration of the Laft moft Dreadful Judgment, it is natural to pafs on to what will follow it. And accordingly we are taught that after Mankind have been judged, || *fome fhall go away into Life eternal, and the reft into* || St. Mat. *Everlafting Punifhment.* We have likewife already 20. 46. feen that thefe Punifhments of the Life to come belong to the Impure. Our Lord fpeaking of Chaftity, fays it is better to mortify ourfelves, and deny ourfelves thofe things which are moft agreeable to the Flefh, * *than to be caft into Hell-Fire,* * St. Mar. *where the Worm dies not, and the Fire is not quenched.* 9. 43, 44. St. *John* declares, † *that the Impure, Fornicators, and* † Rev. *Abominable, fhall have their Portion in the Lake that* 21. 8. *burns with Fire aud Brimftone, which is the fecond Death.* Well then may we believe that the Punifhments of the other World will be exceedingly fevere, when the Holy Spirit fets before us fo terrible a Draught of them, when he fpeaks of Fire, and Brimftone, and Hell, and the Worm that never dies, and the Fire that is never to be extinguifhed. We may judge alfo of the Severity of the Punifhments referved for the Impure, by the weight of thofe temporal Judgments that God has upon certain occafions inflicted upon the Luftful and Licentious. But above all the Example of *Sodom* is moft remarkable; fo that we cannot call to mind this lewd People confumed by Fire from Heaven, without obferving what an Abhorrence

the

the Almighty has of Impurity, and how insupportable the Punishment of this Sin will be.

No doubt it will be pleaded that God did not so terribly destroy this People for the Sins of Fornication and Adultery, but for those other more intolerable Abominations and Impieties that reigned amongst them. And I grant it. But then it is to be remembred that not only this People fell into these dreadful Excesses by means of the other Sins of the Flesh, and so it was Incontinence that brought this Destruction upon them; but besides there is a difference to be made between the State of this People and that of Christians, inasmuch as if the Faults are not the same, neither are the Persons. For Men are not only more or less culpable according to the Flagitiousness of their Sins, but likewise, and perhaps not less, by the Estate, and more or less favourable Circumstances wherein they are set. By this Rule, which yet is most unquestionable, Fornication, Adultery, and all sort of Licentiousness is far more criminal in a Christian, who is instructed by the Gospel, and has before his Eyes the Doctrine and Example of his Saviour, who is so powerfully assisted in order to a Purity of Life, and has solemnly renounced the World, and all the inordinate Desires of the Flesh; Impurity, I say, is far more criminal in such an one, blessed with these inestimable Advantages, than were the Prostitutions of a Pagan buried in Darkness and Idolatry. To commit the Crimes of Impurity in the Church of Christ, is a much higher Provocation than those Abominations which were acted in *Sodom.* And upon this Difference between the Persons it was that our

* St. Mat 11. 24.

blessed Lord so peremptorily declared, that * *those who would not be reformed by his Preaching amongst them, should be more severely punished at the Day of Judgment than Sodom and Gomorrah.* Wherefore I make no difficulty to affirm that impure Christians, and

more

more particularly thofe that give themfelves up to Diffolutenefs and habitual Senfuality, will be more feverely punifhed, than the Vileft and moft excefsively Wicked amongft the Heathens. The Torments of thefe latter will be lefs, and their Condition far eafier to be born ; and for this plain Reafon, That their own Confciences will not fo fharply rebuke them. This ought well to be confidered. When we think of the Heathens, and in particular of this infamous *Sodom*, whofe Diffolutenefs was fo intolerable ; of thefe wicked Cities, whofe Memory will be always execrable, and which perifhed in fo dreadful a manner ; of thefe People whofe Crimes were fo deteftable ; it feems as if thefe were the moft heinous Sinners the World ever bare. But let us not deceive ourfelves ; the Condition of finful and vicious Chriftians will be far more deplorable in the other World, than that of this People.

The Impure will be fhut out of Heaven. Saint *Paul* profefses, 1 *Cor.* vi. 10. That *they fhall not inherit the Kingdom of God.* And we fhall fee in the next Chapter, that they cannot pofsibly be admitted into it ; and that Impurity is an invincible Barr in their way to Eternal Salvation. What Defpair will feize them, for having preferred tranfient and filthy Pleafures, to an Eternity of Happinefs which they might have attained to, but from which they are now irrecoverably excluded, and all meerly through their own fault ? They fhall have their portion with the Devil and his Angels, and fhall roar and languifh under the fame Punifhment with him, becaufe they had chofen to be like this Unclean Spirit, and to do his Will.

But amongft the other Puifhments they fhall have executed upon them, the Shame wherewith they fhall be covered deferves to be peculiarly attended

tended to. They will find themſelves expoſed, by
reaſon of theſe dreadful Sins, to eternal Reproach
before both God and Man. It is moſt certain,
that in this Great Day, when * *God will bring every*
work to Judgment, together with every ſecret thing,
whether it be good or evil ; † *and will bring to light the*
hidden things of Darkneſs, and will make manifeſt the
counſels of the Heart, ‖ *and in the day when God ſhall*
judge the ſecrets of Men by Jeſus Chriſt ; the Crime
and the Shame of theſe Tranſgreſſors ſhall be
made publick. It has moreover been thought,
that in the other Life, the Miſery and the Number of the Reprobate will be known to the Angels
and to Men ; who, as they ſhall obſerve the faithful Worſhippers of our Lord, ſo will they thoſe
that ſhall have forſaken him. Moreover, according
as the Juſtice and Goodneſs of God will be ado-
rable in the manner of his manifeſting and crown-
ing the Innocence of the Righteous ; ſo will
they be proportionably in the Puniſhment of ſecret
Sins, ſuch as the Sins of the Fleſh for the moſt
part are.

As an Inſtance of this, let us call to mind, that
there are divers Perſons whoſe luſtful manner of
Life is not at all taken notice of, nor can they be
charged with any known Immoraſity, and ſo they
paſs under a very different Character from what
they juſtly deſerve ; theſe might be expected
to be found amongſts the Saints in Glory, but
will not be found there, becauſe of that Impurity
wherein they had indulged themſelves in ſecret,
and which had prevented their admiſſion into
Heaven. The Damned in Hell will be greatly
ſurprized, to behold ſuch amongſt themſelves
as had been accounted Good Men, whoſe Virtue
the Wicked themſelves reverenced, and whoſe
Probity, perhaps whoſe Holineſs and Piety, was
had in reputation. Now if any enquire how
theſe

* Ecclef.
12. 14.
† 1 Cor.
4. 5.
‖ Rom.
2. 16.

these came to be punished in the company of the
Profane, Blasphemers, Murderers, &c. he will
find these Men of whom he had so high an opinion, to have been given to Lasciviousness. He
will find his Neighbour whom he took to be so
eminently Religious; had privately addicted himself to brutish Passions, and was really a wretched
Instance of Impurity, and so much the more
culpable in the sight of God, because he had imposed upon Men, by adding Hypocrisie to his
love of Vice, and under an appearance of Vertue
had covered a wanton Heart, and gratified his
own infamous and sensual Desires. Thus will
Misery and Shame be the Reward of those who
suffer themselves to be enslaved to this Passion.

I shall not go on to enlarge upon their doleful
Condition, but shall rather observe of what singular Influence a Fear of Hell is, for obliging to
Chastity. And here the Goodness of God is admirable, in offering such powerful Motives for
reclaiming from Sin; inasmuch as the more intolerable these Torments are, the more ought they
to affright us, and to make us Wise and Continent. So rare a Preservative are they from Carnal Passions, so effectual a Barr to the Allurements
of Lust, and so proper a Means of defeating the
Charms of Temptations. Let us then compare
the false Delights they offer, with the intolerable
Tortures that attend them; let us compare those
shameful and unprofitable Gratifications which are
but for a moment, with the eternal Vengeance of
the Life to come, let us consider, that the Pleasure passes away, but the Pain will never be over,
and then see to what purpose all these Pleasures
serve, for which Men have had so great a fondness, and to which they have sacrificed all they
had, and even their own Consciences with it; or
whether they will administer any manner of Con-
                                        solation.

folation. This may in a good meafure be judged of, by what befalls us in this World. Every one fees, that one only Sickneſs, one fingle Pain, if in any meafure of extremity, takes away our relifh of the Pleafures of this Life, and even caufes an Averfion to them. What opinion then will Perfons have of thefe Pleafures, what regard for them, when they fhall be tormented in Hell? efpecially when they fhall reflect, that they were thefe fame unhappy Pleafures, that by their deceitful Enticements and poifoned Baits, drew them into that deplorable ftate of Perdition.

Wherefore, let all thofe who without any Fear of God, or Reverence for their Baptifmal Covenant, pollute themfelves with the filthy Sins of Lafcivioufneſs, weigh this well with themfelves: Let them bethink themfelves what is like to become of them, and whither their infamous Paſſion will carry them. They fhall one day pay excef-fively dear for the brutifh Dalliances with which they had pleafed themfelves, unlefs they take care to amend their Lives in time, and make due Reparation for their Sins. Thofe that burn with the impure flames of Luft, fhall one day burn likewife in thofe of Hell. Let none of us deceive themfelves; this Sin leads directly to the dark Abyſs. *God will judge Whoremongers and Adulterers.* The Scripture fays not this in vain; and fince it fpeaks fo pofitively and fo affectingly of thefe Torments, they muft neceffarily be both Terrible and Inevitable. I befeech thofe efpecially who are in danger of being drawn into this fo pernicious a Paſſion, and efpecially the Younger Sort, to weigh this Argument well with themfelves; that they may be afraid of following fo deftructive an In-clination, and may prevent that dreadful Vengeance which will be the Portion of all who

* Eccl.   * *who walk in the ways of their own Hearts, and the*
11. 9.   *fight*

fight of their own eyes, and who *remember* not their *Creator in the days of their Youth.* Chaftity is an excellent Security againft all thefe Evils ; and he that whilft Young takes care to acquire and pre-ferve it, faves himfelf a great deal of Remorfe, and lays a good foundation for a folid Happinefs throughout the whole courfe of this Life, and for all Eternity.

CHAP. X.

The Tenth Motive, The Happinefs of the Life to come.

THE Laft Motive to Chaftity, is taken from the Happy State wherein the Bleffed fhall live in the World to come, the unconceivable Felicity whereto they will be advanced in Heaven. I fhall not ftand to defcribe the Greatnefs of this Felicity, either with refpect to its Nature, or to its Duration. I fuppofe it to be the happieft State a Creature can be raifed to ; and that all we can conceive moft defirable in this World, is nothing, in comparifon of the Heavenly Treafures, thofe moft ineftimable Advantages, and thofe unfpeak-able Satisfactions, whereof the glorified Saints fhall be poffeffed in the other Life.

This being fuppofed, I fay, the Expectation of this Felicity, is a very confiderable Engagement to Chaftity. * *He that has this Hope in him, purifies* † 1 St. Joh. *himfelf.* † *Having therefore thefe Promifes, let us* 3. 3. *cleanfe ourfelves from all filthinefs of Flefh and Spirit.* † 2 Cor. St. *Peter,* 1 Ep. i. 3. attributes fuch Efficacy to 7. 1. thefe *great and precious Promifes,* that he fays they are able to raife us above ourfelves, and *to make us*

Q   *Partakers*

Partakers of the Divine Nature, by escaping the Corruption which is in the World through Lust. And indeed, what ought not Persons to attempt, that they may obtain an Interest in the Glory and Felicity of the other Life? Or, what can one that understands the Excellency of that Blessed State, ever set in competition with it? All the Pleasures, all the Charms of Sense, vanish, upon the appearance of these inestimable Promises. Men are touched with Pleasure; and to the Carnally-minded it seems a very hard Lesson, and an unreasonable Task, to require that they deny themselves the Pleasures of Sense. Yet these Pleasures are nevertheless of no great value; they are shameful, they are often-times hurtful, but always are imperfect, vain and transitory. And were they more solid, and more lasting than they are, it were the height of Folly to prefer them before the supreme Happiness of a Future Life: And indeed, not to have a very mean esteem of them, and be ready to part with them whensoever they interfere with our hopes of That. It has been formerly observ'd, and is still to be seen every day, That People are not afraid to deprive themselves of these sort of Pleasures, and to lead a painful and uneasy Life. St. *Paul* affirms, That those who were to *strive for the Mastery* in the Olympick Games, were *temperate in all things,* 1 *Cor.* ix. 25. What *Plato* writes upon this Subject, is proper also to be mention'd in this Place[*]. This Philosopher, speaking of the Laws which were to be enacted against Impurity and Debauchery, says, Though this Abstinence from Pleasures seems very difficult, yet it is not impossible to be effected: And for the Proof of his Assertion, he instances in certain Wrestlers, who,

---

[*] Plat. de Legib. l. 8.

to perform their Exercises the more Manfully, abstained from these sort of Pleasures throughout their whole Lives.   If the Heathens had these Sentiments, and could attain to such Continency, what ought not Christians to do, in order to the Heavenly Glory ?   *If these Wrestlers did so much to gain a corruptible Crown, we should be ready to do much more for an incorruptible,* as St. *Paul* argues.

It is true, if a Man could be received into Heaven, whatsoever Course he takes here, whether he renounce his Lusts, or study to attend and serve them, there would then be no such absolute necessity of Chastity.   But if we would know for whom these infinite Rewards are reserved, and who they are that shall be thought worthy to partake of the Glories of the other State, the Scripture plainly teaches them not to be such as are given to Lasciviousness ; for it excludes these out of Heaven.   St. *Paul* professes more than once, That * *these shall not inherit the Kingdom of God.* And St. *John* says, † *There shall in no wise enter into the heavenly Jerusalem, any thing that defileth, or worketh abomination.*

* 1 Cor. 6. 10. Gal. 5. 19, 20, 21. † Rev. 21. 27.

But to come a little nearer to the Point : Why does God exclude the Impure out of Heaven ? Shall we say barely, because it pleases Him to do it ; and that He thinks it not fit to admit them, though there is nothing to hinder it, if He would ? This Answer is by no means satisfactory.   The Notion we have of God, as a Being infinitely Good, perfectly Wise, and superlatively Just, directs to think otherwise, and to argue with ourselves, That if God has established certain Laws, and enforced them by certain Punishments, it was because the Happiness of Mankind made it necessary such Laws should be imposed upon them, and because Punishments are the natural Consequents of the Violation of his Commands.   We

can

can never be happy any other way, but by the Obſervance of theſe Laws ; and by the Breach of them, we make ourſelves neceſſarily miſerable. By doing what God enjoins, we fit ourſelves, as becomes Reaſonable Creatures, for the Poſſeſſion of the Sovereign Good, which is God, and bring ourſelves nearer to him ; but by Diſobedience to his Divine Laws, we turn away from God and our ſupreme Felicity.

Let us therefore meditate and weigh well with ourſelves what the Scripture conſtantly teaches; namely, That * *God will render to every one according to his doings :* That † *we ſhall receive in the other Life, according to the Good or Ill we ſhall have done here :* That ‖ *each one ſhall reap in the other World, that which he ſhall have done in this :* And that ‡ *without Holineſs, none ſhall ſee the Lord.* All which Paſſages perhaps will naturally put us in mind, that our future Eternal State depends upon our Behaviour at preſent ; and there is ſuch a natural and neceſſary Relation betwixt what we are now, and what we ſhall be hereafter, that without getting ourſelves into a good Diſpoſition in this Life, we never ſhall, never can be, happy in the other. And that ſince Chaſtity is a Diſpoſition that God exacts of us, our Hope and Expectation of that Bleſſed State, muſt be a moſt powerful Motive to the Practice of this Virtue.

* Rom. 2. 6.
† 2 Cor. 5. 10.
‖ Gal. 6. 7, 8.
‡ Heb. 12. 14.

To the end we may enjoy the Heavenly Felicity, we muſt receive and ſtedfaſtly believe the Promiſes which are made to us by *Jeſus Chriſt* ; and muſt ſearch after it, deſire it, and put a high value upon it. Becauſe, Man being endued with Reaſon, no Good, how great ſoever, can make him happy, unleſs he ſeek it, and believe he ſhall find his Account in it. And whoſoever therefore, inſtead of ſetting his Affections upon thoſe Heavenly Treaſures which the Goſpel ſets before him, places

places them rather upon the Earth, and its vain
Delights, hereby incapacitates himself for aspiring
after the Bliss and Glory of the other World ; and
so much the more, because the Heavenly State,
and the Pleasures of the Flesh, are of a quite different Nature. It is upon this Consideration our Blef-
sed Saviour declares, That * *our Heart will necessarily*
be where our Treasure is, and that † *we cannot serve two* * Mat. 6.
Masters. As his Apostle St. *John* also affirms, That 21.
‖ *if any man love the World, the Love of the Father is* † Ver. 24,
not in him. As a Drunkard or Profligate Person 1 S. Joh.
is unable to taste the Satisfaction a Wise Man finds 2. 15.
in the Search and Knowledge of the Truth ; so he
that minds nothing but his Sensual Delights, as
knowing no other Pleasures, can never relish
those Entertainments which are not only of a
different, but quite opposite Nature, such as are
Spiritual and Heavenly Pleasures.

If the Felicity we aim at were to be a Corporal
Felicity, the Habits and Dispositions which are
contracted by a Licentious course of Life, would
be no impediment to the Possession of it ; and so
a Love of Sensual Pleasures would be in some sort
pardonable. But Christians are not to believe
like those Infidels who place their Carnal Pleasures
amongst the Blessings of Paradise. We have
Hopes of another nature, and expect a Divine and
Spiritual Paradise ; and are well assured, that after
the Resurrection, the Pleasures of Sense shall be
at an end. Our Lord himself has told us, That
‡ *then People shall neither Marry, nor be given in Mar-* ‡ S. Luke
riage, but shall be as the Angels of God. And we have 20. 35.
all therefore abundant reason to prepare ourselves
for this State, to aspire after it, and to get as
near it as we can. A Hope to be with God, to
see Him as He is, to be with Jesus Christ, and
with the Holy Angels, to be employed in Exercises wholly Spiritual and Heavenly, and in the

Contemplation of the marvellous Works of the Lord, such a Hope can never be well fixed in a Heart, where Corruption and a Love of Sensuality reign. This Hope calls for pure and virgin Hearts, chaste and innocent Souls ; and to this purpose may be applied what is said in a different sense, *Rev.* xiv. 4. *These who are not defiled with Women, but are Virgins, shall follow the Lamb wheresoever he goeth, these were redeemed from among Men, to be the First-fruits to God and to the Lamb : These shall dwell in the Temple of God, and be Kings and Priests to all Eternity.*

These are the chief Motives to Chastity ; which, were they taken either from uncertain Conjectures, or Considerations of little Importance, it were more excusable not to be prevailed upon by them. But this is not the Case : For nothing can possibly be proposed that is more certain, or of greater consequence. There is nothing in the World more certain than these great Truths; That we shall one day die ; That yet we shall not die like the Beasts, but have a Soul which dies not with the Body ; That there is to be another Life after this, when our Bodies shall be raised from Death, and we shall all be brought to Judgment : and lastly, That after this Judgment, we shall live eternally either in Misery or Glory. These are indisputable Truths, and they are likewise of the highest moment and concern to us. All other Considerations are of very little weight; and next to nothing, in respect of These.

Wherefore, seeing there is no acting like Rational Creatures, without giving way to the strongest Motives, those who are not prevailed upon by these which I have mention'd, though so pressing, and of such weighty importance, should be sure they have other Reasons and Motives of greater force to overbalance them. But what

what can thefe be ? Or, how comes it about that Senfualifts are fo wedded to their Impurity, in fpite of all that is urged to reclaim them from it ? They can pretend but one reafon for it, and that is, brutifh Pleafure, fuch a grofs and fenfual Inclination as themfelves are afhamed of. But is this a Temptation fit to be compared with thofe weighty and important Confiderations, which are drawn from the Will of Almighty God, his Prefence with us, the Life and Death of our Bleffed Lord, the Honour of the Chriftian Name, our own Death, and all that is to follow after it ? Are all thefe Arguments to be looked upon as of no force, and to be defpifed, and thrown afide ? Is it the part of a Man, to fhut his Eyes againft all Means of Conviction, to hearken to nothing that can be faid, but, for the Satisfaction of his Lufts, to run headlong upon certain and irretrievable Ruin ? This is an Excefs of Blindnefs that were hardly to be conceived, and whereof Mankind were not capable, if they would but ferioufly attend to the Motives they have to Chaftity. It is moft certain, People do not give themfelves to Impurity, for any other caufe, than that thefe Motives are not well impreffed upon their Minds ; the proper Means of Chaftity being to think of them ferioufly and often.

Q 4   SECTION

SECTION III.

Of the Means to be uſed in order to CHASTITY.

CHAP. I.

That there are Means of being Chaſt, and that this Vertue is attainable by their Help.

AFTER having in the preceding Section propoſed the principal Motives to Chaſtity, I am in this to treat of the Means to be made uſe of in order to it.

And here I take it to be incumbent upon me, in the firſt place to prove, that it is not at all impoſſible to be Chaſt. I muſt not ſay that all theſe Doctrines of Purity are laudable and juſt, but withal that it is difficult to reduce them to Practice; and Means muſt be found out for enabling Perſons to obſerve them, this being above their Capacity; and a Task fitter for Angels than Men. This is the Libertines Plea whereby they ſeek to excuſe their Diſobedience to the Laws of the Goſpel; but nothing can be ſaid more idly, or more falſly, or more injuriouſly to God and the Chriſtian Religion.

This one Conſideration, That God enjoins Chaſtity, is an invincible Proof that People may attain to it. It is by no means to be imagined that

God

God is unjuſt, or will ſtrictly and under pain of eternal Damnation command the Obſervation of ſuch Duties as he knows to be utterly above our Power. No, he is too Good, too great a Lover of Equity to impoſe ſuch Impoſſibilities upon his Servants. There are Means of performing what he enjoyns, ſure Means of doing it, and the uſe of which is not very difficult. And as it is He who has ordered theſe Means, ſo has he engaged himſelf to ſecond them with his Bleſſing, whenſoever we heartily ſet ourſelves to obey Him.

It is ſtrange that any who call themſelves Chriſtians ſhould make a queſtion of this. We have ſeen that the very Heathens have believed Chaſtity to be a practicable Virtue. The Precepts of their Wiſemen, and the Examples of Continence that occur in Ancient Hiſtories ſuppoſe it. And ſhall Chriſtians have ſo mean an Opinion of their Lord's Doctrine, and the Efficacy of his Grace, as to think that People cannot however live in Purity?

Yet it muſt be granted that this Duty is not a-like eaſy to all ſorts of Perſons; and ſome find conſiderable Trouble in it. But ſo is it in all the other Duties of Morality. There are ſome who, whether from their natural Temper and Conſtitution, or from the bad Habits they have contracted, are violently preſſed on to certain Paſſions, and muſt be at pains with themſelves before they can refrain from them. For inſtance there are thoſe whom an eager Temper and fulneſs of Heat, together with an ill Habit too long indulg'd, have render'd ſo prone to Anger, that they muſt be very diligent and watchful, and always upon their guard, or they will not be able to avoid it. Nevertheleſs it will ill become theſe to pretend this for their Excuſe; for ſo there is no Sinner but would be able to vindicate himſelf. Let him but

be

be throughly engaged before-hand in any Habit of Vice, or subject to any Passion to such or such a Degree, and then he may take his Liberty, and it will not only be to no purpose, but will be unfair to go about to oblige him to a Reformation, and to threaten or punish him if he refuse it.

I yield that divers are strongly pressed to Impurity. But in the first place it cannot be concluded from hence, that there are no Means of preserving themselves from this Passion. If they brought themselves into this Estate by their own Fault, and for want of using the Means that were afforded them in order to Chastity, this is no Evidence that these Means are not sufficient for their purpose. The Case is the same here, as if a Man had fallen into a mortal Fit of Sickness, by not using certain Preservatives or Remedies; which does not shew that he had no Means of Preventing this Sickness, but only that he did not make a right Use of them. I say, in the next place, That God has ordained a proper Means and Remedy for such, whereby to avoid the Excesses of the Flesh, which is Marriage, as St. *Paul* teaches, 1 *Cor.* vii. But I add farther in relation to those who are already entangled in this dangerous Passion, and whose Return to Chastity appears very difficult, that they may yet recover themselves, and many have actually done it. It is true they will find it troublesom at first; but then they should remember that it is but reasonable for them to cross their own Inclinations, and bear with some Inconvenience, to preserve themselves from Destruction. And again, all this Trouble will grow less in time, and by the Use of these Means they will every day become easier, as I hope to shew very plainly.

I lay this down then as a Principle, that there are Means of being Chast; and that whosoever shall make the Trial, will quickly find the Benefit

of

of them. As for those that will not use them, who will do nothing to help themselves, will not Pray, nor Fast, nor keep out of the way of Temptations, nor Watch over themselves, nor Cross themselves in any thing, which is the Case with most of the Unclean; these, I own, will never attain to Chastity, but then they have none but themselves to blame for it. It is their own Fault, and not any Defect in their Religion, that they are in this Condition: And their wilful Negligence will not hinder but that there may be sufficient Means of making the Practice of this Vertue not only Possible, but Easie.

CHAP. II.

What is to be done, in order to Chastity; and first, of Holy Exercises.

THere are two General Means of acquiring Chastity; namely, Holy Exercises, and Watchfulness against Temptations.

The Exercises of Piety and Devotion, are an excellent Preservative against Impurity, and most effectual Helps towards becoming Chast. By which I do not mean barely External and Corporeal Exercises, such as are those of most Christians, which consist only in the Recital of some Prayers, the Reading some good Discourse, being present at Religious Assemblies, and attending the Publick Worship of God. Which Outward Acts and Duties of Religion are both useful and necessary, but yet cannot, without a great Mistake, be thought to be so of themselves, and that they are sufficient to gain a Man Acceptance with God.

So

So far from this, that bare Outward Devotions do but ſet him at a greater diſtance from God, and defile the Conſcience. Here therefore I mean, an Interior Devotion, ſuch Acts of Piety as come from the Heart, and are accompanied with a ſincere Deſire and Endeavour to pleaſe God, and and attain to a real Purity. Without this Deſign, all a Man does will ſtand him in no ſtead.

There are Three Pious Exerciſes that are more eſpecially uſeful, in order to the Virtue we are treating of ; and they are, Prayer, Reading, and Meditation.

I. He that would be Chaſt, muſt Pray often ; Prayer being a moſt effectual Remedy againſt Temptations to Impurity, as having a two-fold Uſe for Purifying the Heart. On the one hand, by Prayer, we obtain of God the Spirit of Purity, and Ability to withſtand the Deſires of the Fleſh ; and prevail with Him to aſſiſt us, and to preſerve us from many Temptations. On the other hand, it is impoſſible that Application and Intercourſe with God ſhould not make us Pure. A Cuſtom of ſpeaking to Him who is Holineſs itſelf, of diſcovering our Hearts to Him, and appearing in his Preſence, will make us Wiſe and Circumſpect. When a Man is about to preſent himſelf before the Lord, or when he goes out from his Divine Preſence, he will not dare to allow himſelf in any Pollution, nor will be at that time ſuſceptible of the Impreſſions of Senſuality : The Comfort he has found in the Exerciſe of Prayer, the Satisfaction ſo pure and ſolid which he enjoys at ſuch a time, makes him leſs attentive to the ſhameful and tranſient Delights of Sin. Thus Prayer ſerves very much to Strengthen and Purifie the Soul.

Wherefore, ſo many of you as deſire to live Chaſtly, preſent yourſelves often before God, lift up your Hearts frequently to Him ; put up to Him,

at

at every turn, and with great earneftnefs, that Prayer of *David*, Pfal. li. 10. *Create in me, O Lord, a clean Heart.* Let this be your firft Thought when you awake in the Morning ; intermix this Prayer with your Bufinefs ; in the midft of your Work have fuch Ejaculations ; and, though fhort, they will not fail of being highly beneficial. Do this when you find yourfelves free and undifturb'd with evil Thoughts ; and when thefe affault you, double your Prayers. Ufe the fame Courfe at Night, before you betake yourfelves to Reft ; and again whenfoever you lie awake : So will it become habitual to you to behave yourfelves as in the Prefence of God ; your Souls will become Pure, and your Temptations will either keep at a diftance, or at leaft will lofe a great part of their Force.

But now if you would have your Prayers produce this happy Effect, you muft Pray with Faith, and through *Jefus Chrift* our Lord ; and muft be fully perfuaded that God will grant the Favour you beg of Him, provided you do your part for obtaining it. This you muft believe, and ftedfaftly too, becaufe hereupon depends the Efficacy of your Prayers, *If any one lack Wifdom,* (fays St. *James*, ch. i. 6.) *let him ask it of God, who giveth to all men liberally, and upbraideth not : but let him ask in Faith, nothing wavering.* And it is our Bleffed Saviour's own Promife, St. *Matth.* xxii. 22. *All things whatfoever ye fhall ask in Prayer, believing, ye fhall receive.* That is a fruitlefs Prayer, which is offered up without this Faith, and at all adventures, and only by the Lips, without minding whether it is like to fucceed or not.

And let not the faintnefs of your Defires difcourage you : Ceafe not to make your Supplications to the Lord, how weak and defective foever they be, provided you be fincere in them. Offer them

up

up with Confusion and a profound Humility, and beseech Him, in the Name of *Jesus Christ*, to pity your Infirmities.   God is of himself so Good, and so ready to do Good to Mankind, that He never fails to answer those who invoke him with any measure of Sincerity. If you take this Course, you will quickly find the benefit of your Prayers, and will see cause to join returns of Thanks with them, and to bless God, when you feel the Bonds that had tied you so fast to the Flesh, and to your Senses, begin to fall off, and that the Allurements of Pleasures are nothing so strong as formerly; And thenceforward you will go on more easily, and be continually making new Improvements in Chastity.

II. The Second Pious Exercise I would recommend, is Reading.   And this is advantageous upon divers Accounts.   It employs Persons, and hereby is an useful Remedy against Evil Thoughts. It suggests Good Meditations, and affords such Reflections as we should not otherwise make ; it excites Devotion ; it takes off our Minds from Sensible things, and raises them up to Spiritual : In a word, it is a great help to Piety, supposing what is read to be Good and Instructive. But for this Purpose, of all Authors whatsoever, there is none comparable to the Holy Scriptures : For besides the Holiness of what is contained in these Sacred Volumes, the Authority of Almighty God speaking in them, challenges a particular Attention and Respect.   The whole Tendency of the Scripture, is to make Persons Spiritual ; and to this end, it proposes to them a great number of Precepts, Examples, and Motives excellently conducing to cleanse them from the Pollutions of the Flesh. St. *Chrysostom* * attributes so great Power

---

* Conc. 3. de Lazaro.

to the Scripture, in refpect to Chaftity, that he
fays, A bare Sight, or Touching of the Gofpel, is
enough to drive away Evil Thoughts. Which
doubtlefs he faid, upon account of the Reverence
and Fear that is apt to arife in the Mind, upon
the appearance of this Divine Book.

To the Reading of the Word of God, that of
other Books may be ufefully added. And in
chufing of thefe, I would advife every one to
felect thofe which he obferves to affect him moft,
and to ftick to them. When a Book has been
read over, and the Reader finds himfelf improved
by it, it fhould be read over again and again;
for it is a great Miftake, to think, the beft way of
profiting by Books, to lie in reading a multitude of
them; and they that are always paffing from one
Book to another, make ordinarily but fmall Improvements in Piety.

Wherefore, I wifh thofe who find it neceffary
to take Pains that they may become Chaft, would
impofe it as a conftant Task upon themfelves, to
read fomething every Day, to fet afide fome certain Time for this, and efpecially that they would
fpend part of all their Days and Times of Devotion
in this Employment. But I have one particular
Direction to give concerning Reading, which is,
that fuch as find in themfelves an indifpofition to
this Exercife, would ftrive hard to overcome it.
People are not always enclined to Reading; but
I beg of them however not to forbear it: They
would do well to offer violence to themfelves in
this Cafe; and they may affure themfelves no
Hurt can come of it, but very great Good may.
If Reading ferv'd only to employ the Mind, yet
fo it were worth the while. Sometimes a Reading begun without Defign, and with fome Unwil-
lingnefs, ferves to excite good Thoughts, and
infpire

inspire the Mind with such Sentiments as it would not otherwise have had.

III. Meditation, is another very good Means of Purifying the Soul. It excites and recalls into the Mind divers good Reflections, prevents Temptations and Evil Thoughts; and whenever they intrude, it abates their Force. And if any one would know what is a proper Subject for his Meditation; I answer, There are very many, very proper and useful; and that in general, there is no Matter of Religion and Piety, which may not be revolved in our Minds to Advantage. It may be very useful also to meditate upon all that has been discoursed in this Treatise, upon both Uncleanness, and Chastity. But there are some particular Meditations that have a peculiar Virtue for dissuading from Pollution. Such is, the Consideration of God's Presence. And we should therefore habituate ourselves to think frequently of it, remembring and well weighing with ourselves, that we are always in His Sight. I wish Persons would often call to mind that great Truth, That God is near them; That he speaks to them, exhorts, encourages them, makes Promises, and denounces Threatnings; That he tries them, and says this and that to invite them to Purity. For all this he does to reclaim People from Sin. These Thoughts would fill them with a Religious Fear; and, considering themselves as before God, they would not dare to take the liberty of Defiling themselves. Of such mighty Influence is a Fear of God, and Reverence for his Presence. *It is by the Fear of the Lord, that Men depart from Evil*, Prov. xvi. 6.

Another proper Subject for Meditation, and a likely Means of making the Soul Chast, is the Life and Sufferings of our Saviour *Christ*. The Life of our Saviour and his Crofs, are a powerful Motive, not to feek our own Eafe, and the Satisfaction of our Senfes in this World.

Our Meditations may be alfo very profitably employed about the Ends of Mankind, their Death, Refurrection, Judgment, and Heaven, and Hell. Thefe are Objects that fhould be always prefent to us, and have an excellent Tendency to keep us from Impurity. The Thoughts of Death, which puts an end to all our Delights here, and not only lays the Body in the Grave, but turns it into a Neft of Worms, muft neceffarily abate the Allurements of Senfual Pleafures. The Thoughts of the Refurrection, will force us to have a regard to our Bodies, and to preferve them Pure. Thofe of Judgment, will ftrike us with Dread and Terror. That of Hell, will fhew the Temptations of Luft to be very dangerous, and put us upon trying all ways for avoiding them. And the Thoughts of Heaven, and its unconceivable Felicity, will put us upon renouncing moft heartily thofe deftructive and fhameful Pleafures, the fhort enjoyment of which, would for ever fhut us out from this incomparably Bleffed State. In fine, The Confideration of that Eternity, which every day draws nearer, and wherein we know not how very foon we may be placed, fwallows up our Thoughts in fuch a manner, that it will fuffer us no longer to hearken to the Enticements of Vain Pleafures, but will caufe us to look upon the Delights and the Advantages of this Life as nothing worth.

Thefe are the chief Subjects of Meditation, which may ferve for a Remedy againft Impurity, and a Means of obtaining Chaftity. I beg leave to add to what I have faid, That by Meditation, I do not underftand only, a continued Courfe of Attention for fome time together, but fuch Meditations likewife as are very fhort, or rather are

R	only

only good Reflections, and holy Thoughts. Men may allow more or less Time to Meditation, according to their present Circumstances, and the Leasure they have for it. But it is of necessity that some Time be set a-part for it; and that, to this Purpose, some Intermissions be contrived in the midst of our worldly Affairs, wherein the Soul being at liberty, and having recollected itself, may have leasure for, and seriously employ itself in these holy Thoughts, and so may considerably improve itself. Besides this, Persons should likewise accustom themselves frequently to reflect upon something that is good, in the midst of their worldly Employments, and often to recall into their minds such Thoughts as are useful for Purifying their Hearts. This may be done, without interrupting their own necessary Affairs and Occupations, and a habit of doing it may be easily acquired. And Labourers, and Artificers, and such others as have their Bodies ordinarily at work, have yet this advantage; that whilst thus employed, they have nothing that can hinder their entertaining themselves with good Thoughts.

To conclude this Chapter: It is of the highest Consequence to Chastity, that the Time which is not spent in Sleep at Night and whilst we are in Bed, be employed in Meditation. This should the rather be observed, because Persons are then more at liberty; and should therefore more especially be upon their guard, for fear of being surprized by evil Thoughts and Temptations.

CHAP.

CHAP. III.

Of the Care that is to be taken for avoiding Temptations.

WHatfoever the Effect of Holy Exercifes be, for difpofing Perfons to Chaftity, they muft neceffarily be accompanied with our own Care and Pains : And this is no more than All will infallibly apply themfelves to, if they once fincerely fet about thefe Exercifes of Piety ; it not being poffible for a Man heartily to defire a thing, without being willing to take fome Pains for obtaining it. And here therefore I am to fhew, what courfe is to be taken for preferving the Soul and Body in Purity.

Our Endeavours then muft be two-fold. For as there are two forts of Remedies, either Preventive, which a Man ufes for fear of being Sick, or Reftorative, and which are defigned for his Recovery after his Difeafe has feized him ; fo are there two different Methods to be purfued againft Impurity, the one for Preventing Temptations, and the other when under them. I fhall treat of the former of thefe in this Chapter and the two next.

I. One of the chief Means of Defence againft Temptations to Impurity, is a Diftruft of ourfelves. This Diftruft proceeds from an opinion of our own Weaknefs, and a fear of being furprized and enfnared by Temptations. Nor is there any one who has not too juft reafon to diftruft himfelf. It were meer Folly to imagine, that People fhall never be expofed to Temptations, or fhall certainly be able to overcome them

if they be. When once any prefume this of themfelves, they are undone ; for thenceforward they
are no more upon their guard, but grow negligent, and fo a Temptation is fure to prevail
againft them : Whereas, did they diftruft their
own Strength, and had an humble opinion of
themfelves, they would not be able to fleep in
fecurity. Diffidence, makes Perfons Wife, Vigilant, Circumfpect, infpires them with Fear, and
makes them avoid the Occafions of Falling. On
the other fide, it directs them to put their Truft
in God alone, and to apply to Him for the Affiftance they ftand in need of : And if God be on
their fide, they will eafily fubdue their evil Defires.

But none have more reafon to diftruft themfelves, than thofe who are enclinable to Impurity, and have often fallen into it, one way or
other. Thefe cannot attend too diligently to this
Admonition. Though they feem to have their
Paffions allayed, they are not however to think
themfelves fafe. Many have fallen, and loft the
fruits of their firft Attempts, by a falfe Confidence,
and by believing too foon and too eafily, that they
had already got the Maftery over themfelves.
Having obferved in themfelves fome beginnings
of Chaftity, fome declenfion of the Heat of Luft,
and having been fome days, or for fome time,
without feeling the returns of their Paffion, they
thought they had already attained to Purity : whereas, had they tarried a while longer, they would
have found themfelves very much deceived ; there
being nothing wanting but an Object or Temptation, and poffibly a very light one, to reduce
them to their former State. Luft is often-times
like a Fire hid under Afhes, which breaks out
again with great violence in an inftant, and
when it is thought entirely extinct. Wherefore,

that

that fuch who are not well confirmed in Purity, may be benefited by this Advice, their State fhould be a State of continual Diffidence and Fear, but yet fuch as is accompanied with Hope and Courage. For it is abfolutely neceffary for them not to be out of heart.

II. This Diftruft will produce Vigilance, which is a fecond Means of Defence againft impure Temptations; and to which the Gofpel invites. Our Bleffed Lord himfelf often exhorts to watch; and the State we are in in this World obliges us to be inceffantly upon our guard. And Watchfulnefs is efpecially neceffary with refpect to the Paffion we are treating of; which is lively and quick, and though its Beginnings may feem weak, it makes a great Progrefs, and does great Mifchief in a Moment. Let it but lie afleep for a fmall time, and it will beget great Falls. It was want of Vigilance made *David* fin; who fell becaufe he did not watch over himfelf.

Now one of the principal Duties of Vigilance, and one of the greateft Advantages it brings, is the avoiding Temptations. The firft and moft certain Means of fecuring ourfelves againft Sin, is to keep off from whatever might probably betray us into it. He that being expofed to Temptation takes care to refift it, does well; but does it not without fome Struggle and Danger. And it had been much fafer to have avoided the Temptation and Conflict.

For avoiding Temptations they fhould be forefeen and taken notice of. It has been already fhewn what are the Allurements to Uncleannefs, and every ones bufinefs is to fhun thefe Temptations and Occafions as much as poffibly he can. I am fenfible he cannot always efcape them wholly, but in a good meafure he may, and then he will be in far lefs Danger from them. For example,

He

He that deſires to be Chaſt, muſt fly Idleneſs, and be always ſome way well employed ; he muſt beware of Intemperance, and live very ſoberly ; he muſt be very moderate in his Sleep, and in things permitted him ; muſt not ſeek too much the Conveniences of Life ; muſt avoid Luxury and any Diverſions wherein is Exceſs. He muſt refrain from going to any Places where he may be like to hear or ſee any thing that may draw him aſide ; and muſt not read any obſcene or wanton Books. But above all things he muſt govern his Eyes with great care, and keep out of the Company of Perſons whom he cannot look upon without Danger. He muſt never be familiar with them, either in his Actions or Diſcourſe, nor uſe any Toying and Wantonneſs, but be Grave and Circumſpect ; and in one word, muſt be upon his guard againſt whatever might occaſion any Senſual Thoughts or Deſires.

But that this Practice may have its wiſhed Succeſs, Two things are to be taken care of. Firſt that Perſons be very exact, and very ſcrupulous, as to every thing that leads to Impurity, and that they do not take too much Liberty, under any vain Pretences. Men impoſe upon themſelves divers ways. Sometimes they think things to be inconſiderable ; wherein they deceive themſelves, not remembring that little things are here of great conſequence, and cannot be neglected without Damage to Chaſtity, as every one may have obſerved. Some things they look upon as innocent ; and that there is no Evil or Danger in venturing upon them ; yet theſe ſame things have oftentimes been the Occaſions of great Falls. It is eaſy to be deceived in point of Converſation. One looks upon another of the other Sex, and thinks there is nothing unlawful in this, and that here is nothing with reſpect to either of them but Eſteem and
Friend-

Friendſhip; perhaps Religion too had at firſt ſome concurrence towards the Kindneſſes and Diſcourſes that paſs between them ; yet by this means a Paſſion has inſenſibly taken hold of them. And the caſe is the ſame with many other matters that are thought innocent.

The other thing I would have obſerv'd is, that ſeeing Perſons are not always expoſed to all the forementioned Temptations, and they have not all the ſame force upon all ſorts of Perſons, every one ſhould make trial of himſelf to ſee by which he is in moſt danger of falling, which Objects make moſt Impreſſion upon him, and upon what occaſions he is moſt apt to be ſeized with ſenſual Thoughts. There are ſome who are very orderly by themſelves, but when they go abroad, the diverſity of Objects they meet with diſcompoſes them, and they cannot be in Company without forgetting themſelves. Such ſhould be very wary, and live retired. There are others who when Sober are Wiſe and Chaſt, but who in their Cups or after a Feaſt are not able to contain themſelves within the Bounds of Modeſty. Theſe are oblig'd upon this particular account, beſides thoſe other Reaſons which engage Chriſtians to live in Sobriety, to be conſtantly upon their guard againſt Intemperance. Others again there are, who cannot go into ſome Places, or ſee ſome Perſons without being enſnared by ſome impure Paſſion. Theſe ſhould be ſure always to avoid ſuch Places and Perſons. And in this caſe it may be requiſite to break off theſe Converſations, in ſuch a manner as may prevent our ever renewing them for the future. Thus muſt every one apply himſelf, to diſcover and avoid whatever may be like to kindle any ill Deſires in him. But ah! how very different is the ordinary courſe of Mankind, who ſeek out, inſtead of ſhunning theſe Occaſions! Many know

very

very well what it is that drives them on to Sin; they know they cannot frequent the Company of such or such Persons, without being subject to some unlawful Desires, and yet they frequent it. They have found by Experience that the reading of some Books are a Poison to them, and yet they will not forbear it. They know before-hand that Wine is apt to have an ill Effect upon them, and make them disorderly, and yet they will not keep themselves sober. When any thus put themselves in the way of a Temptation, and willingly cast themselves upon it, it is not in their power not to yield to it.

CHAP. IV.

Of the Care to be taken with respect to the Body.

THat we may be safe from Temptations, our chief Care must be to watch over ourselves; the Cause and Original of Evil being in ourselves; as St. *James* witnesses, 1 St. *Ja.* i. 14. *Every one is tempted, when he is drawn aside of his own Lusts and enticed.* Occasions and Object seduce us not but through our own Fault. Nor again, do Temptations come always from without; they often proceed from ourselves, without the Intervention of Objects. So that our chief Care is to be laid out upon ourselves, and this with respect either to our Bodies, or to our Souls. The Body being the principal Fountain of Impurity, Lusts are therefore called Bodily or Carnal; and St. *Paul* makes Chastity to consist in possessing the Body in Sanctification. And accordingly there is no preserving

ving

ving Chaftity, without governing the Body. And therefore my Bufinefs in this Chapter fhall be to fhew what is to be done in this refpect.

I. My Firft Advice is concerning its Diet ; and it calls for an efpecial Attention from all that find themfelves inclined to Senfuality. Now here the Gofpel directs two Duties, Sobriety and Fafting.

1. I have already fhewn, when I was confidering the Caufes of Uncleannefs, that Intemperance in Eating and Drinking is one of the chief Caufes of this Sin ; and that confequently all that would be chaft, muft neceffarily be fober. Sobriety allays the Heat of Paffions, that have been raifed by too great Abundance, and too great Activity of the Blood and animal Spirits. By this Virtue it is that People become accuftomed to command their own Appetites, and put themfelves in a condition to refift their other Paffions. But when I fay Perfons muft be Sober, I do not mean they muft only forbear being Drunk, and abftain from Gluttony, and other Excefs of Riot ; they muft farther beware of being dainty, and not feek after what pleafes the Tafte and Senfes, but to Eat and Drink moderately, and to ufe themfelves to the plaineft Sort of Food.

2. And yet the Gofpel proceeds farther, enjoining not only Abftemioufnefs, but Fafting. Which has always been look'd upon as an excellent Inftrument of Mortification of the Flefh ; and was accordingly both recommended and practifed by the Prophets and the *Jews*, by our bleffed Saviour, by his Apoftles, by the Primitive Chriftians, and by the whole Church. Abftinence from Meat and Drink is certainly a Help to Chaftity. But then I mean a rational Abftinence fuited to everyone's prefent State and Need. It weakens the Body, and fo is of great ufe for beating down the
Paffions.

Paffions. Every one feels that he is better able to refift his inordinate Defires, when he has from time to
time denied his Body, not only Superfluities, but
moreover some part of what is Neceffary. A Government of our Appetites is of abfolute neceffity
in order to the Practice of this Virtue ; but when
a Man will not endure to crofs himfelf in this, he
will find a great deal of Trouble in doing it in
other things. In giving the Body always whatever it demands as neceffary, it is eafy to grant it
what is fuperfluous, and after that even what is forbidden. It is natural to have the like Complaifance
for the Body in other things likewife, as well as in
what relates to Food ; and it is therefore needful to
betake ourfelves to Abftinence, if we would tame
the Paffions of the Flefh. If the Impure would
make ufe of this Means, they would prefently expe-
riment the Advantage of it. But it is a great Un-
happinefs, that fuch vaft Numbers entirely negleſt
it to that degree, that the greateft part have no
Notion of this Duty, nor think that they ever
ought to crofs themfelves in Meat or Drink, and
fometimes totally to refrain from them. This is
one of the Caufes of Licentioufnefs, and in particular of Uncleannefs. Men will be wifer than
God. Jefus Chrift has taught us how to mortify
ourfelves, and accuftom ourfelves to deny the Flefh
what it requires of us ; and he has not prefcribed
this without great Reafon. His firft Difciples
were fo fenfible of this, that they conftantly made
it the Matter of their Practice. And it is a melancholick Confideration, That in our Days fo
few will be invited to imitate them in it.

II. Labour is another Means of promoting
Chaftity. And as we would not be drawn afide
by impure Defires, it will extremely concern us
to beware of Idlenefs. Too much Reft makes
People wanton ; and it is too common for them
that

that live without any Employment to be addicted to this Vice. But now Labour is an excellent Prefervative againft it. This brings down the Powers of the Body, and dries up the Springs of many Temptations. Befides that whilft Men are bufied, vain Thoughts do not fo eafily creep into their Minds. Thus therefore fhould every one order himfelf, though always with regard to his own Condition and Circumftances. But generally thofe that have a ftrong Inclination to Senfuality, cannot do better than to employ themfelves as far as they are able, even to Pains, Fatigue, and Wearinefs, without fparing the Body; and they will fee this Paffion will lofe much of its Strength.

III. A Third Means is, Mortification as to what concerns the Body and the Senfes, and comprehends in it two Duties.

The Firft Duty is to refufe the Body thofe things that are pleafing to it. I fay this not only in relation to things forbidden, but I mean that Perfons fhould mortify themfelves in what is permitted, and above all in what they have the moft defire for, as in Food, in certain Conveniences of Life, in Sleep, Cloaths, and lawful Pleafures. In which Cafes the way to mortify onefelf is by abftaining from thefe things, if not altogether, at leaft in part, fo as not to ufe them too frequently, or take all the Liberty in them that might be without Sin, obferving Moderation in the ufe of them, and never being too eagerly fet upon them. I know not what more to fay as to this Point, than that a Complaifance for the Defires of the Flefh, is the deftruction of Virtue and Chaftity. A cockered and pampered Body is a Receptacle of evil Thoughts; and it is therefore of the higheft Confequence to regulate and mortify ourfelves in this refpect.

2. The

2. The other Duty of Mortification is sometimes to contradict our own Inclinations, and accustom ourselves to a painful and uneasy Life. But herein Care must be taken to keep exactly in the middle between the Superstition of such as believe the Practice of excessive, and oftentimes idle and ridiculous Austerities to be Meritorious, and the Indulgence of those who know not what it is to suffer any thing that is painful and afflicting, willingly, and for their Spiritual Advantage. There is no particular Rule to be prescribed in this Case, but each one must observe what suits with his Circumstances, his Strength, and the Need he has of Mortification. For the Necessity of Mortifying ourselves is much greater in some than in others, and all are not alike qualified for taking this Method with themselves. Some being of a weakly Constitution, may justly favour themselves; whilst Others whose Bodies are robust and healthy, must be less sparing of themselves. But whensoever any find themselves enclined to Lust, and a vicious Temper of Mind, it is then high time for them to betake themselves to this Course of Mortification, and make use of Fasting, Watching, and Labour; to Eat little, to take their Rest only when forced to it by Weariness, and when their tired Limbs require it; and not always to Sleep so long as Nature would direct. Yet care must be taken not to favour the Body for false Reasons, and under colour of Necessity, or that it is for their Health. Upon these Pretences Men often indulge themselves in many things that they might well enough be without. They will not shorten their Rest, nor take Pains, nor Fast, for fear of ruining their Health; when would they fairly examine into the matter, they would discover that they herein plainly deceive themselves. After all, it is always the safest course to provide for the most

pressing

preſſing Neceſſity. When the Soul is in danger, the Body is to be leſs favoured ; it being far better that the Body ſuffer, than that the Soul be eternally ruined. But there is no need of this. God would not have us cruel to ourſelves; and it is certain, that we may Mortifie, take Pains, and Faſt without Murdering ourſelves. Beſides, it is obſervable, That ſuch who lead a mortify'd and ſevere Life, enjoy better health, and live longer, than thoſe who have a blind Complaiſance for the Body.

Where is the Chriſtian that makes any doubt of the Neceſſity of Mortification, after the Pattern St. *Paul* has left us of Faſting, who profeſſes of himſelf, I *Cor.* ix. 27. *I keep under my Body, and bring it into ſubjection.* And to prove here is meant ſuch Mortification, as conſiſts in abſtinence from Pleaſures, and a ſtrict Temperance, it is to be noted, that the Apoſtle produces the Example of Wreſtlers who obſerved great Continence, in relation both to their Food, and to their Pleaſures, and abſtained from many things that others allowed themſelves. Thus much theſe words import ; * *He that wreſtles or fights, uſes Abſtinence, or Continence in all things.* And that Paſſage of *Plato* before cited, ſhews that this Continence of Wreſtlers, may be extended to whatever I have been treating of : It was, to mortifie himſelf, aſwell as to promote the Propagation of the Goſpel, that St. *Paul* choſe to ſuffer Hunger, Thirſt, Faſting, Watchings, Poverty, Heat, Cold, and divers other Inconveniences. If this great Apoſtle took this Courſe ; Who will be ſo preſumptuous as to queſtion whether there be need of it ? I conclude then, That it is a moſt effectual Means of ſecuring us from the Infection of impure Temptations, if

---

* Πᾶς ὁ ἀγωνιζόμενΘ πάντα ἐγκρατεύετ).

we

we can but perfuade ourfelves to lead a Life of Self-denial. This kind of Life, though it feem fevere, is the Foundation of the pureft Joy, and moft delightful Satisfactions. A Soul that inhabits a Body foftned with Pleafures, is in a State of Slavery, and is the Prey of Paffions and Remorfe; but that which dwells in a Body tamed and brought into fubjection, is free, happy, quiet, is a true Ray of the Divine Effence, exempt from a thoufand hurtful Paffions, a thoufand mean and fhameful Defigns, and a thoufand Griefs that befall fuch as are not Mafters over their own Bodies.

IV. There is one thing more to be obferved in relation to the Body, whereon alfo Chaftity has a great dependance, and that is, the Government of the Eyes and Looks. This is an Affertion of great weight, and which I have already touched upon * in the former Part of this Treatife. I have cited alfo what our Lord Chrift fays of unclean Looks, St. *Matth.* ch. v. And thofe words of *Job,* ch. xxxi. 1. *I have made a covenant with mine Eyes, not to look upon a Maid.* All that indulge themfelves in impure Thoughts, know by their own experience, that thefe begin almoft always by the Sight. Here therefore are two things to be obferved. The firft, not to feek after Objects that may feduce us; they that do this, are firft in the Temptation; they willingly expofe themfelves to it, and fo muft needs fall by it. The fecond is, not to fix our Eyes upon fuch Objects when they come in our way, but inftantly turn away from them. We cannot be too wary in this refpect, but muft arm ourfelves with a firm Refolution, and muft put it in execution, without taking time to confider, fo foon as ever the Occa-

* *Sect.* I. *Ch.* 7.

fion prefents itfelf ; nothing being quicker than a Look, and the Impreffion it makes upon the Heart ; fo that one Moment is Time enough for it to furprize us. One Look caufed King *David's* dreadful Fall. Let every one therefore lay it down as a Law to himfelf, not to take the liberty to look at every thing that offers itfelf, not to fix his Eyes upon all the Perfons and Objects he meets with ; and to keep his Senfes to himfelf.

Thefe are the principal Means to be ufed as to the Body, in order to Chaftity, and there is none but ought to make what advantage he can of them ; there being none of us but has a Body, and none therefore but ought to be afraid left this Body prove the Caufe and Inftrument of his De-ftruction. But the propereft Seafon for the Ufe of thefe Means, is in Youth, this being the Age wherein the Danger is greateft, becaufe the Body being then in its full Strength, it is fo much the more liable to corrupt the Soul, and draw it into the Exceffes of Impurity. Then therefore is the Time of keeping under the Body. And this alfo will be a Means of preventing the Temptations of Uncleannefs, and continuing Chaft for ever after. And that we may the better improve what has been faid, it will be requifite to add hereto the Reflections which were made in the Third Section of the former Part, Chap. 3; where I have fhewn, Intemperance, Idlenefs, too great Care of the Body, and a Love of Pleafures, to be the ufual Occafions of Uncleannefs.

CHAP,

CHAP. V.

Of the Cares which relate to the Soul.

WHat has been ſaid, does not ſo entirely re-late to the Body; but that the Uſe of theſe Means will prove highly advantageous alſo to the Soul, and will ſerve to keep off many Tempta-tions. But yet care is to be taken in ſome In-ſtances that have a more particular relation to the Soul. If the Body be neceſſarily to be tamed, the Soul alſo is no leſs to be brought into ſubjection. And what is to be done to this end, may be re-duced to theſe two Duties; ſtudying to put away Evil Thoughts, and labouring for Good ones.

I. Evil Thoughts may be put away, either by caſting them off as ſoon as ever they offer them-ſelves, (which will be the Subject of the next Chapter) or by preventing their firſt riſe. Which at firſt ſight appears a difficult Task, and really is ſo to thoſe that have contracted an ill habit of en-tertaining themſelves with theſe ſort of Thoughts. Such know not how to get rid of them, without great Foreſight; and it is what they ought earneſt-ly to labour at, till they have brought themſelves to that paſs, that they ſhall have ſtopt the Spring whence impure Thoughts inceſſantly flow. And theſe are ſome of the ways of ſucceeding in ſuch an Attempt.

1. Perſons ſave themſelves from multitudes of Evil Thoughts, when they avoid the Occaſions and Objects which are wont to produce them; (as I have ſhewn before.)

2. Per-

2. Persons should accustom themselves to fix their Mind, so as that it do not wander, nor be distracted. It is a wicked Liberty, to suffer the Imagination to rove after all sorts of Objects, and to hearken to all the Thoughts that present themselves. Whence it comes to pass, that these Thoughts press such on to divers Miscarriages; and so much the more unavoidably, because after they have once found the way to their Heart, they presently become habitual, and so the more powerful upon this account. More especially this happens, in those Thoughts which gratifie their Sensuality; as is well known to great numbers of People, who have contracted this unhappy Habit. Such commonly entertain themselves with divers foolish and wanton Imaginations; their Soul is full of corrupt and lascivious Idea's, with which they are continually poison'd more and more, and kindle in themselves more and more the Fire of Lust. For Cure of this so great a Fault, and which, if not amended, will certainly ruine them, Persons should settle their Minds, and not accustom themselves to think of too many things, nor busie themselves about what signifies nothing, or what is wicked. And for this cause, it is highly useful to govern well the Senses, and particularly the Sight, to shun whatever makes the Thoughts go astray, not to be too free, and not to talk too much. Reading, Meditation, and good Discourse, are very proper for fixing the Mind, and keeping it from wandring.

3. The Memory is also to be brought into Order, and taught, not to call back those impure Notions and Matters that we may have read of, seen, or heard, or which we may have fansied to ourselves: All these things are to be blotted, as far as may be, out of the Mind; and if at any time they recurr to our Thoughts, great heed must be taken to prevent their stay there, and we

S

must

muft fpeedily eject them, and fet ourfelves to think of fomething elfe.

4. Curiofity being a frequent Caufe of the Wandrings of the Minds and Heart; and a Defire of fatisfying it, being a great occafion of Pollution, this alfo is to be guarded againft. Men defire to hear, fee, read, know fuch or fuch things, which they take to be meer Matter of Curiofity, and that this Defire is therefore wholly innocent; but would they ferioufly examine themfelves, they would difcover fome fecret Paffion that made them thus inquifitive. Wherefore, whofoever would be pure, muft believe himfelf to be undoubtedly concern'd to refift this vain, imprudent, and fometimes carnal Curiofity, that makes us fo earneft to inform ourfelves of what is not at all neceffary to be known.

II. But it is not enough to ward off Evil Thoughts: We muft labour alfo to have Good ones; and to this end, muft give them Entertainment when they prefent themfelvs, and muft feek after them when they do not.

1. I fay, in the firft place, That we muft be ready to admit of, and entertain them, whenever they prefent themfelves. And indeed, it contributes very much to the Purity of the Soul, to make a good Improvement of thofe Moments wherein it is well difpofed. There are divers Circumftances that bring good Thoughts into the Mind, and put it upon ferious and profitable Reflections. As is efpecially evident in Times of Affliction, or when Perfons apply themfelves to holy Exercifes, to Reading, or to Prayer, or when all the Paffions are quiet. When they find themfelves in any of thefe favourable Circumftances, they muft be very induftrious to improve them aright, by cherifhing thefe good Thoughts, dwelling upon them, retaining them as long as they can, and not letting their Minds wander after

other

other Objects. Then is the Time for them to encourage themselves in Chastity, by representing to themselves the Excellency and the Necessity of this Virtue, and considering how happy a Man is when he has got rid of a Voluptuous course of Life, and how miserable and wretched whilst he indulges himself in it. Then that is easie to him, which at another time would be accounted very difficult; and by a good Improvement of these short Intervals, a considerable Progress may be made in Purity.

2. Since Good Thoughts are of such advantage, care must be taken to raise them, and produce them as much as may be. This is worth taking Pains for: For Evil Thoughts spring up abundantly, and there are many things, both within us and without us, that easily give occasion for them. Insomuch, that unless due Care be had to store ourselves with good Thoughts, to set in opposition to so many vain and sinful Thoughts, those will be sure to get the possession of our Hearts. Now the Means of being furnished with Good Thoughts, are, Reading, Prayer, Religious Conversation, Acquaintance with those that are good, and Retirement. It conduces also extremely to this Purpose, to settle our Minds, and govern our Imaginations, (as has been said) so as that they may present us with no Idea's or Desires but what are pure. Our Minds should also have a stock of Arguments, for dissuading from Impurity, and inviting to Chastity; by which means, we should have a Fountain of good Thoughts within ourselves. But it is especially of great Advantage to follow these two Advices; namely, to have good Thoughts in the Morning as soon as we awake; and, to get a Habit of intermixing them with our other Affairs all the Day after.

I add farther, That it is singularly useful, to labour after Spiritual Pleasures, and accustom our-

selves

felves to a fenfe of them ; that fo one Pleafure may drive away another. I wifh none would ever draw to himfelf too inviting a Scene of Corporal Pleafures, nor would delude himfelf into a belief, that it is a peculiar happinefs to enjoy them. On the contrary, they are to be look'd upon as vain, tranfient, and dangerous. And Perfons would do well to reflect, that Death will one day ftrip them of whatfoever they efteem moft charming in this World, and then all their Pleafures will be at an end, and will leave nothing to thofe who are moft enamour'd of them, but cruel Remorfe. A Wife Man and a Chriftian will often think upon this ; and will call to mind, that he has a Spiritual and Immortal Soul, and is call'd to the Poffeffion of Blifs and Glory. He will endeavour after thofe true Pleafures, thofe pure Delights, and that inward Peace, which naturally flows from a Senfe of God's Favour, and an Expectation of the Heavenly Felicity. Thefe juft and wife Reflections every one fhould make, as being highly ufeful in order to an utter diflike of the ignominious and finful Pleafures of the Flefh, and for banifhing foolifh Thoughts and fenfual Imaginations, and raifing the Soul to great Purity.

C H A P. VI.

Of what is to be done when under Temptations.

BY reducing to Practice, what has been difcourfed in the foregoing Chapters, many Temptations are avoided ; yet can they not all be fo prevented, but that the moft vigilant will be liable to them from time to time. Befides that, there are multitudes, who, by having neglected

the

the promotion of Chaftity, and fuffer'd themfelves to be enticed to Senfuality, are affaulted by frequent returns of this Paffion, and are in danger of deadly Falls : So that it will be neceffary to fhew what is to be done when under a prefent Temptation.

I. And here my chief Advice, and which, if duly practifed, were fufficient of itfelf, relates to the Beginnings of Temptations : And it is this ; That as foon as ever any impure Thoughts arife in the Soul, they be inftantly refifted and driven away. This is the moft certain, and at the fame time the eafieft Means of fecuring ourfelves againft Impurity.

1. It is the moft certain Means, becaufe hereby Perfons preferve themfelves infallibly from all the mifchievous Confequences thefe firft Motions might have. The firft Moment almoft wholly determines the Event of a Temptation ; inafmuch as if at firft withftood, it is ufually conquer'd ; but if it be fuffer'd and hearkened to for ever fo little a time, it gains its point. The firft reception of impure Thoughts into the Soul, fhews them to be pleafing to it ; and the longer they are entertained there, the more this Pleafure encreafes ; and when this Pleafure once prevails, the Man is no longer in a capacity to defend himfelf. There is no furer way to prevent a Conflagration, than to put out the firft fpark of Fire ; and it would be weakly done to let it kindle, in expectation of being able to exftinguifh it afterwards : So alfo in Sicknefs, the fafeft way is to provide early againft them, and ftop them at their firft appearance.

2. I noted, That this Means is likewife eafie. The firft beginning of a Temptation, is the time when it is weakeft ; and by confequence, it is then beft dealt with. People complain of the Strength of Temptations, and the difficulty of

conquering them ; but were it not for themſelves, they would neither be ſo ſtrong, nor ſo hard to be overcome. It is true, there is a great deal of trouble in encountring them, when they have been permitted to gather ſtrength ; but it were no ſuch task to ſtrangle them in the birth, for then there needs but little force to oppoſe them, be-cauſe they are of little force themſelves.

But when theſe Beginnings are ſlighted, and wicked Thoughts are ſuffer'd to ſettle themſelves in the Soul, they ſoon get a great advantage over it. Impurity, together with Anger, is perhaps the firſt Paſſion which, above all the reſt, has the quickeſt Motions, and makes the ſpeedieſt Progreſs. Upon any the leaſt occaſion it captivates the Heart, ſo that the Man can neither argue againſt it, nor reſiſt it. It is a Fire which ſpreads itſelf with ſuch aſtoniſhing ſwiftneſs, that its firſt breaking out is ſcarce obſerved, before the whole Houſe is all in a Flame. It is an Enemy that by no means ſeems terrible at the firſt on-ſet, but which makes great advances by the leaſt favour is ſhewn it ; inſomuch that if a Perſon does not reſiſt it at firſt, he will find himſelf overcome almoſt in the ſame inſtant wherein he is aſſaulted : So that we can never be too obſervant of the firſt ſtirrings of Luſt, to get them ſtifled immediately.

Now that it may appear the more diſtinctly how a Man ſhould manage himſelf in the firſt beginnings of a Temptation, I ſay, that he muſt forthwith turn away his Mind from impure Thoughts, without concerning himſelf with them, without ſtaying to conſider them, without weighing which ſide is to be choſen. If he ſtand to parly with his Luſt, he is in a fair way to be taken in its ſnares ; for this ſhews him diſpoſed to hearken to them, at leaſt that he is not fully reſolved to reject them. We muſt therefore be ſure to get immediately at a diſtance from theſe
    ſort

fort of Thoughts, to turn away inftantly our Eyes, our Senfes, and our Minds from whatever we forefee like to feduce us, and, in a word, to flee from it. Some Temptations are to be refolutely encountred; but as to this, the fafeft way is to fhun it; and the honourableft Victory, is not by coming to grapple with the Enemy, but by avoiding the Combat. St. *Chryfoftom* * alledges to this purpofe the Example of *Job*; he notes, that this holy Man, who did not flee when *Satan* came to attack him, but enter'd the Lifts with this dangerous Enemy, fled however at what might poffibly have prejudiced his Chaftity; as thefe words teftifie, *I have made a covenant with mine Eyes; Why then fhould I look upon a Maid?* Job xxxi. 1.

Let us not flatter or deceive ourfelves, by imagining there is no great hurt in the beginnings of a Temptation, that thefe firft Motions do not neceffarily lead to the Sin, or, if they did, they might however be ftopt by the way. This is a trick of the Paffion, by which it deludes us; and they which have fuch-like Thoughts, may learn, by their own experience, that nothing is vainer, or falfer. When a Man has given a Temptation time to grow ftrong, he will not afterwards have it in his power to put a ftop to it. So that the wifeft courfe he can take, is to have a great diftruft of himfelf, and not run the danger of a trial; but as foon as ever he perceives any irregular motion within himfelf, to fall immediately to his bufinefs, without hefitation, or much confidering about it.

II. To this moft important Advice, fome others may be added.

1. The firft is, Not to be difcouraged, when affaulted by impure Thoughts. I do not mean,

---

* Serm. de Continen.

S 4

that

that they should be look'd upon with an unconcernedness, and People should give themselves no trouble about them ; for, on the contrary, they are to be resolutely opposed, (as I have been proving :) But my Intention is, that Persons should not be disheartned, and give over the design they had formed, of keeping themselves clear of this Vice : They must not conceit it will be impossible to succeed in such an Undertaking, nor that they are clearly forsaken of God : Their business is rather, to humble themselves under a sense of their own Corruption, and to resist it, and then to hope in the Mercy and Assistance of the Lord.

2. Besides, recourse must be had, in times of Temptation, to holy Exercises, and Acts of Devotion. Short Ejaculations, whether only by raising up the Heart to God, or addressed to Him with the Mouth when one is alone, are very proper at such a time. And though Persons do not offer them up with Earnestness and Freedom enough, which in truth is very difficultly done in the state they are in at such a time, and especially when they are lukewarm and in trouble, they must not however fail to send them up as they can. It is likewise very useful under a Temptation, to turn the Mind to other Thoughts; for instance, to call to remembrance, that God sees us, and is near to us ; to think of our Lord, and his Sufferings ; or of Death, and the Last Judgment, or any other of the great Motives to Chastity which have been already treated of : Recourse also may be had to Reading, upon these Occasions.

3. Not only Holy Exercises, but other things likewise of no great consideration in themselves, may serve to deliver us from the Temptations of Impurity ; as, not to stay in the Place where we are, nor to take our ease, to apply ourselves immediately

mediately to some sort of business, or get into Company, or fall upon some Discourse. A change of Posture, or Motion of the Body, sometimes suffices to prevent a train of evil Thoughts. There are some things that seem not worth minding, small, and even contemptible, that yet are not without their usefulness this way. But above all these Means, every one must consult himself, and see what is like to make most impression upon him.

·And yet once more I must observe, That all this is to be done resolutely and undauntedly. 1. In the first place, Men must not be discouraged either by their own Weakness, or their Backwardness to set about it. Though these Means are practised but imperfectly and unsteadily, this however will turn to some account, provided it be done sincerely, and with Perseverance. 2. Neither must they be affrighted at the Trouble they find in resisting the Allurements of Lust. To this end let them remember for their Encouragement, that their Conflict will not be long, but if they can but hold out for a few Moments, they will presently be safe, and the Storm allayed ; and after this they will have the Satisfaction of having done their Duty, and will taste an inward Peace rejoicing and strengthening the Soul, and exciting them to a Performance of their Duty upon all other Occasions that shall offer themselves.

C H A P. VII.

Of the Assistance that may be had from Others in order to Chastity.

AFTER the Consideration of what each one is to do in order to Chastity, I am next to shew what Helps to Virtue may be found in others. And this is so much the more necessary, because
                                                              this

this perhaps is the Means leaſt taken notice of, and moſt neglected.

I. Nor have we leſs need to be aſſiſtant to one another, in Matters of Salvation, than in thoſe of this Life. This mutual Help is one of the moſt indiſpenſable Duties of Charity ; and as ſuch is often preſcribed by the Apoſtles. † *Exhort one another daily ;* ‖ *let us conſider one another daily to provoke unto Love, and to good Works.*

‡ Heb. 3. 13.
‖ Heb. 10. 24.

Neither is it to be doubted, but it highly conduces to the promotion of Piety, and more particularly of Chaſtity, to partake of the Company and Diſcourſe of Virtuous Perſons. For as this Virtue is loſt by converſing with the Vicious and Debauched, ſo it is preſerved and improved by Communication of thoſe that fear God. The Example of ſuch is of great weight, and their Counſels of great force for purifying the Heart. Good Converſation is of inconceivable advantage, I mean ſuch Converſation where each Party ſpeaks with an Openneſs of Heart, and with Confidence, and Sincerity. And a Man does not leave ſuch Society without carrying ſome Fruit of it along with him.

2. The Scripture teaches likewiſe that we may aſſiſt each other with our Prayers. The greateſt part of Chriſtians have but little knowledge of the Efficacy of Prayer, and for want of Faith make little uſe of this Means, as taking it to be of no great ſervice to them. But it is moſt certain that * *the fervent Prayer of a Righteous Man avails much with God* ; and he is always diſpoſed to beſtow his Favours, when ſincerely ſollicited in behalf of ſuch an one as greatly deſires them, and to this end deſires alſo the Interceſſion of other good Chriſtians for obtaining them. Whence I conclude that whoſoever deſires to overcome the Paſſions of the Fleſh, muſt beg the Help of his faithful Brethren, and particularly muſt entreat the Aſſiſtance of their Prayers.

* St. Ja. 5. 16.

3. But

3. But chiefly Others may help us by their Advice and Exhortations. It is not to be expressed of what advantage it is, to have a faithful Friend from whom to receive Counsel and Encouragement in time of need, and principally to such as have little Prospect of Success from their own single Endeavours. †*Wo to him that is alone when he falleth,* †Eccles. *for he hath not another to help him up.* A Man is al- + 10. ways in a woful Condition, and in danger of committing great Offences, when he consults none but himself, and relies solely upon his own Understanding. This is true in the things of this Life, and it is no less so in what concerns our everlasting Salvation. One of the chief Reasons why so few make any considerable Progress in Goodness is, because in Affairs of this nature People love to act separately, without asking others Advice, or being willing to be advised by any. But no where does this Observation hold more certainly than in the Case of Uncleanness. Persons will venture to discover something of their other Sins, but will not own this in the least; they are so ashamed of it, that this makes them reserved, and they very hardly prevail with themselves to take Advice concerning it, or to confess their Weakness. Or perhaps they cannot think of one of whom they may prudently ask Advice, or to whom they may disclose their Case, either as to this or any other Sin; this being what the greater part never once dream of.

Yet it is plain this would be an admirable Means of delivering ourselves from many Disturbances and Dangers. Some know not whether certain Actions are allowed or forbidden, and so for want of better Information, they venture, uncertain as they are, to do what perhaps is contrary to Chastity, and even infamous and sinful; and which had it not been evil in its own nature, would yet be so to them, because they act it doubtingly, and

not

not of Faith. Others are sensible of their deplorable State, and have an intention to get out of it, and make some Attempts this way, but without Success, because they have none to assist them. Not to say any thing of those who being guilty of Sins of Uncleanness, have need to consult with such as may instruct them, how to make amends for what they have done. Each of these has need of Assistance. A hidden Evil is always dangerous, but when discovered it is half cured. We may easily have taken notice of such who, whilst obstinately resolved not to ask Advice concerning the State of their Heart, keeping it closely to themselves, have had no Rest, nor been able to free themselves from the Tyranny of their Passions; but who so soon as ever they have had the Courage to disburden their Consciences, and make known what it was that troubled them, found themselves instantly comforted and strengthened, and thenceforward supplied with new Forces in order to their better Progress in Piety.

Why then are People so backward to make use of so beneficial a Remedy? Will they say they do not know to whom they may apply themselves? The number of Wise-Men, and Men of Probity is not so small but that such may be found, either amongst those whom God has ordain'd to instruct others, and guide their Consciences, or else amongst Private Persons. Or is it Shame that hinders their doing it? If so, in the first place, it is not necessary in all Cases to discover what they are most averse to having known, but there are secret Means and Methods of desiring Advice and Counsel, without such a Declaration. Besides suppose by letting their Case be known, they venture some Shame and Confusion of Face, is it not much prudenter and safer, and much better in all respects to discover a Distemper, than live in continual Torment by concealing it, and at length perish

perish by it ? He that has the Courage to make
this acknowledgment, hereby shews himself to be
affected with his Condition, and desirous to get out
of it, and has in truth already made a good step
towards his Conversion. As also the Sinner who is
covered with Confusion in the Sight of God for
his Faults, which he has committed, does not stand
in such Awe of Men, nor is so fearful of exposing
himself to some little Mortification.

II. Since we are treating of the Assistance that
may be received from others, it must be noted
that there are such to be found as may contribute
considerably to the promoting of Chastity, I mean
Publick Persons and Parents.

1. If those in Publick Stations would heartily set
themselves to it, they might in a great measure suppress the Excesses of Impurity, and make the Manners of Christians much chaster than they are. Good
Order both in Church and State would conduce
very much to it. The Ministers of God's Word
may employ themselves both in Publick, in giving
good Instructions and frequent Admonitions concerning this Point, in their Sermons ; and in Private, in exhorting zealously and prudently those
who are backward to their Duty. Magistrates may
also do great Service, by enacting wise and just
Laws against this Sin ; by an exact Observance
and Execution of the Laws thus enacted ; by not
suffering those Places where Youth are corrupted,
and accustomed to Play, to Riot, and to Debauchery ; and in not bearing with those who are the
Promoters of Leudness, and Corrupters of Youth,
and who serve only to introduce Effeminacy, Wantonness, and Love of Pleasures. There are some
places where the Magistrates make this their Business ; and it were heartily to be wished, that all
would do it every where.

2. Fathers and Mothers may also contribute
much to the Chastity of Youth. If they would do
what

what they can in their Families, and what it is not hard to do, there would not be ſo much Uncleanneſs in the World. This I have ſaid before, but cannot forbear repeating it. Parents ſhould bring up their Children in great Purity, and ſhould from their Infancy inſpire them as much as may be with a Senſe of Modeſty, even in the ſmalleſt Matters, and not ſuffer the leaſt Indecency amongſt them, nor allow them to ſay or do any thing contrary to Chaſtity. This might eaſily be done, and with good Succeſs, becauſe theſe Principles of Modeſty enter of themſelves into Childrens Minds, and when well imprinted there, ſerve thenceforward as for an excellent Preſervative from Impurity. Whereas if Children once grow careleſs in point of Modeſty, they ſeldom reſume it afterwards. Wherefore Parents ſhould take heed what Example they ſet their Children, that themſelves be pure, and extraordinarily circumſpect both in their Actions and in their Words ; I ſay, not only to forbear all filthy Diſcourſe, which none will indulge themſelves in that are not utterly void of Virtue and Modeſty, but to refrain from whatſoever is a little too looſe, and never to laugh at any thing that has the leaſt relation to Impurity, but on the contrary to teſtify always their Diſlike and Averſion to whatever hurts Modeſty in any manner of way. Fathers and Mothers ſhould likewiſe teach their Children to mortify their Bodies and their Paſſions, to be contented with little, and always eaſy; they ſhould train them up in great Sobriety, and beware that Idleneſs and Sloth get not the poſſeſſion of them, nor a fondneſs for Pleaſures draw them aſide, and that they read no bad Books. And as they grow up, they ſhould ſtill keep them in a State of Dependance upon themſelves, and have their Eyes upon them, to ſee them well employed, and not let them be abroad at Night, and thoroughly to enform themſelves what Company they keep, and

what

what Places they frequent ; and when they are
put, out, to take all poffible Care that a Wife and
Prudent Perfon have the infpection over them.

CHAP. VIII.

Some Directions concerning the Ufe of thefe Means.

HAving directed to fuch Means, and laid down
fuch Rules as are neceffary in order to this
Virtue of Chaftity, I fhall now apply myfelf, for a Conclufion of the Whole, to fhew how
they may be ufefully reduced to Practice, for the
Inftruction of thofe who defire to be benefited by
them, and chiefly with a Defign to make the Practice eafy.   For it is not fufficient to fay there are
Means of being Chaft, but it is more efpecially
needful to fhew, that when ufed as they ought to
be, there is no fuch trouble as Men imagine in living Chaftly. - And what I have to add in this
Chapter deferves to be confidered with more than
ordinary Attention.

I. The firft Advice I have to offer is, That each
one make ufe of thefe Means according to the
State he is in, there being Three States, in either
of which he may be, in relation to Impurity.

1. There are fome who have no Inclination to
this Vice ; or if they had would take care to keep
themfelves free from it.   Thefe have great reafon
to blefs God ; yet they fhould not fail to make ufe
of the Means here prefcribed, for fettling themfelves the more firmly in this happy State.   None
fhould be remifs and unguarded, becaufe many times
thofe Paffions prefs with great violence, out of the
reach of which Perfons had thought themfelves.   A
moft remarkable Example in this kind we have in
King *Salomon,* who in his Younger Years was an un-

par-

paralleled Example of Wisdom and yet in the latter part of his Life gave way to an infamous Passion, and hereby left himself for a Warning to all the World, not excepting those who have the least Apprehension of falling after the same manner. But here it is also to be remembred, that such who are not subject to this Passion, will find it no difficult matter to preserve themselves from it. It is with these as with Men in Health, who need only Foresight and Observation, to keep themselves so.

2. There are multitudes of Others, that have a deadly hankering after Impurity, and suffer themselves to be sometimes betrayed into it, but yet do not allow themselves wholly in it, but strive against it so far that they not only have escaped the Crime, but have never been brought to an entire Consent of the Will to it, much less to a Habit of it. Those of this second Rank have more need of Direction than the former, and must take more Pains, and strive harder to secure themselves.

3. Lastly, Some are Slaves to this Passion, in whom it reigns, and who have either ventured upon the Sin itself, or if not, are however commonly full of sensual Desires, and defile both Soul and Body by their inordinate Actions, Words, and Thoughts. The Estate of these last is extremely deplorable, and very dangerous; and they have more need to consider with themselves, and make use of those Remedies, which may recover them out of this Condition. I cannot better compare these, than to those Sick Persons whose Distemper is come to that height, that without a speedy Medicine well applied, they must perish. I do not deny but such, who are thus impure both by Inclination and Custom, will meet with difficulty in recovering themselves, and will find, at first, their Sin very hard to be overcome: As all experience, who will undertake to conquer any strong Passion, or any well-rooted Habit. Yet I have two things

to fay, to prevent their suffering themselves to be affrighted from it. The one, That this Difficulty will be of no long continuance, the trouble of doing it being worst at the beginning, and growing afterwards more and more easie. The other, That this Work of their Conversion is not equally difficult at all times, but in some Circumstances is easily effected; as I shall prove, in treating of the next Particular. Wherefore,

II. My other Advice is of such importance, that I dare say it will conduce perhaps above all things to facilitate the Practice of the Duties we are now upon. There is no Time wherein Persons ought not to use their utmost Endeavours for overcoming their Inclination to Impurity; but withal, there are some Times and Opportunities, wherein it is done far more easily than at others. In Matters of Salvation, aswell as in all others, a great deal depends upon a choice of proper Seasons. No body but must have found, that he is not always equally well disposed: Upon some Occasions, a thing will appear almost insuperable, and it cannot be done then without great opposition; which yet will not be so at another time. Take a Man given to any particular Passion, and in the instant when he is seized and transported with it, all you can say to the contrary will make no impression upon him: Yet take the same Man out of his Passion, and when his blood is cooled, and you will see him a very different sort of Person. The Impure have their intervals, and these longer or shorter, and more or less frequent, according as the Habit they have contracted is stronger or weaker. There are some in whom this Passion bears such absolute sway, that they are almost always employed by it; yet such as these have some more favourable Moments wherein they are capable of Reflection, and wherein their Passion allows them some respite.

T   God,

God, who is full of Goodneſs and Love to Mankind, and deſires the Salvation of Sinners, does not entirely forſake them. He ſpeaks to their Conſciences divers ways, and ſometimes they hear his Voice, and are affected with it; they begin to relent, they review the Miſcarriages of their paſt Converſation, and are humbled for them. The Preaching of God's Word, the Uſe of the Sacraments, the inward Operation of the Holy-Ghoſt, the Diſgrace they have ſuffered for their Folly, the appearance of ſome Object, and the Reflection they make at ſuch times when their Conſcience is awakened, may raiſe good Motions in them, they being then in an eſtate wherein to make good Reſolutions, and begin to put them in execution. This therefore is a valuable Opportunity, and may turn to very good account; by their doing then, what they are not like to do at another time.

But more eſpecially it concerns every one to make good Uſe of Times of Affliction. Afflictions, which are an excellent Means, and uſed as ſuch by God, for withdrawing Men from their Iniquities, have a particular efficacy for taming fleſhly Paſſions. And if there be any way to reclaim thoſe who have habituated themſelves to Impurity, theſe will do it, and they are alſo commonly the laſt Means God will try them with. For this cauſe therefore, he ſends Pains, and long and grievous Diſeaſes, which bring them to the very gates of the Grave, and at other times he expoſes them to Ignominy and Diſgrace. And it is obvious to obſerve, that when People are reduced to a ſtate of Affliction and Sufferings, the Fleſh loſes a good part of its Dominion. The Paſſions cannot but be calmed, when the Body and Soul are mortified by Grief. This therefore is a moſt beneficial Circumſtance in order to Converſion, and ought upon no terms to be neglected, any more

than

than all those other like Advantages we at any time meet with.

Sinners and Libertines sometimes reason thus with themselves: When the Precepts, the Counsels, and the Motives of the Evangelical Morality are laid before them, they say, All this is true, and they are well satisfied these Commands are just, and the Means produce their Effect, when made use of: That it is easie to reform themselves, if they will heartily endeavour it ; but the difficulty is, to make Persons willing to amend, and use these Means : That the Inclination which hinders their taking this Resolution, and prevents their Use of these Means, and draws them some other way, must first be rectified ; and, in a word, That they want a Will to set about this Duty. Whereto I answer; God gives this Will ; He allows Seasons and Junctures, in which Men may easily be willing to reform ; when both the Sinners find themselves incited to do it, and besides, God inspires into them a Desire of doing it. I say farther, They ought to make a good Improvement of these Junctures, and the good Dispositions they find in themselves at such a time. I say again, If a Man take but a little Pains with himself, these favourable Circumstances will ever and anon return, and he will not be long before he may have made a considerable advancement in Goodness. So that I can give no better Advice to such as desire to renounce their Impurity, than to take the advantage of those Opportunities and Occasions, wherein they are at liberty, and in a state to make serious and useful Reflections.

III. Let not Persons be discouraged at the Beginning. This Advice is highly necessary for all that have the misfortune to be under the power of Carnal Passions ; because they cannot hope to shake them off all at once, but will be in danger of some relapses ; so that if they suffer themselves

T 2   to

to be worfted, it is certain they will never get free
of them.   It is not unufual for People to have
taken up good Refolutions, and made fome an-
fwerable Attempts, and to have concluded hereupon, that they had gained fome advantage over
themfelves ; but yet thefe being but weak Attempts, they have no fooner felt the returns of
their Luft, but they have prefently yielded to it,
either through Surprize, or Negligence, and have
been difcouraged, and began to think they could
never hope to rid themfelves of this Paffion, and
it was therefore in vain to ftrive againft it, and fo
have given over their Defign, and grown as diforderly and licentious as ever.   But it was a great
failing in them to be fo eafily repulfed: For Habits
are not extirpated all at once ; and if all that have
undertaken to work out their own Converfion, had
given over upon a relapfe, none of them poffibly
had ever been Converted.   There is nothing
of more pernicious confequence, than to be thus
eafily difcouraged :   For when a Man's Courage is
once caft down, and he has taken up a perfuafion
that he fhall not fucceed, he will give over his Endeavours, and ftrive no longer ; he will be fure to
do well no longer, purely becaufe he thinks he
cannot ; and ventures to become a greater Slave to
his Paffions, than ever he had been before.

What a Chriftian does for God and his own Salvation, fhould be done with Refolution and Confidence, and even with Joy. The weakeft of them,
and who have made the leaft progrefs, fhould perfuade themfelves, that their firft Beginnings will
be accepted with God, provided they be fincere ;
and that though they do unhappily relapfe, they
muft yet beware of being difheartned.   It is a
great happinefs, on the other hand, when our Falls
make us uneafie, when they teach us how far our
Paffions have got the maftery of us, and what great
reafon we have to labour inceffantly that we may
over-

overcome them, and may recover ourselves out of the great Danger whereinto they had brought us. These Falls must not be slighted or despised. But I must repeat it again ; They must by no means dishearten us, or take us off from what we were about : But rather we should animate ourselves the more, and strive to get above them, and renew our former Resolutions against them : Which if we do, our Gracious God will infallibly bless our Endeavours, and, for the Love of Christ, will pardon those Falls which are not wilfully persisted in. Whereas, if we be discouraged and faint, we become a Prey to Temptations, and shall be involved in them more and more. A wise Man having happened to fall, would get up again and continue on his Journey ; but he that should choose to lie where he fell, without trying to rise, would be deservedly look'd upon as one who had lost his Senses.

I beseech my Readers to put a favourable Construction upon what I write, and not to misinterpret what I have been discoursing. I have written it for the Encouragement of the Weak, such I mean as act sincerely, though with Weakness, and who meet with some success in their Endeavours of Amendment. For what I say, relates not to those who content themselves with weak and imperfect Resolutions of Amendment, without putting them in execution, and are ready, upon every Temptation, to recede from them. These sort of loose and ineffectual Resolutions are taken up by abundance of Persons, who yet notwithstanding perish in their Impenitence.

IV. To be benefited by these Advices, it will be necessary to pursue them with Diligence and Perseverance ; and not carelesly, negligently, or only for a while : They must be follow'd heartily and earnestly, this being the only Method of attaining to Virtue. Our Lord *Jesus Christ*, and

his

his Apostles, exhort us to *strive that we may enter in at the streight gate*; to *watch*, and *fight*, and *take pains*: But these Endeavours are especially required, when we are to resist such Temptations as entice by Pleasure, and, above all, at the Beginning, because that is the Time when we are to expect the sharpest Conflicts. The Spiritual Life begins with Pain and Grief, unless where Persons have entred upon it in their Youth. When Men begin to think of returning, and taming the Flesh, and bringing it into subjection to the Spirit, and the Bonds which now tie us to Pleasures begin to be broken, then it is that we suffer most, then it is that the Flesh revolts, and that we have need of striving to get the mastery over it. Afterwards our Work becomes much easier; and the greater progress we make, the more does the opposition of the Flesh abate, and the weaker do the Passions grow; till we come by degrees to do well without opposition, and with Delight.

Till Persons are come to this state, they must set themselves to work, and never give over. It is only by Perseverance, that advantage can be made of the Means which are appointed in order to Chastity. It is not to be imagined that these Means will at once produce all the Good that may be hoped for from them; and which they effect only gradually, and by little and little. It is likewise only by Perseverance, that long and settled Habits are to be rooted out. Many have undertaken, and with some sincerity, to depart from their Impurity, and have soon returned to it; because they have not attended to this Advice. They began happily enough; they endeavour'd, for some time, to mortifie their Passions, and with some success; but for want of persevering as they had begun, lost the fruit of all they had done.

V. These Means must be exactly pursued, and with a circumspection reaching to the smallest

matters.

matters. It is not to be thought that any Counsels or Helps to Chastity may be neglected. Nor may any fansie it enough to be exact in the Duties and Counsels which are of greatest consequence, and to abstain from what is sinful, or manifestly leads to Sin ; and that he may slight those Counsels which appear of less importance, and take his full liberty in lesser matters. In the case of Chastity, there is nothing wherein Persons must not be nicely punctual ; nor may they gratifie or excuse themselves in any thing that is detrimental to Virtue, nor neglect any thing of all that may capacitate them to acquire or preserve it.

In all the Passions, but chiefly in this, regard must be had to lesser matters ; because little things lead to greater. By light Faults, a Man comes to great Sins ; and the Observation of lesser Duties, may be a Means of leading to the highest degree of Virtue. Often-times there needs only a want of Watchfulness over ourselves : A Look, a Deed, or a Word a little too wanton, a light Compliance with the Flesh, or other things of this nature, which seem to have no great harm in them ; there needs nothing more, I say, to overturn the Soul, and kindle the Fire of Lust, and this too in a very little time. And again, we as often need only to be attentive and circumspect in relation to some things in appearance of little consideration, to preserve ourselves pure and quiet. A small matter, and which is next to nothing, by the way of speaking it may occasion fatal Miscarriages ; and sometimes again, a very little matter may serve to defend against Temptations. Besides, when People overlook the least Duties, and accustom themselves to violate them wilfully and without hesitation, they expose themselves to the danger of taking the same liberty with those of the highest importance. So that to this purpose may be applied what our Lord says,

St. *Luke*

St. *Luke* xvi. 10. *He who is faithful in that which is leaſt, is faithful alſo in much ;* and what we read in *Eccleſiaſticus* xix. 1. *He who deſpiſeth ſmall things, ſhall fall by little and little.* And yet nothing of all that may conduce to ſo great and ſo excellent an End, as is our Supreme Felicity, deſerves to be accounted ſmall, or of little importance.

These are the principal Means that are to be made uſe of, in order to our becoming Chaſt, and with which I conclude this Treatiſe. And thoſe who will give a ſerious Attention to the Conſiderations I have offer'd concerning both *Uncleanneſs* and *Chaſtity,* may make good Uſe of them. But ſuch over whom a fooliſh and brutal Paſſion has more Power than all Arguments from Religion, their Duty, and their Intereſt, will leave themſelves without excuſe. God grant I may not have labour'd in vain in what I have written, but that my weak Endeavours may ſerve to inſpire all that ſhall read this Diſcourſe with the Love and hearty Deſire of Chaſtity.

F I N I S.

CPSIA information can be obtained at www.ICGtesting.com
Printed in the USA
BVOW08*1819080616

451261BV00004B/6/P